Date Due

FEB 18 1997			
	DISCARDED		

BRODART, INC.   Cat. No. 23 233   Printed in U.S.A

THE WORLD'S PARLIAMENT
OF RELIGIONS

RELIGION IN NORTH AMERICA

Catherine L. Albanese and

Stephen J. Stein,

editors

THE WORLD'S PARLIAMENT OF RELIGIONS

The East/West Encounter, Chicago, 1893

Richard Hughes Seager

Indiana University Press

Bloomington and Indianapolis

The paper used in this publication meets the minimum requirements of
American National Standard for Information Sciences—Permanence of
Paper for Printed Library Materials, ANSI Z39.48–1984.

Manufactured in the United States of America

Library of Congress Cataloging-in-Publication Data

Seager, Richard Hughes.
The World's Parliament of Religions : the East/West encounter,
Chicago, 1893 / Richard Hughes Seager.
p. cm.—(Religion in North America)
Includes bibliographical references and index.
ISBN 0-253-35137-5 (alk. paper)
1. World's Parliament of Religions (1893 : Chicago, Ill.)
2. Religions—Relations. 3. East and West—History—19th century.
4. Liberalism (Religion)—United States—History—19th century.
5. Liberalism (Religion)—Protestant churches—History—19th century.
6. United States—Religion—19th century. I. Title. II. Series.
BL21.W8S43   1995
291.1'72'09034—dc20   94–5510

1 2 3 4 5   00 99 98 97 96 95

For
Katharine Goodell Seager

Classics, whether texts, symbols, events, persons,
or rituals, command attention.
—David Tracy,
Plurality and Ambiguity

CONTENTS

FOREWORD

THE CENTENNIAL CELEBRATIONS for the World's Parliament of Religions, now past, pale when compared with events at the Columbian Exposition of 1893 in Chicago. No effort, however well-planned or well-intentioned, could recreate the sense of excitement, enthusiasm, and curiosity that accompanied the gathering of international religious leaders in the closing decade of the nineteenth century. It was an ecumenical convocation before there was an ecumenical movement. The Parliament, with its representatives from American denominations and sects and also from religious traditions throughout the world, anticipated in unexpected fashion the religious pluralism that would become an increasing reality a century later.

The Parliament of 1893 marks a moment of encounter between Christian and Jewish groups that had long dominated the American religious scene and representatives of Eastern traditions that had roots equally old, or older. The public imagination was aroused by the presence of such figures as an archbishop of the Greek Orthodox Church, a Chinese Confucian scholar, a Shinto priest, a Buddhist from Ceylon, a Hindu—each attired in traditional religious garb. They shared the stage with Protestant Christians, who still formed the largest number of speakers at the meeting, but they stole the show. The 1893 gathering was a small, but significant, step toward the "globalization of American religion."

Richard H. Seager, who has emerged as one of the most astute observers of the Parliament during this centennial period, offers a sobering assessment of the gathering. He argues that the Columbian Exposition—and especially the World's Parliament of Religions held in conjunction with it—exemplified the "Columbian myth." That myth, drawing upon classical, Christian, and patriotic traditions, reflected a triumphalist, universalistic perspective in which ethnocentric Anglo-Protestant ideas and values were filtered through lenses that rendered their ethnocentricity and racism invisible. The ideas and values of the Parliament were presented as transcendent metaphysical truths and as the way things "really" were. The imperialistic and expansionist dimensions of this perspective, however, were unspoken and unacknowledged.

According to Seager, the Asians at the World's Parliament of Religions challenged the widespread assumption about the superiority of the Judeo-Christian tradition and of the West itself, thereby undercutting the Columbian myth. It was those strangely clad Eastern leaders—together with Asian Christians—who seized the moment and captured the headlines, making Americans aware of the existence of alternative religious traditions and opening the door to Eastern missionaries to America. Seager declares the World's Parliament a watershed event, signaling the end of the era of Protestant triumphalism in America and the beginning of a new twentieth-century world of religious pluralism.

It is in this context that Seager's account of the Parliament and his analysis of its underlying ideological commitments show the narrow and self-serving assumptions at the root of what has been called "liberalism." He demonstrates that fact from the statements of the Parliament's participants, and his is therefore more than a bland appreciation of the gathering. It is rather a refreshing, frank analysis of the limitations of the assumptions of its organizers.

Seager exploits to the full the written records of the gathering, and he also makes use of the material culture of the Columbian Exposition and the Parliament. In some of the most engaging portions of this small book, he takes the reader back in time and space to the White City and explores its architecture and public space, demonstrating persuasively how the grandeur and the wonder of the location added to the impact of the gathering.

Not all of the issues surrounding the Parliament are addressed in Seager's study. Some readers may wish to know more, for example, about the ethnocentrism of the Asian representatives; others will desire further reflection on the role of women in the Parliament. The contemporary impact of this unprecedented gathering on the religious population of the nation also remains to be determined. We assume that Seager's work will be joined by future studies addressing these and other significant topics.

Seager's reflections on the World's Parliament of Religions are relevant to the continuing task that occupies students of American religion today, namely, discovering a conceptual model sufficiently inclusive and nuanced to describe and analyze the accelerating religious pluralism of the United States. Much can be learned from his account of the Parliament. It is clear, for example, that any attempt to formulate a pluralistic model that insists on privileging one position or another is flawed and limited, and will be inadequate. Perhaps the concept of a parliament itself, however, is an instructive suggestion.

Catherine L. Albanese
Stephen J. Stein, Series Editors

ACKNOWLEDGMENTS

"A RAPT GAZE into the Millennium" was a working title for this book because I became fascinated by the extent to which traditional ideas about theology, soteriology, and the meaning and end of history underwent radical reevaluations in the nineteenth century. In addition to East/West questions, delegates at the Parliament also contended over issues of tradition versus modernity within particular religions, a struggle fought out at the assembly on the ground of the progressive-millennial ideals that were a central feature of Protestant liberalism, particularly in the United States.

I could not have appreciated these issues had it not been for gifted teachers who, in a wide range of ways, addressed the complex interplay of tradition and modernity. For my understanding of Asian religions, I am indebted to Masatoshi Nagatomi, John B. Carman, Richard N. Frye, Diana L. Eck, and, more than anyone else, J. L. Mehta, who conveyed to me both the depth of the gulf between tradition and modernity and the creative possibilities for synthesis between them. George McCrae S.J., Margaret R. Miles, and Richard R. Niebuhr introduced me to graduate level work in Christian history. A number of highly educated Dominican and Franciscan sisters, most notably Rosemary Parr, early on forged in me an appreciation of how traditionalism could dovetail with contemporary praxis. Marilyn Chapin Massey, Nancy B. Jay, Dorothy Austin, and Stanley J. Tambiah showed me ways to appreciate the dynamism of Christian and post-Christian modernity. The foundations of my understanding of the modern West and the United States were laid down at the University of Wisconsin, where, as an undergraduate, I was fortunate to study under George L. Mosse, Harvey Goldberg, and William Appleman Williams. William R. Hutchison deserves special credit for being the man who oriented me to perennial American questions, encouraged me to synthesize diverse issues and points of view, and allowed me to rail against the confines of the disciplines of the academy without fear of banishment.

Numerous peers in graduate school who are now colleagues in the field have contributed to this book by way of our extended and wide-ranging conversations, the most important being Stephen Prothero, Mark S. Massa S. J., and Bernardino Verastique. Additional conversations came from people associated with the Chicago Parliament centennial, including Swami Sarveshananda, who more than anyone else was responsible for generating early interest in the centennial, Jeffrey Carlson of DePaul University, and Ron Kidd, Executive Director of the Institute for World Spirituality. Joseph M. Kitagawa and Charles H. Long engaged me in a different kind of conversation by offering critical comments on the manuscript that enabled me to make important midcourse corrections. I also want to thank Catherine Albanese and Stephen Stein for their helpful comments on this manuscript.

I also want to acknowledge long-time friends who, by virtue of having lived our adult lives together, made contributions to this book. Many years ago, Pamela Montgomery and I cut our teeth on Buddhism and psychoanalysis; Barbara Hindley has unfailingly encouraged me in my desire to write on contemporary issues related to religion and culture. Special thanks go to William Turner Farrier who, when we were young men seeking wisdom, helped me to explore many dimensions of life in America that bear upon issues raised at the Parliament of 1893.

My wife, Ann Seager Castle, deserves deeply sincere thanks for reading papers and offering thoughtful criticism on a topic marginal to her own interests. Over the years, her patience, generous spirit, and loving humor saved me from the bouts of apoplexy I endured while wrestling with this material.

INTRODUCTION

THE WORLD'S PARLIAMENT of Religions, an event of great importance to last century's Columbiad, was a wholly extraordinary assembly that challenges the most ambitious interpreter. But, the year 1994 provides an excellent perspective from which to proceed. The centennial celebrations of the original Parliament have come and gone, providing us with a comparative perspective on what a global parliament of representatives of the religions of the world can be.[1] The recent Columbiad has also receded into the past, which, given its modest, chastened quality, serves as an excellent counterpoint to the more extravagantly confident celebrations held last century. The 1992 controversy about the relevance of Eurocentricism in an increasingly pluralistic, globalized society is, moreover, powerfully informed by a glance back to last century's Columbiad and Parliament, where the content and boundaries of the traditional canon were limned with unusual concreteness. With the Parliament centennial and Columbian quincentenary fresh in our minds, we can begin to assess the enduring significance of the 1893 assembly.

The Parliament deserves a central place in American and modern religious history. A seventeen-day-long assembly held in September 1893, it was considered by its organizers as the most noble expression of the World's Columbian Exposition, Chicago's great world's fair built to celebrate Christopher Columbus's achievements. The Exposition was dedicated in October 1892, but, due to construction delays and competing celebrations in New York City, its major spectacles, ceremonies, and formal assemblies were held in the summer of 1893. The Parliament makes for an intriguing story, one that deserves to be told and retold from a variety of perspectives, but little scholarly work has been done on it and, as a result, a first account needs to be set into place. There is, moreover, no single story to be told, but many—about growing tensions among Protestants and among progressive and traditionalist Jews and Catholics, the emergence of women as leaders of religious communities, and the exclusion of Native Americans, Mormons, and other sectarians from the proceedings.

But, only one of the many stories is of major importance here—that of the encounter between representatives of Asia and the West at an ingathering of nations and tribes, a unique event in world history. It is not possible, however, to discuss this epoch-making development without grounding it in American cultural and religious history. The East/West encounter at the Parliament was at one and the same time an important domestic and global event, a fact that demands that one consider developments in Chicago, London, Rome, and Bombay simultaneously. It was strictly-speaking a religious assembly, but it also requires that one think about theology, religion, and culture; about the grand sweep of civilization and history; and about issues such as the power of a canon, its claims to authenticity, and its relation to authority.

Our basic knowledge of the Parliament comes from two published sources, John Henry Barrows's *The World's Parliament of Religions: An Illustrated and Popular History* (2 vols.) and *Neely's History of the Parliament of Religions*, edited by Walter Houghton. A third collection, *The World's Congress of Religions* edited by J. W. Hanson, is less complete. Barrows, chairman of the Parliament, claimed to have access to manuscripts of speeches made on the floor, and he published his collection as the assembly's "official history." Houghton claimed to base his collection on stenographic notes taken in the course of the proceedings. Both Barrows and Houghton admit to editing speeches and their collections vary, at times significantly. As a consequence, there is no single authoritative record, although efforts to establish an original text suggest that these published records are more than adequate.[2] The transliteration of Asian terms into English equivalents a century ago was often rough and, at best, done in a style unacceptable by today's standards. In this regard, Barrows was a more careful and informed editor than Houghton, one reason I have relied on his collection. More importantly, the issues bearing on the East/West encounter are so basic that minor textual variations are not, in the main, a serious consideration.

The goals of the Parliament, while liberal and universalistic, were marked by crossed purposes, a fact in no small part responsible for the assembly's complexities. On one hand, it was conceived as an event that would be representative of major domestic and global forces at work in the late nineteenth century. The Chicago committee managed to secure representatives of many constituencies—Protestant denominations and movements from the United States and overseas; Jews, Catholics, and other religious forces in America deemed authoritative and necessary; esteemed representatives of the orthodox Syrian, Armenian, Russian, and Greek churches; prominent scholars in the scientific study of religious history; and representatives from what were then considered to be the ten "great religions" of the world. But on the other hand, the organizers also aspired to have the Parliament exemplify a spirit of national and world religious unity that many thought would characterize the twentieth century. The goal of the Parliament as set forth in two mission statements was "to unite all religion against all irreligion"; to set forth "their common aim and common grounds of union"; to help secure "the coming unity of mankind, in the service of God and man"; and "to indicate the impregnable foundations of theism."[3]

Until very recently, there was little work on the Parliament and some of that is now outdated. An older, influential line of interpretation presented it as an expression of the avant-garde agenda of radical Unitarians. The liberal spirit of its mission statements was more or less taken at face value and, in keeping with the tenor of late nineteenth-century Unitarianism, there was a tendency to see the entire Parliament as an expression of humanistic religious sensibilities. There is some legitimacy to this, but it has distorted the received wisdom as to the nature of the event. For instance, Barrows was not, as an older interpretation had it, a Unitarian, but a leading Presbyterian, an important distinction that points to the actual theological and religious complexity of the assembly.[4]

This older emphasis on Unitarianism has also muted controversies raised by the Parliament both in this country and overseas, the record of which is found in numerous published commentaries. Many observers applauded, often in monotonously celebratory terms, the unitary spirit that frequently gained expression on the Parliament floor. But, others dissented by offering contrary assessments of its significance. The Parliament was seen by some as a sign of the coming fulfillment of missionaries' hopes to evangelize the world, while others saw it as a disaster for missionaries. It was said to prove the superiority of Christianity, but it was also said to prove the superiority of the religions of the East. For some, the Parliament pointed to the coming unity of Christendom, while for others it was a revelation of the forces dividing it. It was alternatively praised as a vision of the Christian millennium and damned as the death knell for pure evangelicalism as the dominant force in America's religious mainstream.

Additional Texts, Institutional Settings, and Interpretive Possibilities

By way of introduction, it is helpful to grasp how the Parliament's significance grows as one delves more deeply into the materials available for study. It was part of a cycle of celebrations held in Chicago in the summer of 1893, and three different institutional settings, all generated by the Columbiad, offer distinctly different views of its meaning. Each institutional setting suggests additional texts and alternative research designs, which further suggest different interpretive possibilities, a brief exploration of which helps to set the Parliament's overall significance in perspective.

A first institutional setting points to the importance of the Parliament as an event in the history of the American religious mainstream. The assembly was a small part of a large series of religious conventions held under the auspices of an organization called the Department of Religion or Congress of Religion. Under the auspices of the Department, some forty American denominations and voluntary organization held meetings in the months of August and September. The Parliament was considered by its organizers to be the culminating event of the entire series; it was held toward the series' end and was considered a "union meeting."[5]

In this setting, the Parliament needs to be read against accounts of other Department conventions, such as the World's Congress of Disciples of Christ, the Columbian Congress of the Universalist Church, the World's Congress of Missions, the Columbian Catholic Congress, the Jewish Denomination Congress, and other published and unpublished papers. The point is to compare how various constituencies presented themselves and what issues they raised in their parochial congresses with their performances at the more closely watched, ecumenical, and politically sensitive Parliament. Perennial issues like the emerging schism between liberals and fundamentalists, the Americanist heresy, the impact of Zionism on the Reform community, African-American religion during the Jim Crow era, and a variety of others, from home missions to the role of women, can be examined in an authoritative setting providing a view of both individual groups and inter-group activities.

Standard interpretive rubrics, such as the distinction between mainstream and non-mainstream or insiders and outsider, can be utilized to create a deeper understanding of relations between the old Protestant mainstream and other groups, some of which were marginalized, others of which were entering into positions of culture authority. One interpretive possibility in this vein has been hinted at by Martin Marty in his *Modern American Religion*[6] and might run like this. The Department of Religion and the Parliament reveal an on-going transformation of the American scene, as Jews and Catholics began to emerge as forces, alongside Protestants, within an expanding mainstream, but at a time when fundamentalists, ultramontanists, and Zionists were also beginning to transform their respective communities. Secondary theses can address the emergence of women as a mainstream force in both Judaism and Protestantism and the way in which African-Americans, although in the religious mainstream in many respects, struggled with the more intractable issues associated with racism. In other words, the Parliament, set within the context of the Congress of Religions and interpreted in the light of standard issues, might well be taken as an epitome of religion in the Gilded Age, a time when a selective broadening was taking place in the American mainstream.[7]

Scholars with interests in denominational and ecumenical history in the American field could explore a great many questions by following this line of analysis. This valuable interpretive possibility, however, does not touch upon the most extraordinary dimension of the Parliament, the encounter between East and West. Nor does it probe the assembly's global significance.

A second institutional setting, the World's Congress Auxiliary of the World's Columbian Exposition, provides a larger frame of reference, suggesting far more ambitious interpretive possibilities. Both the Parliament and the Congress of Religions were parts of the Auxiliary, which was established in 1890 for the purpose of creating international congresses to provide an intellectual and spiritual complement to the Exposition's cultural and technological displays. Like the Parliament, the Auxiliary's leading idea was universalistic and liberal, with a marked Biblical or prophetic tone; its congresses would be "more widely representative of 'peoples, nations, and tongues' than any assemblage that has ever been convened." Its mission was to present a global perspective on state-of-the-art developments in various disciplines and professional fields in order to "bring about a real fraternity of nations, and unite the enlightened peoples of the whole earth in a general cooperation for the attainment of the great ends for which human society is organized."[8]

The Congress of Religion was only one of twenty different congresses held throughout the summer of 1893. Other congresses or departments were devoted to "hard" disciplines such as engineering, medicine, surgery, and an array of the natural sciences and to "soft" ones such as art, music, and literature. Still others addressed questions concerning the public press, commerce and finance, and government. Quite a number were devoted to topics directly connected to the religious sphere, such as the congresses on women's progress, moral and social reform, education, evolution, Sunday rest, and temperance.[9] But, the Auxiliary's organizers understood the Congress of Religion and the Parliament to be the most noteworthy of all the conventions. Charles Carroll Bonney, a Chicago lawyer and layperson in the Swedenborgian church and the inspiration behind the Auxiliary, as well as its president, wrote that the Department of Religion was "the culminating achievement" of all the congresses and the Parliament its "crowning event"[10]

In this setting, the Parliament needs to be read against the many published and unpublished papers by leading scholars and practitioners in a wide variety of disciplines and professionals.[11] Bonney estimated that the Auxiliary hosted some 6,000 delegates, who presented papers that would have filled fifty volumes of 600 pages each. Barrows's Parliament collection filled two such volumes, so twenty-five times more material would be available for study. But more to the point, the texts of the Parliament in this setting represent crowning statements in an encyclopedic system of knowledge generated at the turn of last century, which aimed to be global or universal in scope and progressive and enlightened in disposition. This research design suggests interpretive work well beyond the scope of the normal field of American religious history. It creates the conditions for an historical description of a complex knowledge system, a kind of American Gilded Age variant of Michel Foucault's archaeology, one goal of which could be to uncover the role played by religious ideas and assumptions in a wide variety of disciplines and professions as evidenced in a vast collection of authoritative papers.

Given the liberal tenor of the Columbiad, one interpretive possibility suggested by this line of inquiry could be developed in terms of the authority of the liberal movement in Protestantism, which, in its many forms, was moving into prominence in American society. One might frame a question in terms of the degree to which Protestant liberalism, with its ideas that scripture, nature, science, history, and all great culture were forms of progressive revelation, that the role of Protestantism was to adjust to modernity and to infuse it with its spirit, and that history was moving toward the establishment of the Kingdom of God on earth, informed the knowledge systems articulated in the Auxiliary's congresses?[12] One would not only be alert for explicit faith statements, but for more deeply running structures of thought, such as the use of biological metaphors and evolutionary models, progressive assumptions, and post-millennial aspirations, all of which were prominent in both secular culture and liberal piety. In this hypothetical study, the Parliament is seen as a kind of spiritual capstone in a complex knowledge hierarchy, which, while striving to be global or universal in scope, must be examined to see to what degree it was actually dominated by the assumptions of liberal Protestantism. Less hypothetically, the encounter between East and West appears in this setting to be as much an encounter between complex knowledge systems and civilizations as religions. It also becomes open to interpretation as an encounter among representatives of civilizations and religions on a playing field skewed toward the values of the dominant group in American society.

The third institutional setting against which to read the Parliament is the World's Columbian Exposition itself, the centerpiece of America's tribute to Columbus. The Exposition is not only the institutional setting that informs all others but, given the paucity of scholarship on the Parliament, it is a valuable mother lode of theses that can be used to help set the assembly in its proper historical, cultural, and religious perspective. For instance, the Exposition is seen to have marked, among other things, the culmination of an elite, nineteenth-century "genteel" Protestant sensibility and style, the consolidation of an industrial and philanthropic class in Chicago, and the take-off point for an American imperial urbanity.[13] It is also a trove of additional texts including extensive contemporary comment, much of which suggests the essentially religious meanings of the Exposition, and the voluminous publications of the Exposition Commission.[14] Texts of a very different sort include both the seemingly endless spectacles, rituals, and formal and informal public ceremonies held in conjunction with the Exposition and, most important, its material culture, which is an astonishingly rich collection of symbolic architectural ensembles, hieratic murals, and sculptural allegories.

As the ultimate setting for the Parliament, the Exposition suggests many different interpretive possibilities. In general terms, it provides a backdrop, the grandiosity of which informs the highly ambitious goals of the Auxiliary and Parliament, and a mythic *mise-en-scène* for what was in 1893 the most comprehensive and inclusive assembly of representatives of the various religions in the history of the world. More concretely, an interpretive reading of the Exposition makes it possible to frame questions bold enough to think simultaneously about issues in the nation's mainstream and about the significance of Hindus, Buddhists, and other Asians making formal debuts on the modern and American scenes.

Two theses about the Exposition, which are to be built upon in subsequent chapters, are particularly important in this regard. The design of the Exposition was an expression of an aesthetic with roots in the eighteenth-century classical revival, which became the iconic style for civil religion in the Anglo-Protestant culture of the revolutionary and post-revolutionary decades. The personified virtues, Doric temples, and other classically-inspired art forms from the early national period, once translated into a French-inspired Beaux Arts style, gained a renewed, Gilded Age luster in the Court of Honor at the Exposition.[15] This line of interpretation also points to a well-understood element of nineteenth-century American civil myth—that the nation was seen as both a New Jerusalem and as a successor of the ancient republics and empires, a New Greece or New Rome, being built in the North American wilderness. Columbian rhetoric abounds in antique classical and Christian allusions that reflect two distinct but complementary sides of a national self-identity that Ernest Tuveson found at the foundation of America's "redeemer nation" myth.[16]

The importance of this line of interpretation and its bearing on the Parliament becomes more apparent when a second interpretation of the Exposition laid out by Robert Rydell is considered. Rydell argued that the Exposition was one in a series of American fairs held from

1876 to 1920, all of which assigned a utopian quality to the dominant ideals and values of white America in contrast to those of allegedly less evolved, less enlightened, ethnically and racially distinct peoples. More concretely, the Court of Honor at the Exposition signified this utopian vision by way of a contrast made to a second part of the fair, the Midway Plaisance, where the allegedly lesser civilizations and peoples of the world were on display. The ideological legitimation for this contrast was the evolutionary model, then moving into an authoritative position in liberal theological and social scientific discourses, as a description of both the universal historical process and the relative worth of the globe's religions, civilizations, and races.[17]

The relevance of these two interpretations to the East/West encounter at the Parliament becomes apparent when considered in light of one another. The Exposition signified the dominant culture of nineteenth-century America as embodying a new Greece or Rome, a repristinated Christianity, and the most highly evolved and enlightened civilization in history. These significations point to the authoritative foundations of a myth upon which canonical statements of worth could be constructed about America, the West, the rest of the world, and the meaning and goal of history. Due to the canonical authority of this myth, the facticity of these statements was considered self-evident, but was called into question by the critical observations of Hindus, Buddhists, Confucians, and others at the Parliament who hailed from the fundamentally different civilizations of Asia. As the institutional setting for the Parliament, the Exposition reveals insights fundamental to the East/West encounter that are otherwise easily consigned to invisibility—that the evolutionary model was not scientific and value free; that ideas and values based on Greco-Roman and Judeo-Christian traditions are not universal, but culture-specific; that the idea of "America" was laden with cultural, racial, and theological significations that had a direct bearing on the evaluation of knowledge systems with roots in different civilizations and histories.

The insights gleaned from the Exposition as setting also help to put meat on the bones of the other interpretative possibilities. The idea that the Parliament and Department of Religion were an epitome of an American mainstream—a concept always a bit vague as an interpretive rubric—is rendered highly concrete; there is little in Gilded Age America that can be taken as more indicative of dominant values than those expressed by the Exposition of 1893. The idea that the encounter between East and West was as much about complex cultural systems and civilizations as religions gains a high degree of tangibility; the worth statements implied in the contrast between Court of Honor and Midway were not simply disembodied civil myth, but reflected long-standing theological and philosophical assumptions, the structures of academic disciplines, and the motives and rationales for geopolitical decision-making. These insights also illuminate one major source of the tension between centrifugal forces and the unitive aspirations expressed on the Parliament floor, by revealing the particularistic nature of the foundations of the Parliament's universalistic goals of "uniting religion against all irreligion"; of setting forth "their common aim and common grounds of union"; of helping to secure "the coming unity of mankind, in the service of God and man"; and "indicating the impregnable foundations of theism."

The Exposition and Parliament are the basis for this interpretation, which is intended to be a micro-study of a highly regarded, but little understood, modern encounter between West and East. America and its dominant ideals are necessarily in the foreground and the discussion of the Asians is cast primarily in terms of their interactions with these ideals because they structured the western encounter with the East. I have tried to treat both the western and eastern delegates with an even interpretive hand, a challenge when so much is known about so many of the Americans and westerners and so little about all but of few of the delegates from the East. In this regard, I have been handicapped by my professional grounding in western and American intellectual and religious history. A full scale discussion of the impact of the Parliament in Asia demands a knowledge of the intellectual and religious history of a half-dozen nations of the East, plus a variety of vernacular languages. It is my hope that this initial interpretation will encourage scholars of modern Asian religious history, such as John R. McRae and James E. Ketelaar,[18] to continue to use the Parliament as a touchstone for discussions of the interactions between Asia and the West in general and America in particular. In time, a synoptic interpretation of the Parliament as seen from the eastern side of the question might be forthcoming.

Narrative and Methodology

Parliament, Congress of Religion, Auxiliary, and Exposition are potent cultural and religious phenomena amenable to interpretation through both phenomenological and anthropological disciplines. But, I cast this discussion as a narrative for several reasons. A narrative form enabled me to bring out the drama of the Parliament and the excitement it generated among contemporaries and to develop a line of interpretation that utilized the many metaphors, as well as the religious and theological ideas, used by individuals to assess the assembly's significance. Given the multi-dimensionality of the Parliament, the inter-disciplinary perspective it demands, and the fact that it had consequences on at least three continents, it was also more efficient to cast an interpretation of the event as a story making reference to many developments, rather than as a systematic argument based on a variety of theses grounded in different disciplines, fields, and national histories. In short, I chose a narrative form in order to purchase interpretive leverage, allowing me to move among the numerous issues raised during and after the Parliament in order to make some general sense of its enduring significance and legacy both at home and overseas.

But, at the same time, I have found it useful and informative to evoke familiar methods in an eclectic way to suggest underlying dynamics and to energize the narrative. I use the category of myth, for instance, as in the Columbian myth of America as revealed in the Chicago Exposition of 1893 or as in America's civil myth. My discussion of the Court of Honor and Midway is also framed by Mircea Eliade's understanding of the sacred. Given the profuse religious rhetoric the Exposition evoked, its rich material culture, and its geopolitical significations, it seemed natural to evoke Eliade's ideas of *imago mundi*, even in reference to something as mundane as a trade fair.[19]

I have cast the dynamics of the encounter between the East and West at the Parliament in general terms borrowed from Victor Turner's idea of social drama. The worth statements implied in the contrast between Court of Honor and Midway and the tension between the particularistic assumptions at the foundation of the Parliament and its universalistic goals created an ideological landscape analogous to what Turner called a cultural "field" on which a drama is played out. The Hall of Columbus where the Parliament was convened became an "arena" for a contest over these statements and assumptions, fought out by delegates from East and West acting as partisan players, leading factions, and carrying banners in the name of constituencies, while vying with one another over the final outcome of the assembly.[20]

In order to conceptualize major issues in the East/West encounter, I have relied on Bruce Lincoln's analysis of force and discourse in the

construction and transformation of society. Force is not directly pertinent to the Parliament, although the history of the deployment of
force, both on the domestic and international scenes, indirectly informed the proceedings. For instance, the destruction of native American peoples, the lynching of African-Americans, and the suppression
of the Indian Mutiny, as well as the revolutionary violence of colonial
North Americans, were noted by Asian delegates, both to call into
question American and western claims of superiority and to gain sympathy from the audience for their own revolutionary aspirations. Force
was an important factor in the background of the assembly, convened
as it was in an age of imperial expansion and western triumphalism,
marked by both insurrections and numerous military incidents.

But, Lincoln's understanding of how discourse operates in the formation of social groups is of more immediate relevance. Lincoln describes how verbal expressions, taxonomies, spectacle, gesture, costume, icon, and musical performance are stock elements in any
culture that can be utilized both to maintain and transform a society.
Dominant groups use them as an element in a hegemonic ideology
that works to establish authoritative descriptions of social reality,
elicit support from subordinates, and create a powerful mystique, all of
which serve to bolster their power. Non-dominant groups, however,
can also draw upon these same stock elements to form opposing forms
of social discourse, the intent of which is to implement desired
change. Lincoln's discussion points to the important role of sentiment
and persuasion in the effective deployment of either kind of ideology.
Any group must, first of all, have access to channels of communica-
tion to the broader society. But, more importantly, having gained a
hearing, a group must also employ discourse in a way that persuades, a
quality that depends in part on logical coherence, in part on performance ability, and, above all, on audience receptivity. Lincoln thus
draws attention to the essentially sentimental foundations of societies
and to the fact that the power of a given ideology rests in great part on
its ability to elicit emotional responses that lend it authority and credibility.[21]

Lincoln's perspective illuminates the domestic and global significance of the Exposition and Parliament in a variety of ways. The Exposition, its rich material culture as well as its ceremonies, was a
spectacular manifestation of the dominant ideology of the West, as expressed in the old Anglo-Protestant mainstream of America around the

turn of last century. It not only signified a myth of America, but served as a powerful nexus of symbols designed to elicit the emotions of people, both Americans and visitors from overseas, and to rally them to the allegedly universal values which they signified. The contrast between the Court of Honor and Midway rested on taxonomic categories that attempted to demarcate the highly evolved from the less evolved, the civilized from the uncivilized or less civilized, the progressive from the backward, the modern from the archaic or out-of-date, the enlightened from the superstitious, the truly universal from the merely particular, and the white Greco-Roman and Judeo-Christian from the ethnic, dark savage, or dusky heathen. In short, the Exposition was an immense repertoire of stock elements or signs in a hegemonic social discourse with domestic and global significations available for use by westerners in general and mainstream Americans in particular to bolster their claims to canonicity, universality, and authority. From the perspective of the delegates from the West, the Parliament was an occasion where religious and theological conclusions to be drawn from this taxonomy were given a global forum and put on display.

However, some of these signs were capable of variable, contested meanings that would inform the Parliament debates, an event at which representatives of Asian religions gained a formal, public hearing. The contrast between civilized and uncivilized, for instance, turned out to be unstable: meat-eating was barbaric to a Hindu brahmin; drinking liquor uncouth to a Buddhist; Christian claims to a unique, spiritual freedom anti-social to a Confucian. Stock elements from the repertoire were also capable of being reorganized in novel combinations and utilized by Asians as counterhegemonic strategies. Ideas like "liberal," "modern," and "progressive," which were foundational to the social discourse generated by the Exposition, seemed, to leading Asians, not to be intrinsic to the modern, Greco-Roman, and Judeo-Christian West, but to be amenable to Hindu and Buddhist interpretations. Confounding the taxonomic logic of the dominant discourse, Asians attempted to persuade their audience that progress, liberalism, and modernity, however much a part of the West, had a brilliant future in the East. Even universality was called into question, as the particularistic foundations for universalistic ideas were revealed in the course of debate.

The civil mythology of America itself was also contested at the Parliament. Was America to be a parochial nation, pinned to its western roots and allied to imperial powers, or was it to pursue a more thoroughly universal destiny by embracing the ancient theologies and religions, as well as the modern aspirations, of peoples from the East? In this regard, the Parliament was an exercise in what, in the context of the religious history of the United States, Martin Marty has called "public religion." A creation of the eighteenth-century Enlightenment, American public religion is the invocation of theological and religious values, in tandem with national ideals, in a way that transcends religion, church, denomination, sect, and creed. A powerful force in American history, it nevertheless has often been responsible for blurring the lines between churched Christianity and civil religion and has found expression in such diverse forms as John Dewey's "common religion," Will Herberg's triple melting pot of Protestant, Catholic, and Jew, and the "religion of democracy."[22]

In keeping with the goals of the Parliament's mission statements, Parliamentary delegates from around the world attempted to forge a public religion for a globalizing society. In Lincoln's terms, they sought to create a common discourse for a single community of sentiment for a universal society. But, too many geopolitical issues were at stake, too many theological and cultural variables came into play, and too many particulars hung in the air that could not be tucked successfully into any single framework. Despite often-expressed hopes for and visions of unity, the centrifugal forces on the floor of the Parliament transformed the event into a domestic and global social drama over contested meanings. The central question was nothing less than the relative worth of, and right relations among, the religions of the world at the end of the nineteenth century on the threshold of what many assumed would be the Christian century. But delegates vied, not only for the outcome of the assembly, but to capture the hearts and minds of people, both in America and overseas. As a result, the Parliament was as much a struggle over the content of a myth of America or the shape of a global vision of the future or the meaning of history, as over the particular worth of any one religion or theology.

This brings me to the central thesis that structures my discussion throughout this book. The Parliament was a liberal, western, and American quest for world religious unity that failed. Given the foregoing discussions, it can be no great mystery as to why it failed. The Parliament, however noble its goals and aspirations, was tainted by the same parochialism, ethnocentrism, imperial pretensions, and hegemonic intentions as the entire Exposition. In philosophical terms, it failed because the premises for its universalistic agenda turned out to be particularistic. In crude theological terms, it failed because the God of the organizers of the Parliament turned out not to be quite the same as the Gods of the Asians. In Lincoln's social scientific language, it simply turned out not to be possible to forge a common religious discourse in the Gilded Age among the ten great religions of the world. There is also a corollary to this thesis. Having failed as a liberal quest for religious unity, the Parliament unintentionally turned out to be a revelation of the plurality of forces on the American and world scenes. As a result, it was a harbinger of the rise of the idea of religious pluralism that is alternatively celebrated, studied, decried, and in various ways struggled over in many different quarters today.

So, I invite the reader to become engaged with events that more than any others expressed the spirit of the American Gilded Age.[23] And an odd spirit it could be. It was an age in which prominent Chicagoans, with the help of equally prominent New Yorkers and the U.S. government, could build a world's fair, christen it a new Rome and a New Jerusalem, and then congratulate themselves for having surpassed the glories of antiquity. Toward the end of the summer, the *Chicago Tribune* could entertain the idea, apparently with some seriousness, of landscaping the deserted Exposition with Japanese ivy, to give Chicago a tourist destination and America a world-class ruin.[24] The Parliament is of a piece with the grandiose culture of the age, and I have attempted to interpret its significance in a way that does justice to the idealism in this grandiosity and gives voice to the often astonishing aspirations of the participants in the proceedings, while pointing to the Parliament's enduring religious meaning and historical legacy. Part One: A Millennial City, is a discussion of the World's Columbian Exposition, both the occasion and stage for the Parliament. Part Two: An Ingathering of Nations and Tribes, is a discussion of the encounter between West and East as it unfolded on the Parliament floor. Part Three: Further and Fractious Missions, is a look at the responses of representative figures to the entire proceedings.

A few personal notes are in order to give the reader an idea of my own perspective on issues and events. My original interest in "the East" came from the Protestant side of my family. My first exposure was as a young child, and it came in the form of Canton-ware bowls and Chinese scrolls stored in a drawer of an old Goodell family desk. My second exposure was shortly thereafter, with the arrival in our home of a collection of Egyptian and Near-Eastern seals, which were among the effects of my great uncle Richard, who had been an archaeologist in Crete. Somewhat later, I spent hours in the basement with my father, who was a decidedly post-Protestant man in most religious ways, building a replica of a Japanese pagoda out of balsam wood. Much later, the oriental vogue in the 1960s and graduate work in Hinduism and Buddhism augmented this original interest substantially.

My grounding in Christianity came from my mother's, the Roman Catholic, side of the family. My first real exposure to Catholicism was at seven, the age of reason, when I began to go to Mass. I then spent six years in a Gregorian choir attached to the parish in my home town in the Midwest, and I still count it among my skills to be able to chant the entire Latin funeral Mass. Graduate education in comparative religion and in modern European and American religious history eventually augmented this original exposure to Christianity.

People on both sides of the family have had a strong impact on my development, but the Catholic side, composed of numerous aunts, uncles, cousins, and collaterals with whom I was raised, had the greatest impact on my religious life. In retrospect, I see clearly the way in which the Catholic tradition has provided me with many valuable resources. I also see how my family taught me that religion in general and Christianity in particular are always intimately related to culture, to family systems, and to a way of life. Prior to graduate education, it never occurred to me that the plurality of religions and theologies, any more than the plurality of families, was in any way a serious problem.

Once I discovered this "problem," I was also fortunate to be able to draw on family resources for an answer to it. A few years before my mother's death, we sat up together late one night discussing developments in American Catholicism since Vatican II. She confided in me her recent discovery that when she made the sign of the cross at Mass, the hair stood on end on the back of her neck. She was, I see in retrospect, feeling her mortality. She also told me how much she enjoyed the changes in the liturgy, but how little she cared for Catholic charismatic movements, evangelicalism, and Renew. She had recently read Irving Stone's *The Call*, so eventually the conversation turned to missionaries and the new right revival, then at full steam. The idea of conquering the world for Christ was alien to her, and her views on this matter, which I immediately took to be forthright folk wisdom, became for me a kind of credo, which has helped me to cut through issues raised by a great many kinds of Christian theology. "I love my religion," she told me; "Why would I want to take someone's away from them, when I don't want anyone to take mine away from me?" After years of practicing and studying religion, these are among the few words that, given the opportunity, I would care to carve in stone.

I.

A MILLENNIAL CITY

I

THE COLUMBIAN MYTH
OF AMERICA

"Time's noblest offspring" lives in the West. There do great
energies find their opportunity, there are great cities built in
twenty-five years—and destroyed in two days, there will be
Armageddon. And in the great Occident has been building for
many moons—*nec mora, nec requies*, which being freely translated, means at break neck speed—the greatest of all possible
shows. And on May 1st of this year of grace it was duly opened
with fanfaronades and boomings.

—William Walton, *Art and Architecture: An Official
Publication of the World's Columbian Exposition*

On 1 may 1893, 200,000 people gathered on the shores of Lake Michi-
gan on Chicago's south side to attend the opening ceremonies of the
World's Columbian Exposition, America's quadricentennial salute to
Christopher Columbus. Standing beneath a giant Stars and Stripes,
President Grover Cleveland pressed a telegraph key that set the Exposition's machinery in motion. While Chicago's 5,000 voice Apollo
Choir sang Handel's "Hallelujah Chorus," 700 banners unfurled from
porches on the palaces in the Exposition's Court of Honor, the famous
"White City." Jets of water streamed from electric fountains; drapery
fell from a colossal, gilded statue of the Goddess of Liberty. "When all
these ceased," one observer recalled, "the distant hum of gigantic machinery mingled its low, strong voice with the strains of the national
anthem, played by the orchestra and sung by the people. The World's
Columbian Exposition was underway."[1]

The Stars and Stripes, the Goddess of Liberty, Handel's "Hallelujah
Chorus"—these are such familiar elements in the history of American
pageantry that they seem to have no freshness as cultural signs, but to
be clichés. And yet, they form the foundation of a myth of America—

3

let us call it the Columbian myth of America—which informs the meaning of the World's Columbian Exposition and the World's Parliament of Religions and helps to locate them both in American and world history.

To grasp the essential myth, place the Stars and Stripes, a concrete if by no means unambiguous symbol of patriotism, at the apogee of a triangle. At the base of the left side of the triangle, place the Goddess of Liberty, a symbol of freedom and enlightenment, as she was portrayed in numerous woodcuts and lithographs since first appearing during the rational Enlightenment in the eighteenth century.[2] At the base of the right side of the triangle, place the "Hallelujah Chorus," or more particularly the Christian messiah, whose resurrection on Easter morning Handel wrote his score to commemorate. These are the core elements of the myth.

One element is, however, missing—energy. Set this triangle moving forward driven by the millenarianism implicit in William Walton's statement above, and the myth is complete. Under the sign of the Stars and Stripes, the republic moves forward through time toward its millennial destiny, carrying both the gospel of the resurrected Christ and the Gods of classical antiquity in a modern disguise.[3]

Patriotic, classical, and Christian signs, all infused with millennial energy, are the mythic building blocks of the White City. Its implicit meaning, conveyed in architecture, ceremony, oratory, and song, was that the United States was both the new imperium, a new Greece or Rome, and a New Jerusalem, the City of God and man, toward which Christians had labored for centuries.[4] The republic was, one dared to hope in 1893, on the threshold of fulfilling its destiny. But, as with most myths, there was in the Columbian myth of America a claim to universality that could not bear too close a scrutiny. In this case, the claim was that America, the western classical tradition, and the Christian religion were peerless and unique and, together, were making universal history for all human kind.

These signs are also the building blocks with which we will begin to reconstruct the encounter between West and East at the Parliament, where Asians attempted to introduce alternative signs into the Columbian myth, heathen and exotic signs, with radical meanings. Some signs were place names like Bodh Gaya, the pilgrimage site marking the Buddha's enlightenment. Others were the names of ancient, yet living Gods—the Shinto *kami*, the Divine Mother of the Hindus, and the

Zoroastrian Ahura Mazda. Still others were philosophical ideas such as *Ti, Shen,* or *Shang-Ti* of the Confucians. At issue in the encounter was this: if these sacred places, theologies, and philosophical ideas were given parity with their Christian counterparts and absorbed into the Columbian myth, a wholesale reshaping of the sign configuration at the core of the myth and of the myth itself would be required, which would in turn portend new, alternative meanings of America and its destiny. It would also suggest that universal history might be moving in directions not determined by the forward-driving Christian millenarianism infusing the Columbian myth.

We begin with the Exposition and the Columbian myth of America in order to set a system of symbols and a taxonomic logic into place in a rich ideological landscape replete with domestic and global significations. Later, a drama will unfold on the Parliament floor in the form of a contest over the content and authenticity of this ideology among delegates from East and West, as they labored together to forge a common religious discourse for an emerging global ecumene. Our final destination is the dissolution of the coherence of the Columbian myth of America and the first, dim stirring of the birth of a new one.

The Religion of Anglo-Protestant Civilization

The importance of Christianity to American history is the primary focus of most historians of American religion; cultural historians have attended more to the classical elements in the nation's civilization. So far as I am aware, there has been little attention to both Christian and classical signs and the many ways in which they, together with patriotism, have informed and sustained the American religious imagination for well over two centuries.[5] Mainstream church historians have, moreover, typically thought about religious history in terms of Protestant Christianity and its impact on the secular realm, with little attention to the links between religion and ethnicity. For instance, Henry May has drawn attention to the way in which Protestant religious ideas about the dawning of the Christian millennium and secular ideas about progress became fused in the nineteenth century, giving shape both to the American mainstream and to the nation's exaggerated sense of destiny.[6] Robert Handy called this phenomenon the "religion of civilization"—the attempt on the part of American Protestants to build the kingdom of God on earth through the institutions of the republic, leading them to think of the nation both as "a bearer of civilization" and as a vehicle for "the subjugation of the world to Christ."[7] Neither May nor Handy, however, developed a sustained discussion of the relationship between Protestant Christianity, American culture, and Anglo-American ethnicity as it bore upon the question of who was in and who was out of the nineteenth-century mainstream. Mainstream Protestant phenomena such as the religion of civilization tend not to be understood as expressions of group ethnicity.[8]

The idea of a late-nineteenth-century "religion of civilization" is, however, helpful for understanding the ideological landscape of the Exposition, but it needs to be expanded upon in two ways. First, May and Handy share a descriptive model in which Protestant churches carry a positive religious charge, which became over-identified with secular culture, infusing what should have been religiously neutral with illegitimate religious meaning. Second, they tend not to emphasize, as might a more anthropologically-inclined historian, that culture itself is capable of generating religious meaning and that culture is intimately shaped by ethnicity.[9] Given these qualifications, Handy's religion of civilization is more adequately conceptualized in terms of the fusion of religious elements drawn from both Anglo-American culture and Protestant religiosity. In other words, it is more productive to think about an Anglo-American or Anglo-Protestant religion of civilization, which was a fusion of patriotic, classical, and Christian signs, that formed the core of the Columbian myth as it was generated around the turn of the century in mainstream Protestantism.

To grasp how this fusion could work, consider the poem "Unguarded Gates" published in 1907 by Thomas Bailey Aldrich, one of the influential "genteel" poets and writers of New York City, who played a dominant role in the popular publishing industry around the turn of the century. Technically speaking, his poem is a secular text, although Aldrich and his contemporaries such as E. C. Stedman, Richard Watson Gilder, and George William Curtis were deeply preoccupied with religion, morality, and the fate of the republic.[10] There are few overt Christian signs in the poem because it is structured more around questions of culture and ethnicity; Aldrich wrote it to caution old mainline Americans about the potentially deleterious impact of the massive migration to this country by "men from the Volga and the Tartar steppes, / Featureless figures from the Hoang-Ho, / Malayan, Scythian, Teuton, Kelt, and Slav, / Flying the Old World's poverty and scorn." One of his central concerns, however, was actually religious: these men brought "with them unknown gods and rites / Those, tiger passions, here to stretch their claws." It is not necessary to say that "Unguarded Gates" is a religious rather than a secular poem, but in terms of the Columbian myth of America, it is important to note the way in which classical signs were used by Aldrich to signify American ideals, proper morals and civic values, and an implied threat to the nation allegedly posed by non-Anglo ethnicities.

> O Liberty, white Goddess! is it well
> To Leave the gates unguarded?
> . . . .
>   Have a care
> Lest from thy brow the clustered stars be torn
> And trampled in the dust. For so of old
> The thronging Goth and Vandal trampled Rome,
> And where the temples of the Caesars stood.
> The lean wolf unmolested made her lair.[11]

Or consider a very different text, a theological essay "The Law of Growth," by the influential Congregational theologian, Horace Bushnell. There are in this essay only a few overtly patriotic references, even though Bushnell, like the New York poets and writers, expressed concern about the destiny of the republic and about the perceived threat to the moral and religious authority of mainstream Protestantism.[12] Even so, Bushnell conceived a highly nuanced and sophisticated theology in this essay, the leading propositions of which drew upon and lent substantial support to the essential signs of the Columbian myth.

Bushnell was, first of all, a mainstream American millennialist. He concluded his essay by assuring his readers that the final ascendency of the race was assured, an age of genius had begun, and that America had been called to be its spiritual lawgiver. His essay is Christian; Bushnell saw Jesus and his church as the living link between earth and heaven. We would, however, miss something vital if we did not attend to the important classical themes that he spent a good deal of time developing. Human collective destiny rests not on Christianity alone, he wrote, but on two other forces that have in the past and will in the future nurture and train the race so as to enable it to achieve its ultimate triumph in virtue and liberty—Greek aesthetic beauty and delight in perfect form and the authority, integrity, and nobility of Roman law. "Greek art, Roman law, and Christian faith," he concluded, were "indestructible, incapable of death, must roll on, down through the whole future of man, and work their effects in history. And, if we are sure of this, we are scarcely less sure of an age of law, or of the final ascendency of the intellectual and moral life of the race."[13]

The Chautauqua assembly in up-state New York provides another, very different view of this fusion of signs, one more explicitly linked than Bushnell's to Anglo-Protestant or Anglo-American ethnicity. Founded as a Methodist summer camp for Bible study, the Chautauqua gained influence and fame through its Science and Literary Circle, a study-by-mail program devoted to Protestant religious education and the popular cultivation of the liberal arts. The site of the Chautauqua—the wooded St. Paul's Grove: its temple modeled on the Parthenon, its statues of Homer, Aristotle, and Plato, and the eight-foot iron-clad pillars that at night held "Athenian fires"—evoked both classical and Christian antiquity. The many performances held there—evening Vespers, prayer vigils, theological disputations, patriotic assemblies, and the ceremonial exercises such as Recognition Day—served to inculcate the idea that a good Chautauquan and a good American embodied ideals represented both by classical culture and Protestant Christianity. The way in which the Circle served to link mythic, national, and ethnic identities is revealed in the words of Jesse Lyman Hurlbutt, an old-line Chautauquan, when writing about how students were able to matriculate at any point in the standardized four-year curriculum devoted to the world's great civilizations. The Circle's curriculum "is railroad train on a track with four stations", he wrote; "you can board the train in England, America, or Greece or Rome, and when you have gone the round and reached the station where you began, you have completed the course and receive your certificate."[14]

We would miss a great deal about America in general and the Gilded Age religion of civilization in particular if we did not see that classical motifs derived from the culture served as a rich source for the religious and mythic imagination of nineteenth-century America's Protestant mainstream. Aldrich's poem, the white Goddess, and his more or less explicit xenophobia would simply be dismissed as literary. Bushnell would be considered solely in terms of his being an influential non-ethnic Protestant theologian and minister. Hurlbutt's Greco-Roman, Anglo-American railway would likely be deemed irrelevant or eccentric. We would entirely miss an important element of what these three men held in common, albeit expressed in very different ways—their love and respect for and indebtedness to classical antiquity. We would also fail to see the way in which classical signs play, or at least once played, an important role in the formation of the nation's identity and how these signs conveyed an often quite explicit ethnic meaning to the idea of an American mainstream.

As importantly, we would also miss something vital in the Columbian myth of America and, as a result, we would fail to understand the way in which the White City functioned as a symbol of the ultimacy of the Greco-Roman and Christian West. That would in turn lead us to overlook the foundations of America's mythic claim to universality, as well as the myth's western parochial foundations. Most importantly, we would fail to comprehend why the successful debut in Chicago of delegates from the religions of Asia—the Hindus, Buddhists, Zoroastrians, and others, with their pilgrimage sites, philosophies, and Gods—caused a rousing and important controversy in and around 1893.

Imago Mundi I

The Columbian myth was keyed to optimism, a mood not universally felt across the nation. Radical changes challenged America in the decades between the Civil War and the turn of the century, leading Paul Carter to coin the phrase "the spiritual crisis of the Gilded Age."[15] One change involved a nexus of related developments in the culture—the burgeoning of urbanism, industrial capitalism, science, and technology—which together overwhelmed the agrarian order of the antebellum decades. It was a transition not easily made. America's urban workers battled with industrial capitalists, while the rural economy faced periodic collapse. African-Americans, only recently emancipated, encountered virulent racism in the cities of the north, while, at the same time, Jim Crow legislation was reshaping the face of the south. A sea change effecting all other developments was also underway: when the nineteenth century opened, a vast continent stood before a young coastal republic, but by the time it was over, the Indians had been "pacified," railways linked the Atlantic and Pacific, and, in 1893, the frontier was pronounced closed.

At the same time, a second set of changes more directly pertinent to religious history was revolutionizing western philosophy and theology. Darwinism and related evolutionary ideas were threatening to overturn ancient Biblical views of both history and the nature of human existence, while new techniques of literary analysis threatened to un-ravel the coherence of the Bible itself. In response, the liberal move-ment arose among leaders of Protestantism, both in America and Europe, which sought to adapt Protestant traditions to the spirit of the age, much to the increasing consternation of their more conservative colleagues. For liberals, God and spirit were described as at work in scripture, but also in nature, science, technology, and art. They under-stood themselves to be less members of a particular church than as part of an inspiring Christian movement, one that confidently aimed to in-fuse American civilization with its spiritual principles and, at the same time, to uplift the entire human race.[16]

These many developments all seemed for a time to be unrelated, but by the 1880s and 1890s, they came to be viewed by many in America as parts related in an ominous whole in what Robert Wiebe has called "a framework of jeopardy."[17] Amid vistas of great opportunity and awe-some change, Americans tended to vacillate between over-confidence and despair.[18] One of these national mood swings occurred in relation to yet another major issue—immigration. As immigrants flooded the port cities of the Atlantic coast and poured into the heartland of the old Northwest, one type of American nationalist, "the nativist," grew xenophobic. For these nativists (among whom we can count Aldrich), the many immigrants—northern Europeans, Chinese and Japanese, and, increasingly, southern- and eastern-European Catholics and Jews—seemed to threaten both the morality and the blood lines of the nation. But, a second type of nationalist, "the cosmopolitan national-ist," remained optimistic. These liberal reformers had faith in what would come to be called the American melting-pot, and they remained confident of the Anglo-Protestant mainstream's capacity to absorb, reshape, and reform immigrants, making them into citizens worthy of the nation.[19]

Built in this tumultuous era, the World's Columbian Exposition epitomized the national mood on the cosmopolitan up-swing. It was designed to be a showcase for Chicago, a city rebounding from the Great Fire of 1871. It announced that the city had come of age as the imperial city of the American West—the "Rome of the railroads" and "the Rome that is to be of the new world,"—and that it was seizing its place among the great urban centers of western history.[20] But, in the words of Alan Trachtenberg, the Exposition was also "an oasis of fan-

tasy and fable at a time of crisis and impending violence." For an entire
summer, it seemed to be "the fruition of a nation, a culture, a whole
society." Despite the labor wars, lynchings, teeming slums, bankrupt
farmers, and broken Indians, it seemed to be "the celestial city of man
set upon a hill for all the world to behold. It seemed the triumph of
America itself, the old republican ideal."[21]

The Exposition was also a uniquely modern form of what Mircea
Eliade has called a sacred space.[22] A world's fair, it functioned as a pilgrimage site for millions who, in a young, sprawling, volatile, and
insular society, became enthralled by its evocation of history, its pano-
ramic displays of global culture and modern technology, and its architectural effects that conveyed a sense of permanence and solidity. More
specifically, it was an *imago mundi*, a world picture, that revealed both
mainstream America's image of itself and its image of the rest of the
world, in a decade when the nation was in a time of transition and in
an era when the world was first widely perceived as becoming knit into
a single, global society.

America's grand image of itself (its image of the world we will consider shortly) was revealed in the Exposition's Court of Honor, the famous "White City," a Beaux-Arts *tour de force* created by the nation's
leading architects, sculptors, and muralists. Before construction of the
Court, one local commentator noted that the waste-land shores of Lake
Michigan had been "without form and void," barren like the universe
"in the Mosaic story of Creation on its first night." But, once the work
had been accomplished, another noted how "Apollo and his Muses
with the tinkling of their lyres drown the bells of trains and trolleys
. . . the Hub of the universe is transferred from Boston to Chicago."[23]
Built for a single season out of "staff," a compound of plaster of Paris
reinforced with horsehair and jute, the White City was an American
sacred space, a disposable sanctum sanctorum for Handy's religion of
civilization, and an ideological landscape built upon the classical,
Christian, and patriotic signs at the core of the Columbian myth.

The essential elements of the myth were given architectonic form
in the White City's central axis, which was grounded in the west by
Richard Morris Hunt's Administration Building. Acclaimed as the
most exquisite modern restatement of classical aesthetic ideals, Hunt's
building also functioned as a condensed symbol that called to mind
events that had propelled America and the West into modernity. Inscriptions on its four exterior walls retold the history of Columbus—

his birth, his commission from Ferdinand and Isabella, the landing at San Salvador, and his death in Valladolid prison. Inside, at the base of the building's central dome, lesser heroes of the age of discovery—da Gama, Vespucci, De Soto, Raleigh, and others—were honored with commemorative medallions. Major inventions and discoveries—the compass, printing press, Newton's laws of gravitation, the steamship, and telegraph—were celebrated in inscriptions and murals on panels over each entrance. Friezes above the gallery recalled other ancient and modern advances in mathematics, chemistry, physics, and geology.[24]

Along the axis to the east, monumental statuary in a reflecting pool elaborated on the progressive assumptions in the myth. At the near end of the pool, Columbia stood enthroned upon an antique barge propelled by hieratic women representing the sciences and arts. Fame stood at the bow of the barge with a trumpet, while Father Time worked the rudder at the rear. At the far end of the pool, a colossal, gilded Goddess of Liberty with pike and Phrygian cap gave a renewed luster to the century-old allegory of freedom and enlightenment. Statues of bison, grizzly bear, Indians, and pioneers scattered throughout the Court of Honor served as emblems of the nation's land and history.

The axis was grounded in the east in the Peristyle, with its triumphal arch set in a colonnade of forty-eight Corinthian columns representing the territories and states. The arch was crowned by a triumphant Columbus in a chariot drawn by four steeds, and mottoes inscribed on the peristyle reiterated the nation's commitment to liberty, religious freedom, and risk-taking.

Toleration In Religion
Is The Best Fruit Of The Last Four Centuries.

Civil Liberty Is The Means Of Building Personal and National Character.

To The Pioneers of Civil and Religious Liberty.

But Bolder They Who First Off-Cast Their Mooring
From the Habitable Past and Ventured Chartless
On the Sea of Storm-Engendering Liberty.

And at the apex of the arch, on the cornice just beneath the hooves of Columbus's charging horses, John 8:32 baptized the entire ensemble to Christianity: "Ye Shall Know The Truth And The Truth Shall Make You Free."[25]

The fusion of patriotic, classical, and Christian signs, as well as the energy thought to catapult the republic forward toward its millennial destiny, was explicit in the design of the White City. These also gained expression in essays, oratory, song, poetry, and spectacle, all of which served to create a discourse about America as heir to the western tradition and as apogee of human civilization and to elicit emotional responses from people, which lent that discourse authority and credibility.

Dedication Day was held in October of 1892, a full seven months before the Exposition fully opened to the public in the spring of 1893. It began with a military salute at dawn. At mid-morning, Vice President Morton (President Benjamin Harrison was with his dying wife), members of the cabinet and Supreme Court, senators, representatives, governors of the states and territories, the Commissioners of the World's Columbian Exposition, and members of the Exposition's Board of Lady Managers all rode in a procession to review 15,000 troops. They gathered again at noon under the cavernous roof of the Palace of Manufactures and Liberal Arts in the White City for a formal ceremony. After preliminary prayers and poems, Daniel Burnham, the Exposition's Chief of Construction, presented the artisans and architects of the White City to 150,000 observers, while the Apollo Choir sang Felix Mendelssohn's "To the Sons of Art".[26]

Chauncey Depew, president of the New York Central Railroad, delivered the Columbian oration, in which he fused patriotic and Christian signs to legitimate America's sense of millennial mission. He noted the results of America's experiment of religious freedom—a flourishing practical Christianity, the success of churches independent of the state, and the generosity of a nation that contributed millions of dollars toward the evangelization of the world. His words reveal, moreover, one form of the historical logic that linked the origins of Christianity to the White City. In his oration, Depew noted that like the wise men of the East who traveled west to Bethlehem under a star, so too did the spirit of equality of all men under God and law move westward from Mount Calvary with Columbus to America's shores. It then moved westward again across the continent to the Pacific. The White City, Depew concluded, "condenses and displays the power and fruitage of this transcendent miracle."[27]

Essays in leading national periodicals tended to praise the White City with classical allusions, reflecting what William Cronon called an "imperial cast of mind,"[28] but Christian signs were rarely far beneath the surface. Mrs. Schuyler van Rensselaer, a noted New York art critic, wrote in the *Forum* that the White City was just "a small place" when compared to ancient Rome, but was also the most magnificent and imperial example of modern beauty. Chicago's businessmen displayed their commitment to the "glorification of true art" and to preaching "the gospel of that noble pleasure of the eye through which the mind is cultivated, the heart purified, and the life of the nation enlightened and sweetened." She personified the city of Chicago as saying: "Lo, it is not Mammon you should worship, but the light-bearing gods of intelligence, refinement, and beauty." Van Rensselaer also accused Sabbatarians who lobbied to close the Exposition on Sundays of being "self-styled Christians," who selfishly sought to withhold the fair's "civilizing and uplifting ministrations" from the "mind-hungry, ignorant, but eagerly ambitious masses."[29]

A similar note was struck in the *Atlantic Monthly* in the comments of Henry van Brunt, an Exposition architect and architectural critic, which revealed a very different sort of historical logic than Depew's. According to van Brunt, the White City placed the United States in a direct line with the greatest moments of the past—Elizabethan England, the Reformation, the Renaissance, and Periclean Greece. A comparison with Athens was irresistible: a visitor to the White City would "find himself cloistered as never scholar was cloistered before. No philosopher or disciple of the Academy ever walked and meditated in such porches." The many rostral columns, kiosks, porticoes, and promenades had been arranged to illustrate "that order is heaven's first law." Van Brunt also appealed to scripture to defend the Exposition's great expense; "the alabaster box of precious ointment was not broken in vain at the feet of our Savior, though it might have been sold for three hundred pence, and the money given to the poor."[30]

An extraordinary ceremony in Stanford White's new Madison Square Garden in New York revealed a similar identification of America as heir to Greece and Rome. The artists and architects who had created the Exposition, together with luminaries such as Charles Eliot Norton, William Crary Brownell, Louis Tiffany, and William Dean Howells, gathered in the Garden to honor Daniel Burnham. Following dinner, coffee and cigars, and a program of stereoscopic views of the Exposition, Burnham received a loving cup from Richard Morris Hunt, and those assembled on the platform passed it in tribute to Burnham and the Exposition. When Richard Watson Gilder, editor of *Century* magazine, rose to speak, he read his poem "The White City." "Greece was; Greece is no more," he began. The towns and temples of ancient Greece had been consumed by time, but their ashes bred an "undying seed," first in Rome and then still westward on the "veiled and virgin shore" of America. Greece flowered anew and her temples soared again in Chicago. The White City, Gilder concluded, was a witness to the fact that from the tomb of the ancients, "beauty walks forth to light the world forever."[31]

Liberal Protestant ministers saw in the White City a model for their vision of a God- and spirit-infused civilization. David Swing took the occasion of the Exposition's opening to preach on John 7:8—"Go ye up to the feast." Likening the celebration to a May Day festival, he proclaimed that the White City made "nature seem greater, beauty greater, men greater in genius and sentiment, republics more valuable and religion more simple and true." This day will say to us "we are working out a new politics, a new social science, a renewed religion."[32] Charles Morgan of the Church of the Redeemer took Matthew 16:3 as text for a sermon in which he treated the White City as a "sign of the times." All the world would now hear of the marvels of the nineteenth century and of the "civilization of which the cross is the central sun."[33] Lyman Abbott's *Outlook* took a more social approach, praising the White City as a model of unity in a nation rent by conflict. In design and execution, the Court of Honor symbolized "Greek individuality" subordinated to modern collectivity in "one magnificent temple of all the achievements of man." It was a perfect illustration of the "power of ordered, regulated, and harmonized . . . styles." It was "a National University" that taught the lesson of "the solidarity of the race."[34]

F. Wakeley Gunsaulus, minister at Chicago's Plymouth Congregational and President of the Armour Institute of Technology, saw the Columbiad as suggesting a distinctly modern form of redemption. Speaking from St. Paul's Grove at the Chautauqua, he outlined the role of the Christian scholar for "the Columbians," the class of 1892, urging them to imitate their patron by moving forward from an "old East" into a "some larger West." Be like Columbus, he exhorted them, "seek and ye shall find." His theology, moreover, implied that developments in physics and chemistry had given truth at last to the proposition that "the whole of creation groaneth and travaileth until now." Modern man, he exclaimed, "holds in his brain the very sceptres of divine command," and he exhorted the graduates to go forth with Christian culture as their birthright and gift and to tell the world "that the energies of omnipotence with all the powers and processes of history are vouchsafed to us."[35]

For some, the Exposition was simply a manifestation of divinity. Frederick Noble, a Chicago Congregationalist, noted that "we call this a Columbian Exposition. It is. But it is more—it is a divine exposition." The White City witnessed to "the immanence and infinite resources and loving kindness of God."[36] For literary critic Walter Besant, it was nothing less than the millennial vision out of the book of Revelation. The White City would remain in the minds of the average American as "the vision of St. John," he wrote, "an actual sight of the new Jerusalem; all the splendors that the Apostles described they will henceforth understand."[37]

An Old and Elegant Humanity

School and civic ceremonies emphasized the patriotic elements in the discourse about America generated by the White City. October 12,1892, Dedication Day, was proclaimed Columbus Day, a new national holiday, and it became the occasion for a nation-wide salute to Columbus and the Columbian myth. Francis Bellamy, editor of *Youth's Companion*, outlined a plan for pageants to be held in schools throughout the country to coincide with ceremonies in Chicago, and he drafted for use in it the "Pledge of Allegiance to the Flag." Presidential contenders Benjamin Harrison and Grover Cleveland and the Directors of the Exposition endorsed the idea. The Federal Bureau of Education circulated Bellamy's plan to schools across the nation.[38]

These school celebrations tended to be non-sectarian, appealing to a kind of generic, enlightened theism as the legitimating transcendent sanction for the Columbian myth, similar to that found by Robert N. Bellah and others at the foundation of American civil religion.[39] Theron Brown's "School Song of Columbus Day" was primarily patriotic, and only vaguely Christian.

> Columbia, my land! All hail the glad day
> When first to the strand Hope pointed the way.
> Hail him who thro' darkness first followed the Flame
> That led where the Mayflower of Liberty came.
>
> O Union of States, and union of Souls!
> Thy promise awaits, thy future unfolds.

And earth from her twilight is hailing the sun,
That rises where people and rulers are one.[40]

School programs in New England did include Biblical passages that drew parallels between Americans and ancient Hebrews,[41] but in the Midwest, exercises emphasized Whitman's "Prayer of Columbus" and songs portraying the nation as an object of universal devotion.

O Columbia, the gem of the ocean
The home of the brave and the free.
The shrine of each patriot's devotion
A world offers homage to thee.[42]

There was, however, little question that the theological sanction for the Columbian myth and White City had its ultimate foundation in Anglo-Protestant Christianity. Ceremonies in Columbia, South Carolina, were more or less typical. Exercises began at 9:00 A.M. in the Protestant chapel at Winthrop Normal College. Afterward, the crowd dispersed for programs of historical readings, orations, and prayers in the city's schools. At 11:00 A.M., after a bell rang at the Washington Street school, military personnel, veterans of the Confederacy, members of the School Board and City Council, and the boys of the public schools began their march to the Capitol. They were joined on Main Street by a second group made up of girls from primary and secondary schools and young women from Winthrop College. Meanwhile, the Governor, Secretary of State, Superintendent of Education, and the Mayor of Columbus, together with a variety of local clerics, waited on the platform in the Hall of Representatives in the Capitol for the delivery of the Columbian oration by General LeRoy Youmans, a Civil War veteran.[43]

Youmans wove together patriotic, classical, and Protestant Christian signs with America's millennial destiny in an address that frankly tied the Columbian myth to ethnic identity. He noted that the westward movement of empire, together with all prophecy, poetry, and science, stood as witness to the fact that America combined the "sustained strength of modern energy, the glory that was Greece in her brightest days of intellectual lustre, and the grandeur that was Rome in her most heroic days of patriotism." He compared the Columbian festivities to the great pageants of the past. They were more lavish than the coronations of imperial Rome, the displays at the Eleusinian mysteries, and the festivals in the temples of the mighty empires of the ancient East. They were more grand than the pageants at the Pythian, Nemean, Isthmian, and Olympian games. The Exposition was a concourse of peoples unequalled since the family of man was dispersed at the tower of Babel. It was also a magnificent tribute to the greatest of all Renaissance men—Christopher Columbus.

But America, a nation free from "barbaric pride" and a witness to an "unbounded humanity," was a still greater tribute. Youmans observed that the United States was "a larger and more tolerant Geneva; a larger, less tumultuary and not less patriotic Athens; a larger, freer and more beautiful England." Americans were, he added, "a reincarnation of the old and elegant humanity of Greece, illumined and made to glow by the radiance of a Redeemer and a Revelation." Having "redeemed a continent to the Christian world from the wild beasts and the wilder children of Shem," they then extended over a vast continent "the laws and literature of the Anglo-Saxon race."[44]

Variant Readings

The discourse about America generated by the essays, oratory, songs, poetry, and spectacles occasioned by the White City was forged in the Anglo-Protestant mainstream, and it functioned for those custodians of culture as what Bruce Lincoln called an "ancestral evocation." This White City discourse was, however, not monolithic, but worked within certain boundaries, some fluid, others more or less fixed. The nation in the Gilded Age was composed of a variety of major sub-groups, some allowed to engage with the Columbian myth and share in what Lincoln called "officially-sanctioned sentiments of affinity,"[45] while others were not.

Sabbatarians were one sub-group within the Protestant mainstream who, whether conservative or liberal, sought to maintain the tradition of Puritan Sunday observances. They lobbied and protested to close the Exposition on Sundays, but forces aligned against them were powerful and the issues involved sufficiently complex to thwart their victory. Nudes on canvases in the Palace of Fine Arts, the sale of beer and liquor on the grounds, and the right of workers to attend the Exposition on their one day off in the week were hotly debated in Congress and the press. Complex legal questions returned the issue to the courts seven times until, on July 3, 1893, the Exposition was declared legally open on Sundays. A Sabbatarian boycott of the Exposition ensued.[46]

Despite their disappointment, Sabbatarians retained a love/hate relationship with the Exposition. The fact that it remained open on Sundays suggested that the Exposition contravened the Christian sign in the Columbian myth, but, at the same time, it seemed to epitomize Christian America. The ambivalence of John Henry Barrows, Chairman of the World's Parliament of Religions and an avowed Sabbatarian, indicates the way this sub-group could selectively choose to identify with the Columbian community of sentiment. On one hand, Barrows did not want the Exposition's gates to open. "Over every closed gate on Sunday morning," he told members of the Christian Endeavor Society, "I would inscribe in letters of gold, for all eyes to see, the immortal statute wherein is wrapped up the future of America and of the world: 'Remember the Sabbath day to keep it holy.' "[47] But, at the same time, he was also enamored of the White City, viewing its exhibits as so many "instrumentalities" for the progressive enlargement of the kingdom of God. He later recalled walking in the Court of Honor, thinking how "it would be easy for the Biblical student to find appropriate scriptural words to write on every structure in the World's Fair." Below the dome of Hunt's Administration Building, he would inscribe Isaiah— "The government shall be upon his shoulders"; over the door to the Transportation Building—"Make straight a highway for our God." He considered "He hath not dealt so with any nation" suitable for the United States Government Building, while the Exposition gates deserved the prophecy: "The kingdoms of this world shall become the kingdoms of our Lord and of his Christ."[48]

The Roman Catholic Church officially participated in the Columbian Catholic Congress, in the extensive Catholic Educational Exhibit in the Palace of Manufactures and the Liberal Arts, and in the World's Parliament of Religions.[49] It represented another sub-group that could choose to include itself in the national community of sentiment, by selectively retailoring the Columbian myth to suit its own purposes and by seeking to mute tensions with the Protestant mainstream. In the first case, P. J. Muldoon, Chancellor of the Chicago Archdiocese, simply claimed the White City as a "new gem in the crown of Mother Church." Speaking before a Catholic audience, he noted that there had been none but the Roman church when Columbus set sail, and four hundred years later "the White City waves its flags in joy, and Columbus, the saintly Catholic mariner, in a triumphal chariot comes to greet you." He told them how in Chicago they seemed to "enter upon a soil permanently your own," and he asked that they listen for the voice of the Jesuit missionaries to the Huron and Iroquois saying, "Thank God you follow where I have led. Chicago should be the home of Catholicity before all else."[50]

James Cardinal Gibbons, the liberal leader of the American church, expressed similar sentiments by christening Chicago with a new name. "Let me call her Thaumatopolis," he declared, "the city of wonders, the city of miracles." Gibbons's enthusiasm for the White City was, however, informed by what he considered a distinctly Catholic theological sensibility. Most visitors came to admire the wonders of human invention with an interest that was merely material, he claimed, while Catholics came to study man "with the image of God stamped upon him." But, he encouraged Catholics to avoid the kind of exclusivism and triumphalism that had for so long divided Protestants from Rome, noting that there was a "vast field of free discussion" between "the calm and luminous region of faith and the dark and chaotic region of error." Catholics should proceed with courtesy, charity, and forbearance.[51]

Jews officially participated in the Jewish Religious Congress, the Jewish Women's Congress[52], and the Parliament. They formed a third sub-group that could claim a legitimate place in the officially sanctioned community of sentiments, even if the idea of a Christian America made the situation somewhat unstable and precarious. One source of this instability was noted by the *Reform Advocate*, when it observed that many of the people expected to attend the Jewish Congress would not be Jews, but the sort of Christian who regard Jews as "a curiosity, a freak, or an archaeological specimen." These Christians loved Jews, the *Advocate* complained, but would "have Israel at last accept its true glory, now stubbornly rejected."[53]

Emil Hirsch, a Reform rabbi of Chicago, approached the situation by evoking a liberal Jewish theism that fit comfortably on a spectrum from Catholic to Protestant to vaguely post-Christian, which he linked to the classical sign in the Columbian myth. For him, the White City symbolized an age that "has at last fructified the Promethean spark." The Greek's Prometheus, who was chained to rocks and exposed to vultures, symbolized the spirit of man in the age of slavery. But, in the nineteenth century, Prometheus had been unbound; he was no longer opposed to God but worked in harmony with him: "No chain is clanking; creative energy is ours, the lightning spark is ours; the gift does not doom us to slavery, but destines us to freedom." Hirsch concluded that the American Prometheus "sets aglow with signal brands the hilltops of idealism and hopefulness."[54] Rabbi Solomon Hecht, in a sermon preached at Temple Emanu-El in Milwaukee, took a more traditional tack, calling the White City "the grandest of all temples" and "the most sublime worship which man ever offered unto the Omnipotent One." He saw the art and culture on display there as allies of religion, and he suggested Jews learn from them ways to create more uplifting styles of worship. For him, the meaning of the White City was captured by Isaiah 57:1—" 'Awake, awake, put on thy strength, O Zion, put on thy beautiful garments, O Jerusalem.' "[55]

African-Americans, however, formed a sub-group that was excluded. Racism was institutionalized in the Exposition, a major goal of which was to recreate a national community of sentiment after the Civil War. Although a number of blacks such as Benjamin Arnett, a bishop of the AME church, participated in major Columbian assemblies like the Parliament, there was only one African-American among the 108 Exposition Commissioners, and he was appointed an alternate from Missouri only as a direct result of political pressure. Blacks were also barred from the Exposition's police force and from most of the Exposition's committees, and their exhibits were subject to approval by whites, resulting in few of them making their way into the palaces of the White City. Many blacks boycotted "Jubilee" or "Colored People's Day," one of the official Columbian celebrations for American ethnic groups, in a protest against what many considered a condescending gesture by the Exposition's racist administration.[56]

More generalized racism was also endemic. "Even the United States government," a caption in a souvenir photo album noted, "was not adverse to a little comedy." The comedy in question entailed a comparison of two types of recreational fishing that, in its own modest way, spoke volumes about racial ideas in the American mainstream in the Gilded Age. Two display mannequins in a room of exhibits of fishing implements from around the world presented a contrast that was meant to be "a neat little bit of realism." The first mannequin was a tall, slim, white fisherman dressed in a tweed sport coat and hat, wearing hip boots and a creel, skillfully casting a fly in a trout stream. The second was a barefoot African-American in his disheveled Sunday best, fishing with a crooked stick, a string, and a bent pin. He was, the caption noted, "sound asleep, evidently enjoying the heat of the sun," seeming so life-like that "one almost expected to hear the sonorous snoring of the somnolent fisherman."[57]

Less official commentary in the *World's Fair Puck* and *Harper's Weekly* stretched the comedy to an ugly extreme. *Puck* focused its wit on an imaginary Colored People's Day in which Africans and American blacks joined together in "a Grand Parade of the United Sons of Ham." " 'Tis a glorious sight, and all goes right, the ranks are firm and hold," the cartoon quipped. But "a Georgia coon, named Major Moon" set up a watermelon stand—"the Darkey's theme and dream"—next to the parade route. Arriving at Moon's melon stand, the procession became completely undone. *Harper's* published a series of White City cartoons that lampooned black ethnicity. In one, when an African-American man greeted an African tribesman on the Midway, his wife chastised him: "Ezwell Johnson, stop shakin' hands wid dat heathen! You want de hull fair ter t'ink you's found a poo' relation!' "[58]

Robert Rydell has suggested that black exclusion rested on the assumption made by whites that African-Americans were incapable of appreciating the utopian lessons of the White City.[59] As much to the point, blacks were denied the opportunity to participate in the Columbian community of sentiments because, although overwhelmingly Protestant Christian, there was no officially-sanctioned niche on its legitimating theological spectrum for black theism. Frederick Douglass was forced to announce that it had been the hope of African-Americans to tell visitors from abroad that "progress and enlightenment have banished barbarism and race hate from the United States." We would like to say that in America "the souls of Negroes are held to be precious in the sight of God, as are the souls of white men." Such was not possible. "Morally speaking," Douglass concluded, the White City was for black Americans "a whitened sepulchre."[60] At the Congress of Representative Women, Mrs. A. J. Cooper, the corresponding secretary of the Colored Women's League, noted that black women felt that the cause of all women was one, but "that not till the image of God, whether in parian or ebony, is sacred and inviolable; not till race, color, sex, and condition are seen as the accidents and not the substance of life . . . not till then is the woman's lesson taught and the woman's cause won."[61]

The Columbian myth of America and the White City were expressions of a white, mainstream, American ideology sanctioned by a theology forged in the old Anglo-Protestant mainstream, but flexible enough to be, alternatively, broadly theist, civil, Jewish, Catholic and generally Judeo-Christian. This public Columbian theology, however inadequately it may have expressed the particular aspirations and convictions of different American religious constituencies, provided a broad, consensus-based platform for a selectively expanding religious mainstream in the Gilded Age. It signified, moreover, that the nation was heir to both the ancient classical world and the Christian or Judeo-Christian tradition, a myth that served to create a national identity and to evoke a sense of emotional community. But, the inability of this ideology and myth to be inclusive of African-Americans points, not only to an injustice in American history, but to a gross distortion in the myth's claim to true universality and inclusivity.

2

THE MIDWAY PLAISANCE AND THE
MAGIC OF THE WHITE CITY

The Midway Plaisance is an object lesson that will not fade
from the memory of those who are permitted to study it. Its
teachings are impressive in character and calculated to inspire
the thoughtful mind with a sense of what men owe to freedom
and Christian enlightenment. . . . We may see at this Midway
Plaisance that millions are yet between savagery and civilization, and that a stupendous work has yet to be accomplished
before the race, as a whole, shall be fit for self-government and
permanent civilization.

—*Los Angeles Times*, Editorial, September 20, 1893

THE WHITE CITY revealed white, mainstream America's preferred image of itself, but the Midway Plaisance, a living ethnographic display
that formed a second great part of the Exposition, revealed America's
image of the rest of the world. Together they created a complete *imago
mundi*, a universal world picture, based on a set of interrelated religious, cultural, and racial assumptions that, in the worldview of the
Columbian myth, could serve as the ideological foundations for a common discourse about global community. These assumptions, however,
were replete with value judgements and stereotyped caricatures about
the peoples of the world, which were legitimated by evolutionary theories. On the authority of these theories, a discourse universal in scope
but grounded in parochial assumptions was generated and deployed, in
which "other" peoples were given subordinate signs, ones less august,
less worthy, and often more amusing than those assigned to people
who, figuratively speaking, inhabited the White City.

The ideological landscape formed by the Exposition was based on a
set of contrasts between the White City and Midway, which amounted
to a taxonomy whose nomenclature was imprecise and whose range

extended well beyond distinctions drawn between West and East, often displaying its Anglo-Protestant pedigree. Frequently used categories included "ethnic," "picturesque," "exotic," "semi-civilized," "heathen," "barbaric," "savage," and "primitive." But, the coherence of this taxonomy was less important than its intended meaning. The White City signified the highly evolved, the progressive, the modern, the enlightened, the West, or the truly universal, while the Midway stood for those who were the less evolved, the backward or out-of-date, the unenlightened or superstitious, the East, or the merely particular. In the Exposition's world image, "other" people were incorporated into and subordinated to the White City to create a single global community, in which the Midway peoples were portrayed, in the logic of the *Los Angeles Times*, as lacking freedom and Christian enlightennment, hence "between savagery and civilization" and unfit for "self-government and permanent civilization."

Imago Mundi II

Ninteenth-century evolutionary theories, among them a popularized version of Darwin's on the origins of the species, were put to the service of prevalent forms of racism and liberal, often deeply Christian, ideas about progress and civilization. This gave rise to now discredited, psuedo-scientific theories about a global hierarchy of races and peoples thought to ascend from "primitive man" to the highest form of human culture—modern, western, Christian civilization. To make the World's Columbian Exposition truly universal, anthropologists from institutions such as Harvard's Peabody Museum and the Smithsonian Institute sought to assemble this hierarchy in Chicago, by bringing peoples from around the world to live on the Midway Plaisance for the summer of 1893. The racism explicit in both theories and displays was compounded by the overall design of the Midway. Ethnographic installations under the authority of academic anthropologists stood on a mile-long strip of Exposition grounds cheek by jowl with commercial amusements run by concessionaires.[1]

The peoples exhibited on the Midway ran the gamut from picturesque European ethnics, who tended to be placed closest to the White City, to semi-civilized heathens to savage primitives, who stood at respectively greater distances down the evolutionary ladder replicated on the Midway.[2] Representing ethnic survivals from the West's own pre-modern past was an Irish Village, containing a replica of Castle Blarney, exhibits of lace-making, bog oak carving, and Celtic jewelry-making. A German Village contained a feudal castle, cottages built in forty different regional styles, a concert hall, and beer gardens. Quaint outdoor cafés in Old Vienna became fashionable spots for Exposition visitors to relax over late-night dinners in the continental fashion. Panoramas of Pompeii and the Bernese Alps and models of the Eiffel Tower and St. Peter's in Rome, as well as evocations of other popular destinations on the Grand Tour, were thrown in for good measure. There was no Anglo-Saxon Village on the Midway.[3]

Further down the Midway from the ethnics stood the exhibits of the semi-civilized, non-white, non-Christian peoples—the infidels and heathens. A Java Village covered four acres and consisted of thirty-six traditional huts that housed 120 Muslims and Hindus. It included a bazaar, a theater troupe that performed shadow-puppet plays, and an exhibition of sarong dyeing. A dance troupe from the court of a native prince performed sacred dances in the village temple, and, in the course of the summer, priests performed weddings and funerals for village residents.[4]

The exhibits in the Chinese Joss House, a Confucian hall of culture which was a commercial rather than an ethnographic display, included paintings of the Buddhist hells and images of figures in Chinese folk religion, including Grandfather Kwan and Kuan Yin. In the Chinese Theater, a Confucian play called God-in-Heaven was mounted three times daily with actors in brocade robes performing to the accompaniment of flutes and gongs. Outside, a Chinese soothsayer, identified by official Exposition historian Rossiter Johnson as a "kwa t'sim," read fortunes for the public.[5]

Near Eastern and North African civilizations were represented by Algerian, Tunisian, and Turkish villages, all of which stood adjacent to the most popular exhibition of Muslim culture, Cairo Street, where visitors could drink espresso at cafés or purchase curios from the Holy Land at one of sixty-two bazaars. Camel and donkey rides through the Casbah became a popular Exposition pastime, and, at selected times throughout the day, a Muslim wedding procession wound its way through its narrow streets. For a small, extra charge, visitors could enter a re-creation of the Temple of Luxor to view mummies reputed to be those of famous Pharaohs and to "be awestruck by the rites of Ammon-Ra, Morit, and Chons," performed by leopard-clad priests of Isis.

In the Turkish Village, Sultan Abdul Hamid II built a replica of Constantinople's Saint Sophia mosque, staffed with *muezzins* and *imams*, to serve the needs of Muslims on the Midway.[6]

Authentic re-creations of the social lives of so-called savages and primitives, including Dahomeyans, Samoans, Laps, Inuits, and other American Indians from a variety of tribes, represented the bottom of the hierarchy. Sixty-nine men, women, and children from Benin lived in the Dahomey Village in thatch and plaster huts. Stewart Cullin, Superintendent of the Exposition's Division of Folklore, was impressed by their authenticity, reporting that village residents sacrificed a bull on an altar housed there to ratify their contract with the Exposition Commission. Samoans, Fijians, and Wallis Islanders performed traditional dances at the center of a re-creation of a South Sea island village. The Lapland Village exhibited reindeer and sledge dogs and twenty-seven people, including seven children, who spent the summer displaying techniques for tanning and dressing pelts and woodcarving. Penobscot Indian families, along with other North American Indians, camped just off the Midway in wigwams. Inuits demonstrated whip-lashing and spear-throwing and lived in bark-covered huts, but, to the disappointment of visitors, they refused to wear their fur parkas during August. Mexican Indians lived in a replica of an Aztec ruin and spent the summer weaving serapes.[7]

Other exhibitions more thoroughly mixed both commercial entertainments and ethnography. Twenty-two men came to Chicago from Tcheraz and Teheran to display rug-weaving techniques, but when the exhibition went bankrupt half-way through the summer, concessionaires paid them to perform in the more lucrative exhibition of dancing girls in the Persian Palace. The Ottoman Hippodrome, staffed by Maronite Christians and Bedouin marksmen and equestrians, gained renown as the oriental equivalent of Buffalo Bill Cody's Wild West Show. In the International Dress and Costume Exhibition, more popularly known as the World's Congress of Beauties, women from around the world modeled native costumes. As described by Julian Hawthorne, thirty or forty "belles" were "ranged in pens round a big showroom, like cattle in a show."[8]

Most descriptions of the Midway residents were voyeuristic in tone, but a respectful, intimate glimpse of west Asian religious life was published in a notice of the Yom Kippur services held by Turkish Jews. The Kol Nidre service on September 19 was held in the Saint Sophia mosque on Cairo Street. Women sat behind a carved wooden screen; men sat cross-legged, covered with prayer shawls, as the cantor intoned Hebrew prayers. "The services lasted long into the night, and when silence reigned all over the White City, when the robe of night and sleep covered the kaleidoscopic Midway, these Jews from the land of the Wise Men were still worshiping." The crowd of Midway residents on the twentieth was too large for the mosque, so the Cairo Street bazaar was converted into an outdoor synagogue, with an improvised altar and ark. On the Midway streets outside, "the fakir's cries, the clang of symbols, the din of tom-toms . . . and the strains of martial music from the German village mingled together, while inside rose the shema, "Hear, O Israel! The Lord our God, the Lord is one."[9]

More typically, contemporary observers considered the Midway in much the same light that *World's Fair Puck* and *Harper's Weekly* had African-Americans. Hawthorne wrote in the *Cosmopolitan* that on the Midway "you have before you the civilized and savage world to choose from—or rather to take one after the other." "To my mind," he added, "the half-civilized is the most delectable, then the savage, then the civilized."[10] Julian Ralph, a correspondent for *Harper's* called the Midway "a side-show at a World Circus" and "a place of great and genuine wonder"; it was "a bit of Fez and Nuremberg, of Sahara and Dahomey and Holland, Japan and Rome and Coney Island."[11]

Humorist A. J. Dockarty in *Midway Plaisance: The Experience of an Innocent Boy from Vermont* had his young hero say how he saw "a lot a fellers as was blacker than a pair o' shoes on Sunday morning." Some were Hindus, the narrator noted, and were "all rigged up in sheets and pillar cases." Others were Muslims, and when they turned east to face Mecca, "you can't tell whether they're at prayer or a dog fit, but I suppose its all the same in Arabia."[12]

Novellas inspired by the Exposition took a more genteel approach, but with a similar effect. In Clara Burnham's *Sweet Clover: A Romance of the White City*, the heroine Mildred met a Hindu delegate to the World's Parliament of Religions whom she took to calling "Pink Turban." He talked to her of transcendental philosophy in the purest English, while she found him to be "a totally novel *sauce piquante*." As the two of them stood together talking in the White City, Mildred mused to herself that "Pink Turban [was] splendid in his unconsciousness of being regarded on all sides as a sort of embodied apotheosis of the Midway."[13]

Souvenir albums typically offered magisterial pronouncements on the relative worth of the various Midway peoples. Describing what it called a "Midway Congress of Races," one album, in a caption under a photo of two Africans, noted that these men had come to Chicago with "a strange but purely scientific motive"—to contrast "the extreme of barbarity in contact with the highest type of civilization." It observed that Africans persisted in the "horrible customs" of "fetishism" and "cannibalism," but were a "strong, athletic people," "so liberty-loving that they would not submit to slavery, preferring death to servitude." The Lap were deemed "curious folk," but "specimens of a remarkably brave race." Hindus were described as "mild mannered, small of stature, and as musical as they are industrious and frugal."[14]

Commentators most often took an essentially liberal tack when evaluating Midway peoples, by including them in a universal vision of a common humanity, albeit occupying lesser niches within a single evolutionary perspective on human worth and destiny. Unintentionally anticipating theological issues raised by the East/West encounter at the Parliament, J. W. Buel, a popular and prolific journalist, commented upon a photograph of Anagarika Dharmapāla, a Theosophist and Buddhist reformer from Sri Lanka; J. J. Modi, a Zoroastrian businessman from Bombay; and Vivekananda, a young Hindu ascetic and reformer from Calcutta, as they all stood together on the Midway. These men, he noted, had come to Chicago from Asia to proclaim their faith in the common fatherhood of God, who is "the actuating essence of all religions."[15]

Statements about the relative value of peoples were not limited to writers of popular novellas, magazine articles, and souvenir books. Frederic Ward Putnam, curator at Harvard's Peabody Museum and the head of the Exposition's Department of Ethnology, compiled his own authoritative portrait gallery of people he thought of as Midway "types," such as a Turkish Jew from Cairo Street he called "Faraway Moses," whose portrait he included as an illustration of "the persistence of the Jewish type." Additional types exemplified the characteristics of other peoples—the "French Peasant Girl"; the "Hungarian Gypsy"; the "Javanese Carpenter"; the "Greek Brigand"; the "Algerian Musician"; and the "Egyptian Donkey Boy." In Putnam's taxonomy, however, there was no "Prince of the Pulpit type," no "Entrepreneurial Magnate type," no "Anglo-Saxon Artistic type." The only American sufficiently typical for inclusion in what Putnam called the "mimic world" of the Midway Plaisance was the "American Cowboy" from Buffalo Bill Cody's Wild West Show, performing in Chicago for the summer.[16]

Columbian Inclusivity

The Columbian image of the world found expression in more than exhibits based on dubious racial theories and questionable ethnic humor. The process of incorporating and subordinating ethnically and racially distinctive peoples and non-Christians into the Columbian myth also found ritual expression, as a result of the Exposition's Committee on Ceremonials having designated special days on which to salute people in America's immigrant communities and in other nations. Historian of immigration John Higham has written about American civic rituals and pageants that bear a strong family resemblance to those held at the Exposition. He described these pageants as "solemn dramas" in which immigrants performed their folk dances "in an offertory spirit before a white-robed figure of America." These reflected what he called a liberal "contributions theory of assimilation," which considered the traditions of European ethnics as having the capacity to enhance, rather than simply to undermine, the genius of the republic.[17] Operating on similar principles, the festival days at the Exposition served to enhance the White City and to reinforce the Columbian myth, by portraying other peoples as ancillary players who supported America's leading role in the unfolding of universal history. They amounted to picturesque signs in a global discourse about history and culture, God and religion, race and ethnicity, which invariably worked to support the authority of the White City.

On Sweden Day, held on the date of the Midsummer Festival in the old country, 12,000 people from choral societies in Swedish communities across the country marched into the Court of Honor in a parade with tableaux on floats depicting Vikings, Valkyries, Valhalla, and pioneer Swedes who fought in the American Revolution. Turkish Day, held on the anniversary of the Sultan's accession to the throne, began with prayer in the Midway's Saint Sophia mosque followed by a parade of camels, donkeys, and Bedouin horses into the Court of Honor. On Italy Day, 3,000 Italians marched through the streets of Chicago, but the climax of the day's festivities was a concert of music by Italian composers in Festival Hall and gondola races on the lagoon abutting the palaces of the White City.[18]

Wales Day coincided with the International Eisteddfod of 1893, and, by the authority of the Archdruid of Wales, the Cymrodorion Society of Chicago convened a week-long series of ceremonies on Government Plaza, between the United States Building and the Palace of Manufactures and Liberal Arts. A large, unhewn stone, a *gorsedd*, surrounded by a circle of twelve smaller stones formed a sanctuary where bards in robes and oak leaf headdresses engaged in responsive chanting, harp-playing contests, and choral competitions. The climax of the festivities was the initiation of green-robed "ovates" into a Druid confraternity. In its report of the event, the *Los Angeles Times* noted how the "mystic circle" of a people who had withstood the armies of Rome found a proper home between the "greatest palace of commerce the world has ever built" and the government building of the "youngest and greatest republic the world ever knew."[19]

German Day, held on the anniversary of the coronation of Kaiser Wilhelm II, drew 40,000 Germans from Chicago, St. Louis, Milwaukee, Cincinnati, and other midwestern cities. A program published in the *Chicago Tribune*, which in honor of German Day was run in both English and fraktur, outlined in detail the process by which Old World symbols and New World ethnic communities were ritually incorporated into the Columbian myth and White City.[20]

On the morning of German Day, a mile-long procession composed of German national fraternities, choral groups, gymnastic clubs, and benevolent societies formed in the streets of Chicago behind a lead float carrying a statue of Columbia surrounded by thirteen German-American girls representing the colonies. The second and third floats carried tableaux representing German heroes in the American Revolution and Civil War. The fourth carried a log cabin from Germantown, Pennsylvania, reputed to be the first German colony on the continent. Toward the rear of the procession, floats depicted Teutons defeating the armies of Rome, Germany's liberation from Napoleon, and allegorical figures of Bacchus, Father Rhine, and Germania Enthroned.

A midday program included German-American songs performed by the World's Fair Chorus and an address by the German ambassador to the United States in the German national building. Afterward, the assembled crowd processed down Columbia Avenue, the main thoroughfare in the Palace of Manufactures and Liberal Arts, into the Court of Honor for a program of symphonic music by German composers, "The Star Spangled Banner," and patriotic orations. That night the climax of the celebration consisted of a three-hour concert of German martial music under the direction of John Philip Sousa and firework displays of Germania and Columbia over the reflecting pool in the White City.

The process by which other peoples were incorporated into the Columbian myth was underscored more powerfully, if less formally, when the Midway's residents themselves were invited to parade into the White City. As a result of both the Sabbatarian boycott and widespread rumors that the Exposition was incomplete, attendance in early summer remained low. The Directors of the Exposition also grew concerned that the Court of Honor was too high-minded for the general public. In response, they organized a Midway festival in mid-June to promote the Exposition. Due to its great success, Midway residents appeared in similar events throughout the summer, such as the open air balls, reported by the *Chicago Herald* as featuring "Revelers from Nokomis to Nippon" and "Dancers from Dahomey to Damascus," which helped to boost attendance by relieving the austerity of the White City.[21]

The June Midway festival, a "great parade of the nations," captured front page headlines:[22]

NATIONS IN REVIEW
People of the Plaisance Parade Through the Fair
BARBARIC BAND MELODY
It Adds Interest to the Kaleidoscopic Procession
ICELAND WALKS WITH INDIA
Horsemen of the Desert Show Their Wonderful Skill
THOUSANDS VIEW THE PAGEANT

Reports mixed tantalizing fragments of anthropological description with a large dose of sensationalism. "Women in Paris gowns and women in none to speak of" marched side by side with "half naked savages from the South Sea Islands and fur-clad men and women from Lapland." Chinese in robes "riotous with Oriental colors" and "black-scarred Dahomey Amazons" amassed on Midway Avenue amid a jungle of noise made by the "rattle and rasp of barbaric instruments" and the "wild chant which has struck terror in the hearts of French soldiers in the wilds of Africa." Hawaiians carried the banner of Pele, the goddess of Kilauea; South Sea islanders bore "heathen fetiches." Egyptian temple priests "carried aloft the sacred utensils of their rites," while a dancing phalanx of Africans wore "all manner of queer trophies." The "queer barbaric banner of Algiers" and the flags of other nations fluttered over Midway Avenue, along with the Stars and Stripes.

By noon, crowds had amassed to view the spectacle, and at 2:30, the assembled Midway residents, led by a mounted contingent of the white-gloved Columbian Guard, moved up Midway Avenue out into the White City. "Smiling damsels" playing castanets and riding on Columbian Rolling Chairs joined Arab women with infants in their arms. Brawny Persian wrestlers, "their great muscles standing out in knots and their brown bodies, rubbed with oil, shining in the sun," walked with Samoans, "tall, muscular, chocolate-colored men and women, their wooly hair standing out far from their heads and wearing only cloths about their loins." Swiss guards carried banners announcing to the crowd that the Vatican was "a part of the great conglomera on Midway," and "fat bare-legged men in blue and red robes tramped through the dust, holding aloft standards reading, 'Pray for the Peace of Jerusalem.'" Red-fezzed Turks threw out oriental sweetmeats into the clamoring crowd, while Bedouins rode horseback "with a wild reckless freedom which told the story of their lives." Finally, accompanied by their own contingent of the Columbian Guard, the World's Congress of Beauties rode in a long line of carriages at the rear.

After a lengthy circumambulation of the White City, the Midway's residents came to rest on the banks of the reflecting pool to play games and hold donkey races and wrestling matches. A hundred thousand people watched the Midway procession, "and when it passed they knew better than ever before the vital interest which lies forever in the proper study of man." The festival had been a "great lesson of human brotherhood" in a city "reared in token of the proudest triumph of peace." As a result of the festival, Rossiter Johnson reported that the White City's fame spread throughout the nation.[23]

A Grotesque and Glorious Fourth

The contrast between White City and Midway, and the logic of the ethnic and national pageants, functioned to bolster the message conveyed by the more formal rhetoric and spectacles associated solely with the White City. Thus, the Exposition as a whole served as a vast repertoire of signs available for use in a discourse about the superiority of the West in general, but white mainstream America in particular, while lending to that discourse a mystique of canonicity, universality, and authority. But, like the theology that sanctioned the Columbian myth, these signs were open to variable meanings. In addition, the universal scope of this discourse and the Exposition's inclusivity, however back-handed, created opportunities for the unauthorized appropriation of signs and the creation of reverse significations, dissonant with the overall tenor of the authorized meaning of the Columbian myth and White City.

The Fourth of July was the Columbian high holiday, and it served as the occasion for one such reversal, when an unauthorized theological sign was evoked as a sanction to legitimate the proceedings. A kind of breach in theological etiquette or protocol, this reversal served to underscore the parochial foundations of the Columbian myth and White City. As importantly, it anticipated an important turn of events on the Parliament floor later that summer, when Asian delegates created similar reversals by appealing to America to legitimate their revolutionary religious aspirations and to gain its imprimatur for their philosophies, religions, and Gods.

All America looked to Chicago with great anticipation and high expectations for the Columbian Fourth, and the Committee on Ceremonials went to great lengths to see nothing was amiss. By order of Congress, John Paul Jones's flag, the original Stars and Stripes, flew in the White City. Flowers massed on the podium came from Thomas Jefferson's grave. Stonewall Jackson's sword lay at hand for a ceremonial salute. Cannons on barges in Lake Michigan sat ready to fire barrages during the singing of the "Star Spangled Banner" and the doxology. The Columbian Liberty Bell inscribed with the words of Jesus—"A New Commandment I Give Unto You, That You Love One Another"—rested undelivered in a forge in Troy, New York, but was set to toll there at the touch of an electric switch on the dais. The roster of officials included John Henry Barrows; Carter H. Harrison, the Mayor of Chicago; and Adlai E. Stevenson, Vice President of the United States.[24]

The Concessionaires Club made less grand, but equally fastidious, plans for Midway festivities. The Irish village planned to open its celebration with the performance of jigs. German and American music filled a day-long program for the beer halls in the German Village. The Javanese Village was hung with bunting and its residents had been instructed to dress in red, white, and blue. Wallis Islanders had trained for several weeks to perform their dances while singing "America" in Samoan, and in the China exhibit, "God-in-Heaven" was rewritten to include Chinese actors dressed as Washington, Jefferson, and Hancock, who were to perform clog dances while holding the Declaration of Independence transcribed into Chinese script. Animal trainers at Hagenbeck's Menagerie planned to carry the Stars and Stripes with them into the wild animal cages. One journalist, anticipating a splendid Midway Fourth, reported that all the arrangements followed "rules that had been in force since the days of Washington and Jefferson." At a noon flag-raising, he noted, "Buddhists, Muslims, and heathen will join Christians in raising a shout just at this stage of the proceedings."[25]

It was at eight minutes past noon on the Fourth that a Civil War veteran raised the flag on the parade ground on the Midway before a crowd of 25,000, to music played by the Iowa State Marching Band. One journalist reported that "strange faces and strange costumes were there; there were Mohammedans, Buddhist, and Jews; there were people whose fathers were cannibals; there were Laplanders and South Sea Islanders, all gathered . . . to do honor to the flag which stands for freedom and a Christian nation." J. R. Burton, an Exposition Commissioner from Kansas, delivered a typically expansive address that ranged from the philosophers of ancient Greece to the heroes of Concord and Lexington. "From the isles of the sea and the most remote corners of the earth," he exclaimed, "comes every tongue, and with joyous shout salute our flag—the Nation's ensign and the emblem of humanity." Old Glory floated out on a gentle south wind, the reporter noted, "over a motlier gathering of people than ever assembled in the history of this country to do honor to the glorious Fourth of July."[26]

But, through an oversight of the Committee on Ceremonials, no Protestant minister had been scheduled for the Midway service. As a result, an *imam* from the Saint Sophia mosque on Cairo Street, Jamal Effendi, officiated. The *Chicago Tribune* reported that Effendi "was attired in the full ceremonials of priesthood, a dark blue robe embroidered in gold bullion, and as he turned his face toward the East and raised his hands in supplication, a silence fell upon the crowd. He began chanting a prayer to Allah for his blessing on the United States, the flag above him, and the Exposition in Chicago. At every break in his prayer the Mohammeddans united in a loud amen in old fashioned Methodist style." Following Effendi's prayer, the Cairo Street men led a rousing cheer for the United States.

The next day the *Tribune* was uncertain what to make of it all. It had been disconcerting to see "half-naked Soudanese, long-gowned Arabs, Chinamen, and Turks" participate in a quintessentially American ceremony. It was "rather funny too" to see an *imam* petition Allah for a blessing on a Christian nation. It seemed to the reporter that all these people had participated in an event they did not understand, even though they seemed "as patriotic and loyal in their cheering for all that as people who were born under the Stars and Stripes." All in all, the Midway Fourth had been a great celebration, "patriotic and beautiful," he reported, but at the same time "grotesque."

The grotesque spectacle of Asians celebrating July Fourth and of an *imam* calling on Allah to bless America stemmed from the fact that Effendi and the others had included themselves in the Columbian community of sentiment without official sanction, creating in the process a fundamental reversal of meaning by claiming for the Columbian myth a theological legitimation drawn from alien territory. Such a breach of theological protocol threatened to undermine the taxonomic logic implied by the contrast between White City and Midway and to imply further that other religions and their Gods might be introduced into a myth about America, which would require a dismantling of the Columbian myth itself, suggesting in turn alternative meanings of the nation and its destiny.

But this July Fourth reversal negotiated by Effendi and his companions was easily dismissed as an anomaly, and by nightfall, a glorious, if more predictable, Fourth was celebrated in the White City. Headlines in the *Chicago Tribune* on the fifth told the story.

ITS CLIMAX AT NIGHT
Fitting Culmination of a Celebration Unparalleled.
TOLD IN LIVING FLAME
WITNESSED BY MULTITUDES
SCENE IS BEYOND IMAGINATION

Over the course of the day, the *Tribune* reported, an estimated 200,000 people poured into the White City "to spend an hour within the gates of paradise." 50,000 people jammed the lake front. 10,000 packed the Casino pier. Thousands more reclined on the lawns and promenades in the White City. Hundreds of yachts and launches rode at anchor in the lake, while invited guests gathered atop the Peristyle in the shadow of the triumphant Columbus. As darkness fell, people awaited firework displays, while orchestras and choruses on floating barges led the crowd in song—"America the Beautiful," "Home Sweet Home," "Nearer My God to Thee." Arc lamps swept the throng, lighting now on battleships anchored in Lake Michigan, "now upon the palaces of that vision that Chicago made real."

At the climax of the evening's ceremonies "the lights of nature were turned off and the grandest spectacle earth ever saw was full upon the stage." Amid roving search lights and cannon fire, a monumental portrait of George Washington burst into flame emblazoned with the motto, "First in War, First in Peace, First in the Hearts of his Countrymen." Then, while rockets and bombs were fired off the roof of the Palace of Manufactures, the Great Seal of the United States illumined the night sky. Finally, as the crowd cheered and "the sky was filled with golden hail," Old Glory unfolded from an aerial balloon floating 3000 feet above the White City, with every star and stripe ablaze. "A shrill triumphant shout beat up against the sky," the *Tribune* recalled the next morning, "as must have taught the listening nations in the White City what it means to live under the flag of universal freedom." All in all, the White City Fourth had been "a night for Titans."

The Magic of the White City

Out of wild scrub and dunes on the shores of Lake Michigan, the architects and builders of the Exposition created a transient sacred space that revealed America's image of itself and of the world. The rhetoric used to extol the White City and the ceremonies performed within its precincts proclaimed the nation to be the scion of ancient republics, the vehicle for actualizing the millennial dream, and the agent of universal history. For many, the experience of standing in the White City must have been akin to what Eliade called the periodic reactualization of mythic time, when one lives again in the divine presence.[27]

In *Harper's Weekly*, journalist Richard Harding Davis likened the White City to Venus rising again from the waters of Lake Michigan. He confessed that he was unable to convey adequately in words its ineffable wonder. All he hoped to do was "to give his 'testimony' as the awakened one does at a revival meeting, in the hope it may turn some brother in the right direction."[28]

Richard Watson Gilder, in his poem "The Vanishing City," praised the spiritual quickening the Exposition provoked in people, and he sought to fix its transient splendor in an eternal reverie.

Enraptured memory, and all ye powers of being
        To new life awaken! Stamp the vision clear
On the soul's inmost substance.

The vision that so enraptured Gilder was the White City.

So shall these domes that meet the heaven's
curved blue,
And yon long, white imperial colonnade,
And many-columned peristyle, endue
The mind with beauty that shall never fade.[29]

Charles Mulford Robinson wrote that when an individual first entered the White City his "faculties were all alert; he forgot himself or felt the limits of his own personality slipping away, extending widely, boundlessly, until the whole scene was in his own soul." How little seemed the figure of man, he recalled, but how "far reached and soared his divinity." At night, the flood lights that played upon the palaces, lighting first upon the triumphant Columbus, then upon a monumental caryatid or Columbia's antique barge, "made silvern paths as bright and as straight as Jacob's ladder; the white stream flowed towards heaven until it seemed the holy light from the rapt gaze of a saint, or Faith's white, pointing figure." When one gazed upon the Peristyle, with its tributes to liberty, religious freedom, and Christian truth, Robinson testified that "all one's Americanism surged over him . . . with a patriotism, half love, half pride."[30]

The White City was an unforgettable ensemble of American patriotism, classical beauty, and Christian faith, but it was also a modern technological wonder, the power of which superseded the dreams and visions of all other civilizations in world history. Powerful talismans of the fabled East, like the genie of Aladdin's lamp, J. W. Buel wrote in his *Magic City*, have long since ceased to roam the world. Yet here was proof that there were still real magicians whose work rivaled "the proudest conceptions of imaginary demons with realities as splendid as ever oriental fancy painted." The nineteenth century was not an age of miracles, but one of works in which "the powers of human genius transcend the beauty and opulence of Arabic dreams." Chicago's Exposition, with its many exhibits of races and peoples from equatorial regions and hyperborean climes, was an object lesson in intellectual advancement, possessing a moral of infinite value to all the world's peoples—"the blessings of Christian civilization, and the loving direction and kindness of God."[31]

The Exposition was a ideological landscape replete with signs, all of which worked to confirm the universality of the Columbian myth. The American flag stood for the nation, but as Burton noted on the Midway Fourth, it was "the emblem of humanity." The Stars and Stripes meant both "universal freedom" and "Christian nation." The inclusion and subordination of other people in the Columbian community of sentiment played a critical role in creating the mystique of the White City. Without them, the Exposition would have been little more than an in-group celebration by the imperial nations of the West at a trade fair hosted by a young comer eager to break into front rank. With them, the Exposition became an image of the world that suggested to many Americans how truly liberal, progressive, and enlightened they had become. Dazzled by their accomplishments and charmed by their own magic, most Americans were not prepared to experience the East/West encounter at the Parliament in world-historical time, but in the forward-driving realm of the Columbian myth.

Few observers in the mainstream seemed to care about the parochial foundations of the White City discourse about America and the world or to notice that its signs were subject to variabilities, reversals, and alternative meanings. African-Americans, Christian or not, had been radically marginalized, more or less barred from the community. Mainstream Jews and Catholics merely fine-tuned the dominant discourse and tinkered with the officially sanctioned theology to suit their own needs. Asians at the Parliament, however, presented a challenge of a wholly different order and, the ethnic, racial, cultural, and religious implications of the evolutionary hypothesis and the back-handedness of Columbian inclusivity not withstanding, it was Jamal Effendi who pointed the way.

II.

AN INGATHERING
OF NATIONS AND TRIBES

3

CHICAGO'S PENTECOST

This day the sun of a new era of religious peace and progress
rises over the world, dispelling the dark clouds of sectarian
strife. This day a new flower blooms in the gardens of religious thought, filling the air with its exquisite perfume. This
day a new fraternity is born into the world of religious progress, to aid the upbuilding of the kingdom of God in the
hearts of men.

—Charles Carroll Bonney, Welcome to the Parliament

ON THE MORNING of 11 September 1893, the Columbian Liberty Bell,
only recently installed in the White City, tolled ten times in honor of
what many considered the ten great religions of the world—Confucianism, Taoism, Shintoism, Hinduism, Buddhism, Jainism, Zoroastrianism, Judaism, Christianity, and Islam. At the same time, seven
miles uptown in the Memorial Art Palace (today the Chicago Art Institute), more than sixty religious leaders from around the globe stood
together on a single platform in the Hall of Columbus to convene the
World's Parliament of Religions.

In a fundamental way, the Parliament was another Exposition showcase, albeit one intended to be uniquely sublime. It was designed to
display the universal and transcendent truth to be found in religion, or
perhaps in only one religion, one religious tradition, or, ultimately, in
the value system of one ethnic group: distinctions frequently glossed
over due to the nature of the assembly's goals and design. The Parliament also functioned, like other Columbian spectacles, to elicit the
emotions and sentiments of Americans and to rally them both to the
Columbian myth and to a sense of community. Its organizers conceived of the Parliament as a formal event, with carefully selected delegates presenting papers on particular themes on designated days. But,
in the press of the moment, when some speakers arrived late and others

unexpectedly, and as issues arose that its organizers had not anticipated, it took on an unpredictable life of its own. Charismatic and controversial figures emerged from the pack, becoming familiar to and
popular with the audience, and as events unfolded, the assembly was
followed closely by Chicago's daily press.

In its most exalted reaches, the Parliament was a liberal quest for
world religious unity, whose goal was to forge a common religious discourse or a common community of sentiment for what was widely
perceived to be an emerging global society. The Exposition's vision of
a common humanity created a dramatic but ambiguous *mise-en-scène*
for the proceedings. On one hand, the inequities intrinsic to the Columbian world-picture reflected not simply an American civil myth,
but long-standing, deeply-ingrained western assumptions about the
relative worth of West and East that had concrete ramifications both in
the intellectual realm and in geopolitical history. On the other hand,
the tenor of the Columbiad was so grandiose and so deeply infused
with millennial aspiration that it served to encourage the hope in
many quarters that the Parliament's audacious undertaking might actually succeed.

It failed for a number of reasons—naiveté, ethnocentrism, racism,
and flawed theological premises, among other things. At the outset,
however, it is important to note that part of its failure rests with the
fact that delegates had different ideas of what ends could be achieved
by participating at the Parliament and that the East/West encounter,
however important to the assembly, was not at the center of most concerns, but nearer the periphery. For the Roman Catholic delegation, the
Parliament was an unprecedented opportunity to fulfill a long-standing desire to gain a wider hearing in the Protestant-dominated American mainstream.[1] To this end, eighteen Catholic men, forming the largest delegation after the Protestant delegation, spoke on ecclesiastical,
theological, and scriptural issues and on a range of domestic concerns
including education, race, marriage, science, social reform, and the
civilizing role of the Christian church in American society and history.
The most prominent figures in the Catholic delegation were progressive "Americanists," and the entire delegation reflected only a narrow
ethnic range, primarily Irish, of the Catholic nationalities in the
United States. Three papers dealt directly with world religious unity
and the religions of the East. Like their Catholic counterparts, the Jews
also had predetermined expectations of what they hoped to accomplish

at the Parliament. Composed of distinguished leaders, both men and women, the Jewish delegation's main concern was to underscore their inclusion in the mainstream community by emphasizing the contributions of Judaism to western religion and theology, Jewish views on social issues, and Jewish/Christian relations. Three of their papers mentioned East/West issues, but only in oblique, highly generalized, or idealized ways. The two official African-American delegates limited their comments to race issues in American society and made little direct contribution to forging a common discourse for a global society, which is of no great surprise, given their marginal status in the entire cycle of Columbian ceremonies.

The Parliament was widely praised for its impressive delegation of women, twenty-three of whom spoke on a wide range of subjects including suffrage, crime, Judaism, women in India, American ideals, ecumenism, and race. Papers on the relations between the sexes and marriage outlined liberal, Swedenborgian, and evangelical perspectives on the question. Several women brought moderate forms of nineteenth-century feminist criticism to bear on theological concerns, while two others spoke on the role of women in the pulpit and in scripture. Most female delegates hailed from the liberal end of the Protestant spectrum, and in keeping with the tenor of the Columbiad, they tended to advocate liberal theologies, but only three addressed East/West questions with any specificity.[2]

The Protestant delegation was large and comprehensive but primarily Anglo-American, with conservatives, evangelicals, and liberals of many different types. So overwhelming was their presence that one alarmed commentator later observed that, due to the diversity of Protestant points of view expressed on the Parliament floor, there seemed to be little coherence to the tradition as a whole. But, reflecting their status as the custodians of American culture and de facto hosts, Protestants more consistently than others addressed questions about world mission, religious unity, and the basis for a common religious discourse for a single global community. But even so, the East and Asian religions often entered into the Protestant discourse as after-thoughts, foils, or illustrations of more general statements being made about universal truth and the transcendence of religion.

However, in this account of the Parliament, the Asians and their religions are placed at center stage, which demands that attention be paid to where they were located, as signs in western theological discourse, and to what was said about them in metaphor and by implication, as well as in more direct forms of address. As a result, the Exposition and the White City discourse about mainstream America and the world, with its patriotic, classical, and Christian signs and its secondary signs for subordinate, less evolved peoples, can serve as a broad ideological landscape against which the East/West encounter can be read.[3] This provides what Victor Turner called a cultural "field," which structured the East/West debate. The Hall of Columbus was the "arena" in which a contest over the content of this discourse and its theological sanction was played out. The Parliament was a "social drama" between delegates from the East and West who, as partisan players who were leading factions and carrying banners for constituencies, attempted to forge a common religious discourse, while they vied with one another for the outcome of the assembly.[4]

Parliamentary Ground Rules

The institutional, ideological, and financial link between the Exposition and the Parliament was a mediating organization called the World's Congress Auxiliary. Charles Bonney proposed the establishment of the Auxiliary in September of 1889, the idea being that "something higher and nobler" than the Exposition was "demanded by the enlightened and progressive spirit of the age."[5] In October, a committee of Chicago businessmen, clerics, and educators issued a plan for a convention global in scope, the leading idea of which was grand: to "surpass all previous efforts to bring about a real fraternity of nations, and unite the enlightened people of the whole earth in a general cooperation for the attainment of the great ends for which human society is organized." Some topics under consideration for discussion were suggestive and ambitious, but vague, such as "the grounds of fraternal union in the language, literature, [and] domestic life . . . of different people." Others were more practical and concrete—questions of international copyright law and a common language for commerce, for instance—even while they advanced the general Columbian themes of globalization, fraternalism, and unity.[6]

Under Bonney's direction, the Auxiliary grew to comprise twenty different departments, whose conventions were convened throughout the summer. To house them, the city of Chicago, the Chicago Art Institute, and the Exposition Corporation constructed the Memorial Art

Palace downtown at the cost of $600,000. The Auxiliary's administrative expenses were estimated at another $100,000, and 15,000 people acted as advisors on its committees. The Committee on Foreign Relations in the Senate and the consular offices of the State Department lent their aid in overseas recruitment, and eventually, 1,000,000 circulars were sent out in search of delegates. 5,974 writers and speakers served as delegates, whose papers, Bonney estimated, would have filled fifty octavo volumes of 600 pages each.[7] The Auxiliary sponsored 200 different conventions that drew an estimated 700,000 people in the course of the summer. Of them all, the conventions of the Department of Religion, the Parliament in particular, drew the most attention, the most applause, and the best press.[8]

Bonney chose John Henry Barrows, minister of Chicago's prestigious First Presbyterian Church, to be the chair of the Department of Religion. He headed a local committee consisting of P. A. Feehan, Chicago's Roman Catholic archbishop; Emil Hirsch; and fourteen Protestant ministers from as many denominations. Jenkin Lloyd Jones, a liberal Chicago Unitarian, was named Executive Secretary. Eventually some forty denominations and organizations, such as the World's Evangelical Alliance and the Free Religious Association, together with special interest groups, such as Jewish women and black Catholics, held meetings under its auspices.[9] In the midst of these, the Parliament was scheduled to be "a series of Union Meetings."[10]

The Department of Religion worked for three years with a board of advisors to clarify the Parliament's mission, in the course of which they articulated in various ways its officially-sanctioned theological rules of play. In an early report inspired by Bonney and distributed internationally, the Department set as the Parliament's goal the public expression of a common unity presumed to exist among the religions of the world. It defined the assembly's goal as seeking "to unite all Religion against irreligion" on the basis of the golden rule and to present "the substantial unity of the many religions in the good deeds of the religious life." It was to be a forum in which the religions of the world could set forth "their common aims and common grounds of union." This statement rested, however, on distinctly Judeo-Christian theological ground. Delegates were asked to consider the "evidences of the existence of God," the "evils that are to be shunned as sins against God," and the "moral law" that is the "will of the Creator." Protestant denominational concerns, a drive toward unity, and an eagerness to press toward a Judeo-Christian, public religion consensus were conspicuous. The Parliamentary ground rules would be such that "the Christian, believing in the Supreme Divinity of Christ, may so unite with the Jew who devoutly believes in the Jehovah of Israel; the Quaker with the High Church Episcopalian; the Catholic with the Methodist; the Baptist with the Unitarian; etc."[11]

Just over a year before the assembly convened, however, the committee shifted gears on two issues, the first being the goal of unity. The revised mission statement redefined the Parliament as merely seeking to set forth "an accurate and authoritative account of the present condition and outlook of Religion among the leading nations of the world." It would be "a grand international assembly for mutual conference, fellowship, and information" that sought "to promote and deepen the spirit of human brotherhood among religious men of diverse faiths . . . while not striving to achieve formal and outward unity." The report also attempted to broaden the theological ground rules by instructing delegates to consider only the "impregnable foundations of Theism."

These shifts, however, neither squelched the universalism that informed many aspects of the Columbiad nor dampened the sense of expectation aroused by the proceedings. In the second report, Barrows wrote that "it is our expectation that the Parliament of Religions will be the most important, commanding, and influential, as surely it will be the most phenomenal fact of the Columbian Exposition." He promised it would be "so noteworthy as to make an epoch in history, and be prophetic of that unity of nations which the English laureate [Tennyson] foresaw in singing of a coming golden age: 'When the war-drums throb no longer, / and the battle-flags are furled, / In the Parliament of man, / the Federation of the World.'"[12]

In the end, the theological ground rules of the Parliament were as flexible as those which sanctioned the Columbian myth and White City. The content of this officially-sanctioned theism, its liberal sentiments, and the classical, Christian, and patriotic signs that served as its foundation are revealed in two untitled illustrations in the March, 1893 issue of the *Cosmopolitan*. They framed an article, "The Great Congress at the World's Fair," by Ellen Henrotin, the influential vice president of the Women's Branch of the World's Congress Auxiliary.[13]

The first is a theological model for religious unity and can be considered the "denominational" foundation for the Parliament quest for world religious unity. In the background of the design, the White City stretches into the distance, a symbol of the highest achievement of western, or as many would have confidently said a century ago, human civilization. In the midground, there is a Roman fasces whose bundled sticks each represent a church: Episcopal, Reformed, Swedenborgian, Methodist, Quaker, Catholic, Baptist, Unitarian, Presbyterian, Universalist, Congregational, and, finally, with an awkwardness revealing the somewhat unstable nature of the theological situation, "Synagogue." The fasces is labeled with the ideals of the liberal movement in theology then on the rise in the Protestant mainstream, "Fatherhood of God" and "Brotherhood of Man," and the entire bundle is tied with a cord drawn tight by two muscled arms emerging from clouds of incense rising from braziers. Bearing a shield emblazoned with the legend "Equal Rights for All Men," the fasces is flanked by a Salvation Army sister and a Catholic nun and stands behind an American eagle that grasps in its beak a serpent labeled "Intolerance."

The second illustration represents in a more general way the liberal vision of a God and spirit-infused civilization. In this design, another arm emerges from swirling clouds of chaos to hold aloft a scepter, at the base of which is a cross inscribed with the word "Inspiration." Near the top, three orbs are labeled "Religion," "Research," and "Science." The scepter is topped by a glowing electric bulb, the light of which sheds its rays back upon the clouds and, in doing so, dispels the bats and owls of chaos, ignorance, and superstition.

These illustrations give a comprehensive picture of the Parliamentary rules of play—the confident superiority of the West; its united "churches"; a generally inclusive but patriarchal theology; the inspiration of the cross; and the enlightening of the world through science and technology, tolerance, and egalitarian fraternalism. This nexus of values served as the foundation for an attempt to forge a common religious discourse, and it set the pace for a contest between East and West on the Parliament floor. According to these ground rules, the Asians and their religions could only operate as secondary, subordinate signs in a global discourse. They were the Parliament's underdogs in the very nature of things, according to the rules of fair play.

Unity, Diversity, and New Dawn

In the light of subsequent events, it is clear that the organizers of the Parliament did not foresee the deeper complexities in their undertaking. Delegates presented some 216 papers in which they advocated a wide variety of theologies, philosophies, creeds, and religions and explored the relationship between religion and music, literature, ethics, morality, ritual, history, and art. Sixteen papers expressed the concerns of Buddhists, thirteen those of Hindus, eleven those of Jews. Confucians, Taoists, Shintoists, Jains, Muslims, and Zoroastrians all gained a voice at the Parliament. The assembly's internationalism was impressive, reflecting the concerns of those in seventeen nations. Eighteen papers came from the Indian subcontinent, seventeen from Japan, sixteen from England, and five from France. Armenians, Belgians, Canadians, Germans, Greeks, Russians, Swiss, Syrians, Thais, and Turks all spoke before the assembly.[14]

The event also reflected the growing complexity of the domestic scene, as is suggested by a breakdown of participants based on Robert Baird's well-known distinction between "evangelical" and "nonevangelical" forces in the antebellum religious mainstream.[15] Parliamentary Protestants whom Baird would have dismissed as "nonevangelical"—Unitarians, freethinking liberals and naturalists, Swedenborgians, Quakers, Shakers, and other sectarians—numbered about fifty. Christians whom he deemed to be "nonevangelical," such as Catholics, Armenians, and Orthodox, numbered twenty-seven. There were eleven Jewish delegates. The largest non-Christian Asian delegation was that of the Buddhists with twelve, and the Hindus were next with eight. Others brought the total for the Asian delegation to thirty. Thus, "nonevangelicals" at the Parliament totaled about 118, or 61 percent of the assembly.

Amid this diversity, the challenge set before the delegates was to forge a common religious discourse for both America and the world. But, with global and domestic philosophical, theological, social, and religious issues being aired simultaneously, it was difficult to maintain a focus for the proceedings. The mission statements of the Department, moreover, set a call for authoritative accounts of the world's religions against a search for a common ground for unity. However, no single account could be made of any one religion. Every effort to articulate common ground only pointed to the fact that the unity in question—Anglo-American, American, Protestant, Christian, Judeo-Christian, or world unity—could vary and that the ground under discussion—ethical, moral, spiritual, theological, or humanistic—was constantly shifting. This plurivocalism was muted to a degree by the transcendental cast of the Parliament's ground rules, which meant that delegates' particular concerns tended to be expressed in terms of common and broadly universal themes. But, this created another problem insofar as God, who was recognized by most parties as the authoritative ground for any common religious discourse, was said to be revealed through history, culture, and science; morality, ethics, and inspiration; the Bible, the Quran, the Vedas, and the grace bestowed by the guru. Taken as a whole, the proceedings displayed an elliptical quality, with visions of unity and claims of uniqueness alternately seizing the spotlight, and while the assembly elicited emotions from a great many people, it ultimately worked to rally them to different communities. As the drama unfolded, the Parliament's overall significance remained ambiguously—some would later say dangerously—protean and obscure.

But the confident optimism of the White City discourse and Columbian myth proved to be fertile ground for the production of ingenious ways to reconcile unity and diversity. One such expression was popular American idealism. Only two days into the Parliament, a front-page headline in the *Chicago Tribune* expressed sentiments that would be reiterated time and again with reference to the Parliament.[16]

MEN OF ALL FAITHS
TRIUMPH OF LIBERALISM

Earlier in the week, the same newspaper praised the spectacle of races and creeds standing together "under a common banner of hope." People from the four corners of the earth had come to advance the cause of a common humanity "here and hereafter" and to demonstrate the "vital power of that universal spirit which drives men everywhere to look upward at a star." The World's Columbian Exposition had found its ultimate fulfillment in a "peaceful gathering of the warring creeds.[17]

Another, more magisterial, expression was the mysticism of Bonney, the reigning spirit behind the assembly. Bonney framed his expectations for the Parliament in what Diana Eck called " 'new dawn' rhetoric,"[18] which was infused with the liberal spirit and millennial hope that was the Columbiad's stock in trade. His faith rested on the gospel of John and the "true light which lighteth every man that cometh into the world," a text he interpreted in Swedenborgian terms to mean a universal "influx" into the human mind from God, which prompts people to worship and which must be obeyed. For him, this did not mean that all religions were of equal worth or that anyone should yield one's convictions, but it did mean that religious unity could be established only if people acknowledged and respected differences. Bonney expressed his convictions frankly before the Jewish Congress in August. "We know that you are Jews, while we are Christians and would have all men so." He then tempered this statement of his convictions with an affirmation of the American ideal of religious freedom as the most precious of all liberties, which he linked to the golden rule. "My Master has commanded me that whatsoever I would have another do to me, I should also do to him. What, therefore, I ask for myself as a Christian, I must give to you as a Jew." In this way, we "will more and more make the whole world one in brotherhood and service, and finally in one religious faith."[19]

Still other expressions came from Jenkin Lloyd Jones and Barrows, Bonney's two colleagues in the Department of Religion, who cut the issue of diversity and unity in different ways, implying new dawns for very different days. Jones was a liberal theist, but one convinced that the key to religious unity was not theology, but the ethical and spiritual aspirations natural in and common to all people. After the Parliament, he took issue with what he thought to be a doctrinal bias in Barrows's record of the event; Jones claimed that Barrows had given the Parliament a "Christo-centric" cast, while its entire spirit had been "homocentric." Not the supernatural Christ, he wrote, "but the natural soul of man was the center around which the Parliament moved." It had both "unsexed" and "unsected" the human soul. Jones published his own collection of Parliament addresses, which he heavily edited in order to bring out the common aspirations and theological themes expressed by delegates from different religions. For him, the Parliament's opening day was a revelation of the oneness of humanity, the harmony of all the world's prophets, and "the mysterious in the infinite, the thought of God." On its closing day, people had passed into "Pentecostal heights from which they understood the message that seemed to be spoken by many and divers faiths." The Parliament was a "millennial milestone."[20]

Barrows was a liberal Presbyterian who advocated the reinterpretation of traditional Protestant creeds in the light of modern knowledge, but he remained convinced of the necessity of salvation through conversion. He worked to implement the guidelines of the Department of Religion, but understood them to point to what he later called the "conquest" of Asia by Christ. In July of 1892, before 16,000 members of the Christian Endeavor Society in Madison Square Garden, he praised the White City as "an immense opportunity" for tent preaching and open-air revivals to display to the world "the splendid vitality and vigor of the missionary spirit which is the greatest feature of the grandest century since Jesus commissioned his disciples to evangelize the world."[21] In Carnegie Hall the same summer, he revealed his expectation that the Parliament would be an opportunity to know the "heathen mind" better in order to more readily "supplant" their religions with Christianity.[22] When he published his record of the assembly, he made his own understanding of its significance absolutely clear. Having transformed the many-hued rainbow of the religions of the world "back into the white light of heavenly truth," the Parliament "ended at Calvary."[23]

Delegates from the West

New dawn rhetoric was also conspicuous on the floor, as delegates from the West laid out their contributions to a common religious discourse. For many, Christian unity was of primary concern and the spectacle of representatives from the long-divided religion suggested the dawn of a new day for Christianity. Evangelical church historian Leonard Bacon later wrote that "since those seventeen wonderful September days of 1893," the sky had been "red with promise" for the reunification of Protestantism with the Roman church,[24] and octogenarian Philip Schaff, a widely respected evangelical, provided a template for church unity on the floor. Evoking the idea of an "invisible church" only outwardly rent by schisms, he praised Unitarians, Universalists, and others "who are accounted heretics" for their many contributions to Christianity. Acknowledging that only the Greek or Roman church could provide Christendom with a center of unity, he asked Pope Leo XIII to "infallibly declare his own fallibility in all matters outside his communion" and to invite Greeks and Protestants to a council of reconciliation with Rome in the city of Jerusalem.[25]

Schaff and many other western delegates did not directly address issues involved in the East/West encounter, but those who did ran the gamut of theological positions officially sanctioned by the Parliament's ground rules, more often than not, with little overt references to race and ethnicity.

Protestant conservatives tended toward theological and religious exclusivism.[26] For them, Asian religions had nothing to contribute to a common religious discourse, and the hope for a global community of religious sentiment necessarily rested on the conversion of the world to evangelical Christianity. Their powerful rhetorical strategies and compelling metaphoric language played an important role in the East/West encounter, by sharply cutting the issues and eliciting strong emotions that lent drama to the assembly. Chautauquan William Wilkinson asserted that Christianity preached mercy toward people in a "false religion" but insisted that its attitude toward the religion itself was "universal, absolute, eternal, unappeasable hostility." James Dennis, historian of Protestant missions, asserted that Christianity is not intolerant of "cultured heathenism," but it is "uncompromising because it is true." It was the "steel hand of truth" in the "velvet glove of love." Boston's Joseph Cook evoked the image of the bloody hand of Lady Macbeth asking, "I turn to Mohammedanism. Can you wash our red, right hand? I turn to Confucianism and Buddhism and Brahmanism. Can you wash our red, right hand?"[27]

Catching the attention of the *Daily Inter-Ocean*, George Pentecost homologized Asians to the ancient pagans over whom Christianity had triumphed in antiquity.[28]

TAKES UP THE CUDGEL
HINDOOISM AS IT IS
He Paints Its Abominations in
Strong Language

Pentecost called Christianity "a fighting religion" that brandished the sword of spirit and stood ready to conquer the world. "Where were the religions of Greece and Rome with their Pantheon of gods? . . . Like Dagon before the Ark they have fallen before the cross of Christ." Christianity is the *"only possible universal religion."*[29]

Far more typically, western delegates took a more moderate theological position that nicely dovetailed with the inclusivist world picture of the Exposition. In this inclusivist position, all the world's religions were considered to be good in their own way, but found their ultimate fulfillment in Christianity.[30]

Roman Catholic Bishop John Keane, the liberal rector of Catholic University in Washington D.C., presented a Catholic form of inclusivism based on a sweeping theological interpretation of history and the idea of a primitive revelation given in the past when "man was taught of the Divine by the Divine." Keane argued that since the time of the "golden age," and through all the wandering of the nations and tribes, ideas about God, a fallen race, and a redeemer had been retained in all religions in the garbled form of legend and myth. He also argued that the stream of ancient revelation had long ago split in central Asia; it was to the East where the tribes had gone astray. As a result, Asian theology degenerated into the "mystic gloom" of "emanationism," and life in the East came to be seen as a tedious struggle that "metempsychosis dragged out pitifully." In Asian theology, the idea of a redeemer suggested one who recognized more clearly than others that life was a curse to struggle with and could guide others to escape from it. In the West, however, primitive revelation had flowered into true philosophy and religion. The Hebrew patriarchs and prophets, Greek sages, and Roman sibyls all had pointed toward the God-man Christ, in whom the Infinite Author and his finite creatures had been finally and uniquely linked as one. Climaxing in a blaze of proof-texts, Keane concluded with a plea to the Asians: "Come to the fullness."[31] John Gmeiner, a priest from Minneapolis, argued in more or less the same way, concluding: Beyond "mists and clouds of prejudices, ignorances and antipathies, there will be always more clearly seen the heavenly, majestic outlines of that house of God, prepared on the top of the mountain for all to see, into which, as Isaiah foretold, 'all nations shall flow' . . . —the Holy Catholic Church."[32]

For Protestant delegates in the liberal movement, inclusivism, which gained expression in a wide variety of ways, was the strategy of choice for dealing with the Asians. Lyman Abbott, an American leader of the movement, argued a position that could be called moral inclusivism. "We recognize the voice of God in all prophets and in all times," he noted, but stated with equal force his own conviction that "no other revelation transcends and none other equals that which was made to man in the one transcendent human life that was lived eighteen centuries ago in Palestine." God's love in Christ was the most complete revelation of the moral refulgence, implying that the gospel of love was the surest ground for union. Charles Briggs, a leading authority on scripture, linked inclusivism to scriptural concerns and Protestant Biblicism. Calling the New Testament a "full revelation," he pointed to the "incompleteness" of the Hebrew Bible to underscore the way in which Christianity revealed the "gradualness" of divine truth. Christian scripture contained wisdom to guide men "in every stage of religious advancement"—the "dark-minded African," "dull Islander," and "subtile Asiatic." For the Christian, the sun dawned in the Pentateuch, rose in the Psalms, and reached its zenith in the gospel of Jesus, while the sacred texts of other religions were but "torches of varying sizes and brilliancy lighting up the darkness of the night."[33]

Comparative philosophy and theology formed the basis of the inclusivism of James Lee, an Episcopalian from St. Louis. There was too much God in the religious philosophies of India, he argued, and too little God both in the ancient philosophies of China and in the modern, naturalistic philosophies of Spenser and Kant. But, Christian theology got it just right. "In God as Father the idea of transcendence is met," he observed, "and thus we have the truth of monotheism." In Jesus Christ as God the son, "the idea of an indwelling God is met, and we have the truth of polytheism." In the Holy Spirit, "the idea of God pervading the world is matched, and we have the truth of pantheism." "The whole movement of God looks to the organization of the human race in Jesus Christ, the reason, the Logos, the plan, and the ideal framework of the universe."[34]

Many Protestant liberals based their inclusivist views on the evolutionary model. Henry Drummond of Great Britain noted how the evolutionary perspective had "swept over" the old creedal propositions of Christianity, leaving them "untouched except for the better." The old clockmaker God of eighteenth-century natural theology had been swept away; doctrines of the incarnation and revelation were now seen to apply to the whole order of nature, science, and history. Sin might soon come to be seen as a relic of the human past, he suggested, "the undestroyed residuum" of animals and savages. A. B. Bruce of Glasgow concurred, noting although man was the final product of a process that had begun with protozoa, it was not for savages that all creation had been in travail, but for "man the civilized, man the completely Christianized." William Martin, an American missionary in Peking, drew out one logical conclusion to be drawn from this perspective. In the era of the steamboat, telegraph, and electricity, Asian religions were simply out of date. Deeply indebted to China for silk, tea, and porcelain, America had a duty to export Christianity "to make her people partakers with ourselves in [its] blessings."[35]

The Jewish delegation, while chiefly preoccupied with other issues, addressed the Asian question either through an inclusivism based on liberal Reform theism or by way of rabbinic knowledge. Henry Mendes, a traditionalist from New York's Sephardic community, insisted that separatism must remain a hallmark of Jews, but he also noted that Judaism taught cooperation with the world's great faiths. Citing a rabbinic legend of the fall, he called each of the world's religions a brilliant gem that had once been set in the gates of Eden. "In God's own time, we shall, all of us, fit our fragments together and reconstruct the gates of Paradise." Kaufmann Kohler, a prominent leader of the Reform movement, developed his position on the parable of the rings in Gotthold Lessing's *Nathan the Wise*. A king once gave a ring to each of his three sons, who then quarreled over which of them possessed the one ring representing the father's true love. Like Lessing, Kohler directed his primary attention to the relations among Christianity, Judaism, and Islam. But, he also asked: "What, then, about the rest of the creeds, the great Parliament of Religions? . . . Either all the rings are genuine and have the magic power of love, or the father is himself a fraud."[36]

Emil Hirsch offered a stirring vision of a coming universal faith for all the world. He argued that Judaism, Buddhism, Islam, and Christianity had all transcended their original geographical boundaries to become universal religions, but that one day they all would be eclipsed by one yet greater, which was the destiny of the race. All creeds would then become outdated; character, conduct, and conscience would be "the keynote of the Gospel in the Church of Humanity Universal." Flaming tongues would descend once again as on Sinai, and all the sacred books of the world would be read in spirit, not in law. Hirsch concluded his address with the legend of Jacob's pillow in which all the stones of the desert formed one great rock, Beth El, the Gate of Heaven, on which Jacob rested his head. In like manner, all the religions of the world would one day become "the pillow of man, dreaming of God and beholding the ladder joining earth to heaven."[37]

A significant number of western delegates based their contributions to forging a common religious discourse on non-sectarian theism. In his address "The Sympathy of Religions," Unitarian Thomas Wentworth Higginson argued that enlightened theism was the only ground for world religious unity. For him, all religions—Protestant and Catholic, western and Asian—were doors that released people from superstition. The only true religion, he concluded, is "the Religion of Ages, Natural Religion." In the end, "all will come out at last upon the broad ground of God's providing, which bears no man's name." Paul Carus, a scientific naturalist, argued that science was forcing all religious mythologies to give way to a higher stage of evolution. He admitted that the wreck of traditionalism had been traumatic, but science was now "a revelation of God." W. L. Tomlins, the director of Chicago's Apollo choir, discussed the pedagogy he used in choir school. He compared a child's personality to a bell; if one muffled a child's individuality, he or she could produce no music. But, a child could also learn that he or she was a child of God and discover a "governing center," which allowed him or her to sing more beautifully and more freely.[38]

The revered Julia Ward Howe, who followed William Wilkinson on the platform, contributed a dramatic moment to the proceedings, prompting the *Chicago Herald* to call her "a doughty and staunch fighter." When Wilkinson concluded, the audience "cheered and clapped by turns, while from the hands of women floated a sea of handkerchiefs," but when Howe took the floor, "an instant stillness permeated the vast hall. So quiet was it that one could hear chirping birds in the sunshine outside." The *Herald* reported that Howe began, noting, "'I can never agree with any person, no matter who, who enunciates such principles.'" She continued by saying that Christ's sacrifice was "not one of exclusion but of an infinite and endless and joyous inclusion."[39] But, she also warned delegates from what she called "the ethnic faiths," noting that magic is not religion but "mischievous irreligion, and I think this parliament should say, once for all, that the names of God and the names of His saints are not things to conjure with." The substance of Howe's address, however, was an appeal to all religions to aspire to the divine in the human, to human dignity, to equality among men and among the sexes. "From the parliament let some valorous, new, strong, and courageous influence go forth, and let us have here an agreement of all faiths for one good end, for one good thing—really for the glory of God . . . the salvation of humanity from all that is low and animal and unworthy and undivine."[40]

A few western delegates suggested alternatives to the officially sanctioned theology of the Parliament's ground rules. Daniel Offord recalled that Ann Lee, founder of the Shakers, preached the motherhood of God, and Marion Murdock, an ordained Protestant minister, pointed to recent innovations in language that allowed for the discussion of the "mother heart of Deity." Adolph Brodbeck, a German university professor, appealed to non-theistic transcendental idealism as "the new religion." We are not heathens, Jews, or Christians. We are not atheists, agnostics, deists, theists, or spiritualists, he declared. We "are called Idealists." Idealists strive "for the ideal of science and art, for the ideal of civilization, for the ideal of all virtues, for the ideal of family, community, society, and humanity in all forms."[41]

Chicago's Pentecost

The delegates from the West, even as they attempted to forge a common discourse and common community of sentiment, vied with one another over a variety of western theological issues, for the outcome of the assembly. But, standing together on the Parliament floor, outside the normal boundaries that hedged in and separated church from church and faith from faith, most of them were certain that God spoke through the first ingathering of nations and tribes in the world's long history, near the climax of its most marvelous century, even if they differed as to who he was and what precisely he (or she) was trying to say. Under the aegis of the spirit of the Columbiad, they could create dramatic, sweeping visions of future possibilities, which, despite their varied theological contents, suggested that the dawning of a new religious age was underway.

E. L. Rexford, a Christian Universalist from Massachusetts, captured one vision of the new dawn in his fourth-day address, "The Religious Intent." He called the White City a witness to the fact that God worked in human life, not through dogmas, creeds, books, and sacraments, but through the gradual and progressive revelation of universal natural law. As chemistry had emerged from alchemy and astronomy from astrology, so too the religions of the world were in the process of emerging from an era of separate infallibility into an era of evolutionary unity: "The very gods seem crowning all the doctrines of the past with the imperial dogma of the *Solidarity of the Race*." The Parliament was "the most significant hour in the history of the religious development of the race." It was a "larger Pentecost" in which a greater variety of people than of old are telling in their various language[s], custom[s], and achievement[s], of the wonderful works and ways of God. . . . Welcome in the great and all-inclusive name of God, the common Father of all souls."[42]

Rexford suggested that all the peoples of the world were in the process of returning to the primordial state of unity they had known before the fall. "God-Consciousness, to borrow a noble word from Calcutta" was the goal of all the great teachers of the world. "It is still before the nations. There in the distance—is it so great?—is the mountain of the Lord, rising before us into the serene and cloudless heaven. Let all the kingdoms and nations and religions of the world vie with each other in the rapidity of the divine ascent."[43]

An equally dramatic vision with a more distinctly Christian cast was offered when John Keane and Baptist George Dana Boardman brought the Parliament's business sessions to a close. Keane's address, "The Ultimate Religion," was a diplomatic plea for religious unity in which he never explicitly addressed the question of the authority of Rome, even as he directed his remarks to two distinct audiences—the "separated children of the Church of Christ" and the "long divided children of the family of Noah."[44]

For him, the Parliament was a "memory of sweetness" that recalled bonds of affection broken since the days of Babel. It also recalled the church's heroic Mediterranean past by exposing atheism, deism, agnosticism, naturalism, and "mere humanism" as nothing but ancient Epicureanism in nineteenth-century disguise. The Parliament had also shown conclusively that "the only worthy and admissible idea of God is that of monotheism"; polytheism was a "rude degeneration"; pantheism was "no religion at all." Keane also concluded with a plea for religious unity in the church as "a living organism, imparting the life of God to humanity." He praised its diversity—its "limbs innumerable," its "strong, majestic branches," its "individual twigs"—while he insisted at the same time that "the world's craving for unity can never be satisfied by mere aggregations and confederations of separated bodies." Loyalty to Jesus Christ the son of God must always come first, and the question must always be, "Is this the Vine, the Body, fashioned by the Saviour of the world? And if history shows that it is not, then to all the pleading of kith and kin the loyal Christian must exclaim as did the apostles of old: 'Whether we should obey man or obey God, judge ye.' "[45]

Finally, American Baptist George Dana Boardman took the floor, delivering the assembly's concluding new dawn vision. "ENVOYS EXTRAORDINARY AND MINISTERS PLENIPOTENTIARY IN THE KINGDOM OF GOD—MEN AND WOMEN—The hour for the closing of this most extraordinary convention has come." All honor to Chicago, he exclaimed, "whose beautiful White City suggestively symbolizes the architectural unity of the One City of our One God. All honor to this noble Chairman—this John the Beloved, whose surname is Barrows." For Boardman, the Parliament was the "Pentecostal day again." Dwellers from Mesopotamia, Asia, Pontus, Libya, and Crete, Jews, Arabs, and Greeks—"we do hear them speaking, every man in his own language, and yet as though in one common vernacular, [of] the wonderful works of God." The Parliament, the "crowning glory of earth's fairest Fair," fulfilled, moreover, Joel's prophecy of a day even more august than Pentecost: "I will pour forth of my Spirit on all flesh; and your sons and daughters shall prophesy, and your young men shall see visions, and your old men shall dream dreams."[46]

While Keane had developed the theme of the multiform organicity of the church of Christ, Boardman witnessed to the all-encompassing personality of Jesus as the Son of Man. "Jesus of Nazareth is the universal Homo," he proclaimed. He is the "essential Vir"; the "Son of human nature"; the "archetypal man"; the "ideal hero"; the "consummate incarnation"; the "symbol of perfected human nature"; the "sum total of unfolded, fulfilled humanity"; and "history's true Avatar." Jesus' inclusivistic and universalistic nature was the key to world theological unity, transcending considerations of geo-politics, race, and ethnicity: "See how he blends in himself all race marks. . . . See how he illustrates in himself all essential human capacities. . . . See how he absorbs and assimilates into his own perfect religion all that is good in all other religions."[47]

Boardman claimed that while all other religions were bound by geography, Christianity was the universal religion of all mankind. There was the "Hero religion of Greece," the "Institute religion of Palestine," the "Valhalla religion of Scandinavia," and the "Buddha religion of Burma," but the religion of Jesus alone had been transformed from a national religion into a religion of the universal man. "How majestically the Son of Abraham dilates into the Son of Man," he exclaimed. How heroically Paul carried out his Master's call "to become the founder, under the Son of Man, of a universal brotherhood and a cosmopolitan religion." Boardman allowed that Buddha was in many respects a very noble character; "no Buddhist can offer him a heartier reverence than myself." Yet, what had Buddhism done for the unification of humanity? Mohammed taught some noble truths, but his religion was "fragmental" and "antithetic." Jesus was "the one nexus of the nations," the "great vertebral column of the one body of mankind," and the "one majestic temple-body" of the race.[48]

Boardman concluded his address and closed the Parliament with a forecast for the future of the religions of the world, and he prophesied that the swinging pendulum of the ages drew the millennial hour near. "There, as on a great white throne, serenely sits the swordless King of the ages—himself both the Ancient and the Infant of Days—calmly abiding the centuries, mending the bruised reed, fanning the dying wick, sending forth righteousness unto victory. . . . There he sits, evermore drawing mankind nearer and nearer himself. . . . I see them dropping the spear, waving the olive-branch, arranging themselves in symmetric, shining, rapturous groups around the Divine Son of Man."[49]

4

ON MARS HILL

I believe the spirit of Paul is here, the zealous missionary of
Christ whose courtesy, wisdom and unbounded tact were
manifest when he preached Jesus and the resurrection beneath
the shadow of the Parthenon. I believe the spirit of the wise
and humane Buddha is here, and of Socrates the searcher after
truth, and of Jeremy Taylor and John Milton and Roger Williams and Lessing . . . I believe that the spirit of Abraham Lincoln . . . is not far from us, and the spirit of Tennyson and
Whittier and Phillips Brooks.

—John Henry Barrows, Welcome to the Parliament

IN HIS DISCUSSION of the politics of myth, Bruce Lincoln has described
the mythic past and mythic future as sites of contests among people
engaged in a struggle over the shape of social relations in the present.
At the Parliament, one such contest was waged over the story of Mars
Hill as recorded in Acts 17: 1–34, in which Paul, the great missionary
to the gentiles, is portrayed as preaching to Athenian pagans about the
God they already worship, but ignorantly conceived.

> 22. Then Paul stood in the midst of Mars hill and said, Ye men
> of Athens, I perceive that in all things ye are too superstitious.
> 23. For as I passed by, and beheld your devotions, I found an altar
> with this inscription, TO THE UNKNOWN GOD. Whom therefore ye
> ignorantly worship, him declare I unto you.

This story, like that of the Pentecost, was a Biblical model with which
many western Christian delegates, liberals and conservatives alike,
could mythically identify to explain the significance of the assembly.[1]
One set of important issues related to the surface meaning of this
story, the role and authority of Christian missionaries and the legitimacy and substance of their mission overseas, emerged on the Parliament floor. But, on a deeper level, the story of Mars Hill also pointed

63

to contested questions of a more fundamental nature, with a bearing on the mythic future—which religious party would have the authority to define the terms of what was true and false in a common religious discourse and what shape would relations take among the different religions in the emerging global community.

The emotional force of the story of Mars Hill as it bore on the present was powerfully reenforced, replete with geopolitical significance, by an historical dimension of the Columbian myth. Implicit in the myth was an analogy drawn between the world of the late nineteenth century, increasingly knit together by western imperialism, and the imperial ecumene of classical antiquity, the setting for Christianity's birth and initial victory. This analogical frame of reference was at work in many of the allusions to antiquity elicited by the White City, but was at work at the Parliament as well, which helps to explain the presence of the statues of Demosthenes and Cicero on the floor.[2] It can also be sensed in many addresses, such as when Wilkinson attacked Asian religions as latter-day "Olympianism" and T. E. Slater prophesied that "the temples of Vishnu and Siva will be deserted as surely as have been the temples of Jupiter and Apollo."[3] Orthodox Archbishop Dionysios Latas of Zante, an island in Ionia, saw this analogical linking of past to present, when he remarked on a visit to the White City—"I seem to be in Olympia. It is as though the American soil had opened up and had sent again into life the souls of my ancestors, and had made them rebuild in a new land all the white snow splendor of the Acropolis."[4]

The political importance of the appeal to myths points to an emotional component in the encounter between East and West, about which little can be said in a formal analysis of theology, philosophy, doctrines, and creeds. Augustine Hewitt, leader of the Catholic Paulist order, and William Torrey Harris, the United States Commissioner of Education, presented tightly-wrapped philosophical theologies on the floor, but they had little bearing on the outcome of the assembly.[5] It was the more dramatic performances by delegates like Pentecost and Keane, with their unambiguous metaphors of conquest or sweeping descriptions of the goal of history, that captured the mythic dimensions of the Parliament, clarified fundamental issues, and conveyed the power of the moment to those assembled in the Hall of Columbus. The inclusivism of Howe, Hirsch's vision, and the virtuosi performances by Rexford and Boardman with their eclectic, free-form theologies, were important in a different way. Their broad liberality, theological expansiveness, and oceanic suggestions about the religious possibilities in globalization helped to create an ambiguous realm of ideas on the Parliament floor, well beyond the formal grammar of normative religious discourse, in which both a contest was waged and a creative encounter took place between West and East.

A Bottom-Line Theology

To begin by evoking contest and ambiguity is not to dismiss the substantiality of what Paul Carter called the "consensus-rhetoric" of the Parliament, particularly when focusing upon the discourse generated by western delegates, reserving for the moment the contributions of the Asians.[6] Ida Hultin, a Unitarian, and Anglican Alfred Momerie could both agree that the essence of all religions was ethics. Creeds and theological speculation seemed to both of them to be vanities, what Momerie called "questions of millinery."[7] Baptist Crawford Toy stated the prospects for ethical universalism most clearly: the field of ethics was concerned with social relations, religion with the relations between God and man. The task at hand was to link ideal ethics to an adequate theology in a way in which all the religions of the world could agree. This, Toy concluded, "is our hope of unity."[8]

Walter Eliot, an American Catholic priest, and Laura Chant, a British Protestant laywoman, could both agree that religion was a question of spirituality.[9] Eliot did base his discussion on the God-man Christ, the church, and the inner witness of the Holy Spirit, while Chant pointed to a spirit that moved more expansively through nature, art, and poetry. But, the idea that the longing for the spirit was a universal human instinct was itself an assumption well-nigh universal at the Parliament, and the tenor of the assembly—and this was no small matter a century ago—pointed toward a consensus that a positive, spiritual element was to be found in every religion, at least every great religion, on earth.

Ultimately, however, all such convergences were fraught with a high degree of theological ambiguity. When Eliot spoke of "the elevation of man to union with God," he remained wholly within the bounds of traditional Catholic theism. Chant, however, evoked both Goethe and Shelley's "Prometheus Unbound." Hultin moved easily between evocations of God, father, and the "Infinite Self," while Toy too moved easily between God, deity, and the "extra-human power of the universe."[10] It was easy to run rough-shod over theological nuances at the Parliament, and the apparent consensus on the floor rested on the fact that theological contradictions were masked by an appeal to the fatherhood of God, the theology of choice of the Columbiad and a foundation of turn-of-the-century liberal Protestantism.[11]

The fatherhood of God served as a bottom-line theology at the Parliament, which provoked few women to dissent. Delegates did critically examine the impact of religion on women, but gender, like ethnicity, was rarely directly related to theology.[12] More typically, the transcendental, universalistic tenor of the proceedings relegated sex and gender distinctions to the realm of the transient and secondary, such as when Marion Murdock, after advocating the motherhood of God, concluded: "It is not man or woman in the Lord, not man or woman in the spirit, not in the ministry of the spirit. It is the divine, it is human unity."[13] A similar elision of gender difference is apparent in the remarks about the Parliament's opening day in the *Daily Inter-Ocean*: "The fair sex were there, too, and they were not neglected. But sisterhood in such a gathering was superfluous. The air was full of brotherhood, and it was of the generic kind, such as fits both sexes."[14]

As a result, if "father" had theological content for a delegate, it tended to signify generic universality. For Kaufmann Kohler, the father meant a universal Reform theology—"In trumpet tones resonant with joy and hope, peals forth the great truth of the Brotherhood of Man based on the Fatherhood of God."[15] Belgian priest and scholar Monsignor Charles de Harlez thought people of all religions would one day come to praise with a single tongue "our common Master and Father."[16] For Presbyterian David Burrell, the American republic, indeed all constitutional governments, rested on "the Fatherhood of God, expressing itself in the brotherhood of man, through the Gospel of that Only-begotten Son who is the Brother of all."[17] The fatherhood of God was presented by Fannie Williams, a black Chicago clubwoman, as an antidote for American race relations, by Lady Somerset of Britain as an ecumenical theology, and by James Dennis as a "signal code" in an exportable Protestantism which would speed the evangelization of the world.[18] Walter Eliot perorated, "I go to the Father, because the Father is greater than I," while Laura Chant pictured "God, our Father, answering the prayer of the Japanese in the Japs' own language."[19] On each of the Parliament's seventeen days, moreover, morning worship opened with a prominent male delegate—Schaff, Pentecost, Barrows,

Keane, Gibbons, and Hirsch, together with the Hindu reformer P. C. Majumdar—leading those assembled in the Lord's Prayer, the Catholic "Our Father," which on these occasions was called "the Universal Prayer."[20]

When Barrows published his history of the Parliament, he had the cover emblazoned in gold with the text of Malachi 2:10: "Have we not all one father? Hath not one God created us?" It was a noble sentiment, frequently expressed by liberals and conservatives alike with varying intents, and it would have undoubtedly been easier to hold the image of the father as a theological bottom line had the Parliament been simply a broad church assembly of Jews, Christians, and liberal theists. But, epoch-making developments in the history of religion were taking place at the Parliament, an event chiefly remembered for its role in popularizing the insights of the science of religion and in serving as a formal western debut for the religions of Asia.[21]

Apologetic Scholars and Scholarly Missionaries

The comparative study of religion, which at the end of last century was considered among the new sciences to emerge from the Enlightenment, played a complex and varied role at the Parliament. First of all, there is the question of the contributions of professional scholars to the discourse generated on the Parliament floor by other western delegates. As importantly, there is the question of the way in which many mission-minded delegates, both Christian and Asian, used comparative religion as a kind of "applied science" to engage either in a gentlemanly form of theological trench warfare or in a creative, if at times aggressive, attempt to interpret religious traditions in the interest of forging a common discourse for a global society.

Among western delegates, the science of religion served to buttress the theological options embedded in the ground rules of the Parliament. Prominent European scholars, none of whom attended the assembly but had their papers delivered by proxies, lent their prestige to the assembly and helped to soften the hardest edges of Christian exclusivism. But, seen in a global frame of reference, they stood alongside Christian missionaries as delegates from the West, and their contributions did not depart radically from the broader western and Christian quest for an inclusive theology. Scholars and at least the new generation of missionaries both tended to be political and theological liberals.

Both tended to share a universalistic outlook rooted in the evolutionary model and to see ethical monotheism as the highest form of human religiosity.[22] The similarity between the two was heightened at the Parliament by virtue of the fact that little distinction was made on the floor between the study of religion as a science and as a theological activity. Scholars were often apologists for western religious and theological ideas, while missionaries were often informed scholars of comparative religious history. Together they tended to advocate broadly compatible religious points of view, wholly western in outlook, whether or not they made reference to traditional creeds and theologies.[23]

An absolute distinction can be drawn between missionaries and scholars only by way of contrasting representatives drawn from the extremes. A paradigmatic expression of the liberal missionary spirit is found in the person of Dionysios Latas, whose authoritative air moved the *Daily Inter-Ocean* to comment that with his beard and mitre, "he completed a figure suggestive of Aaron as he might present himself before Jehovah in the holy of holies of the Jewish Tabernacle." At the climax of his address on the Greek church, he uttered Paul's familiar words before the assembly: "Ye men of Athens, among the objects of your worship I found an altar with this inscription, 'To The Unknown God.' Whom therefore you worship in ignorance, Him set I forth unto you." Latas then continued with Jesus' admonition, "Go ye into all the world and preach the gospel to the whole creation," and concluded— "Almighty King, most High Omnipotent God, look upon human kind; enlighten us that we may know Thy will, Thy ways, Thy holy truths; bless Thy holy truths; bless Thy holy church. Bless this country."[24]

The only paper advocating non-theological, strictly empiricist principles for the science of religion was that of Jean Réville, a professor at the recently secularized Sorbonne. He rejected all distinctions made between revealed and natural religion and between monotheism and polytheism, and he disallowed all developmental schemes like those of Hegel and Comte. The science of religion was to have no link whatsoever to any speculative motive, philosophical agenda, or religious creed. Scholarship was to be limited to an analysis of religions as "living organic products of the human mind, in perpetual flux, even when they seem fixed." Religions must be seen as intimately connected to a particular civilization and are studied in isolation from other aspects of social history simply as a matter of convenience. Réville concluded by noting that the "only scientific classification is the historic. This springs from the facts instead of being imposed upon them. It is easy to understand these rules—in the present state of science it is hard to apply them."[25]

Other scholars typically suggested a more ambiguous meaning of the new science by advocating a theology that ranged from broadly theist to specifically Christian while, at the same time, pointing to the apologetic task more typically associated with missionaries. Religious ideas derived from the western tradition were, at very least, woven into a discussion of science, as in the paper presented by C. P. Tiele of Leiden. Tiele reviewed the gradual emergence of the young science from apologetics, but he defined the scholar's task as an "unprejudiced historical-psychological" study of dogmas, texts, rites, and creeds in order to "know from what wants of the soul they have sprung."[26] More speculative theological concerns were at the forefront of Albert Réville's "Conditions and Outlook for a Universal Religion." For Réville, religion was a universal phenomenon, whose key feature was "the postulate of a supramundane power" acting in human life. He found "augustness" even in "uncultured" faiths, but predicted the demise of tribal religion and polytheism due to the dominance of western civilization. He also suggested that the doctrine of a future universal religion would be the consubstantiality of God and man and concluded his paper with the hope that the Parliament was "the first step in the sacred path that shall one day bring man to the truly humanitarian and universal religion."[27]

Specifically Christian theological concerns were more explicit in the papers of Unitarian J. Estlin Carpenter and F. Max Müller of Oxford. Carpenter began with an old legend to establish an irenic spirit: "One is born a Pagan, another a Jew, a third a Mussulman. The true philosopher sees in each a fellow-seeker after God." His aim was to formulate a universal concept of revelation free from all doctrines and creeds, but to do this, he turned to the example of Paul on Mars Hill, to Jesus' prayer to his father, and, above all, to ancient Greek philosophy, the *logos*, and the gospel of John. "So many voices! So many words!" he concluded, "each soul a fresh word, with a new destiny conceived for it by God." With revelation thus conceived, Carpenter argued that the science of religion could gather "up into itself the history of human thought and life. It becomes the story of God's continual revelation to our race. . . . May this Congress, with its noble representatives of so many faiths, hasten the day of mutual understanding, when *God* by whatever name we hallow him, shall be all in all!"[28]

Müller, making a similar theological appeal but in a remarkably more conservative fashion, called for "not simply a reform, but a complete revival of religion, more particularly of the Christian religion." Making no comment on the religions of the world, Müller looked to Clement, Origen, and other early fathers, who had recognized "the perfect realization of the Divine Thought or *Logos* of manhood in Christ, as in the true sense the Son of God, not in the vulgar mythological sense, but in [its] deep metaphysical meaning." This theology, he wrote, could give "a truer conception of the whole world, showing that there was a purpose in the ancient religions and philosophies of the world." Alexandrine christology could also provide the basis for "a true revival of the Christian religion and a reunion of its many divisions . . . I have no doubt that your Congress of Religions of the World might do excellent work for the resuscitation of pure and primitive ante-Nicene Christianity."[29]

A thorough mix of scholarly and religious preoccupations was equally conspicuous in the papers of two American scholars, Unitarian Elizabeth Sunderland and Catholic Merwin-Marie Snell, the secretary of John Keane. They both linked scholarship and liberal, western theological ideas to the apologetic agenda of missionaries. Sunderland based her paper on Matthew Arnold's concept of culture as "the best that has been known and said in the world." Yet, the substance of her address was a rangy discussion of the history of religions, particularly Christianity, which she concluded on an apologetic, if inclusivist, note: "Christianity has gathered contributions from many lands and woven them into one ideal large enough to include all peoples, tender enough to comfort all, lofty enough to inspire all—the ideal of a universal brotherhood bound together under a common Divine Fatherhood."[30]

In two brief papers, Snell defined the science of religion as nothing less than the history of all religions, theologies, dogmas, and rites, which in its highest reaches became a "speculative science" of religious philosophy. He also argued that all missionary training schools should be colleges of comparative religious history. "The first requisite of successful mission work," he observed, "is a knowledge of the truths and beauties of the religion to be displaced, that they may be used as a *point d'appui* for the special arguments and claims of the religion to be introduced."[31]

It was a small, if significant, step from scholarly papers amply riddled with western theological assumptions to the more overtly apologetic papers of professional missionaries. William R. Hutchison commented that missionaries' attitudes toward Asian religions at the
Parliament were ethnocentric and condescending, and he observed that
their theological one-upmanship was based on "ex parte evidence, circular reasoning, and, too often, substantial and stubborn ignorance."[32]
His judgment in this matter is in many respects correct, but as importantly, missionaries saw themselves as practitioners of an applied science and as bringing the work of Tiele, Réville, Carpenter, and other
scholars full circle to ground their scientific data and loosely-construed
theological sentiments within the more coherent, systematic framework of full-blown Christian theology.

Milton Valentine, a professor at the Lutheran Theological Seminary
at Gettysburg, reviewed Egyptian, Chinese, Indian, Zoroastrian, and
Druidic religion and found in them all a "strong witness" to monotheism, the personality of God, and the ethical attributes of Deity. Only
in Christianity, however, did he find the love of God leading to redemption from moral evil. "As I see it, other historical beliefs have no element of true theistic conception to give to Christianity what it has not,
but Christianity has much to give others."[33] Conrad von Orelli, a professor from Basel, argued that all examination of the religions of all the
nations and tribes led to the conclusion that the only satisfying religion was one in which man was reconciled to God by offering himself
as an absolutely pure victim: "Christ satisfies all the desires and ful-
fills all the hopes which had moved and inspired the ages of heathen-
ness with relation to God."[34]

T. E. Slater, an evangelist with the London Missionary Society in
Bangalore, pointed out elements in Hindu scripture he considered to
be gospel "foreshadowings" that could serve as valuable *points d'appui*
for the introduction of Christianity to India. He noted, for example, the
Hindu reverence for Prajapati, a demiurgic figure slain to create the
universe, and suggested that it serve as the basis for the introduction
to India of Jesus Christ, "the Lamb slain from the foundation of the
world." Slater brought C. P. Tiele's scientific investigation of dogmas,
texts, rites, and creeds to "know from what wants of the soul they have
sprung" to a logical conclusion in the form of an applied science in the
service of creedal Christianity. A careful comparative study of religions brought out striking parallels in other religions that only Chris-

tianity could satisfy, Slater noted; the Bible "meets the questions raised in the philosophies of the East, and supplies their only true solution."[35]

Circular reasoning is an apt description of the logic of the missionaries, and more importantly, it is an apt description of the spirit of the Parliament itself, insofar as the event was dominated by inclusivist Christian theists and their more daring colleagues, who tended to advocate forms of western theism only a step or two removed. Liberal western theism echoed Christian theology more than contradicted it, and the task of the scholar, like that of liberal-minded missionary, was easily construed as broadening and correcting western and Christian theistic ideas to give them true universality. One form of this circular reasoning was marked in Barrows's words of welcome, when he said that he considered Jews to be Old Testament Christians and Christians, New Testament Jews.[36] A more universal form was implicit in the frequently-made remark that God had not left himself without a witness in the many nations of the world.

Scholars and missionaries did not make identical contributions to the Parliament; there is little question that J. Estlin Carpenter was both more informed and more conciliatory in his approach to the religions of the world than Milton Valentine. But, Jean Réville stood alone among the scholars by advocating a science of religion that was not hinged to theism. Far more typically, scholarly and apologetic points of view tended to dissolve into one another on the Parliament floor, creating in the process a western theological discourse that, very much in the spirit of the theology of the Columbiad, could alternatively signify a broad, liberal, enlightened theism or a dogmatically and doctrinally-specific Christian or Judeo-Christian God. This discourse provided western delegates with a theological version of what Edward Said called "an accepted grid," a kind of epistemological filter through which scholars and missionaries alike sifted their knowledge about the East, in order to incorporate it into western consciousness.[37]

The Missionary Question

"The East" was at the time not a Cold War construction but a protean concept pointing to a vast stretch of territory extending from the Balkans and Aegean, through the Near and Middle East and central and south Asia, to Siberia, the Far East, and the Pacific. Thus, Asians at the Parliament included Armenian, Syrian, Turkish, and Russian Christians, Christian converts from India, China, and Japan, and delegates from the continent's great religious traditions. They formed a substantial minority of 43, or 22 percent, of the 194 participants at the assembly. Thirty of these, or 15 percent of the total, were, as many people at the Parliament called them, "cultured heathen"—intelligent, educated, and spiritually-earnest individuals, who were neither white nor Greco-Roman, neither Jews nor Christians.[38] As a result, the East/West encounter at the Parliament was about many things—the myth of the "white man's burden," the normativeness of western Christianity, and the dependence or autonomy of Asian Christians on western missionaries. But, the central drama turned on the two Mars Hill themes—the set of issues surrounding the missionary question and the questions of authority among and relations between the religions of the world in the emerging global ecumene.

The mission question quickly emerged as a controversial issue, and American Protestants, as the hosts and dominant group at the Parliament and the primary custodians of the national mainstream, bore the brunt of Asians' criticisms. At about this time, they were, moreover, engaged in their own, broader debate with European Protestants about the strategies to be used by missionaries overseas. The question was not, should "heathen" be converted, but, how should the process of conversion proceed? The traditional method had been strictly evangelical—to preach the Bible to gain conversions, Christianize the world, and civilize the Asians—while a newer strategy, more in keeping with the liberal movement, emphasized civilizing Asians first, through western education, social reforms, technological assistance, and medical missions, as preliminary steps to their ultimate Christianization.[39] It is against the background of this presumption about the legitimacy of the Christian mission that the analogy between the Parliament and Mars Hill both gains its force and reveals its inadequacy. Unlike the story of Paul on Mars Hill, in which the Stoics and Epicureans of Athens are portrayed as having little to say in rebuttal to Paul's charge that they were too superstitious, at the Parliament, the Hindus, Buddhists, and Confucians, together with Asian Christians, came to the defense of their religious traditions and ideals, and in so doing, galvanized the assembly.

Controversy among the delegates from the Christian camps of west Asia raised the missionary question in terms of the ethnocentrism explicit in conversion strategies. On one hand, Mardiros Ignados, a Protestant convert and minister from Turkey, praised the "great and palpable results" of the mission which had placed Armenian Protestants in what he considered to be the vanguard of Asiatic Christianity. Liberal theological ideas and modern education in languages, sciences, and liberal arts had proved mightier than tradition and ritualism. Ceremonials, rites, lenten fasts, pilgrimages, and the use of icons in worship were being abandoned, giving what Ignados considered a more "elevated" religious life to Armenia.[40] But, on the other hand, Minas Tcheraz of the London School of Modern Oriental Studies and a representative of the Armenian church strongly disagreed. He criticized "foreign missionaries who find it convenient to preach Christianity to the faithful of a church nearly contemporary with Christ." They must reconcile respect for the past with the exigencies of modernity, but only destruction could result from "those who waste their time inculcating Puritan simplicity on the brilliant imaginations of an Eastern people." In its perennial struggles with Islam, the Armenian church had discovered sound reasons for maintaining its ancient traditions, even if they separated it from other Christian churches. "The liberal spirit with which all the churches are today penetrated gives ground for hope that tolerance will be shown it [the Armenian church]," he concluded, "as it shows tolerance to its Orthodox, Catholic, and Protestant sisters."[41]

Similar concerns were expressed by Protestant converts among the Japanese. Horiuchi Kozaki, the President of Doshisha University, saw a need for Christians in Japan to build a church on the basis of the national spirit, in order to blunt charges made by Shintoists, Buddhists, and other nationalists that Christianity was not suitable for Japan. Such a move, however, entailed a greater degree of tolerance for traditional Japanese values than was normally allowed by foreign missionaries. "Japanese Christians will never be contented to work under missionary auspices. To be useful to our country the missionaries must either cooperate with us or join native churches, and take their place side by side with native workers."[42] Nobuta Kishimoto, a Japanese layman, agreed. Atheism, agnosticism, and materialism were quickly becoming the prevalent attitudes of the educated classes in Japan. Confucianism, Shintoism and Buddhism all faced this challenge; so too did Christianity. Answers were to be found, according to Kishimoto, in the Christianity of the Bible, nay the Christianity of Christ. "We do not want the Christianity of England nor the Christianity of America; we want the Christianity of Japan."[43]

Sharp resistance to the autonomy of the Japanese churches came from a Congregationalist missionary by the name of Haworth, who took exception to these pleas. "Christians of America will not give money to maintain missionaries in a land where they can be only subordinate helpers, utterly impotent in solving the questions of the church," he noted. "With 40,000 baptized Christians out of 40,000,000 people, with the rate of annual increase in the church diminishing rather than increasing, with all these unsolved problems pressing upon the infant church, let not Christian America listen for one moment to one who would say that our work for Japan is done."[44]

Asian non-Christians more pointedly challenged the legitimacy of the idea of mission, particularly because they understood it to be intrinsically connected to assumptions rooted both in western racism and in the imperial agenda of western nations in the East. Delegates from Japan, India, and China made critical observations on the missionary question that attempted, in effect, to put brakes on the western, Christian drive for unity as it headed East. On the third day of the Parliament, the headline of the *Chicago Tribune* read:

CRY FROM THE ORIENT
JAPANESE PRIEST STARTLES THE RELIGIOUS CONGRESS

The "priest" in question was Hirai Kinzō, a Buddhist layman, whose address the *Tribune* called "the sensation of the day and of the whole Parliament so far."[45] Hirai's paper was considered so inflammatory that, according to one eastern source, Barrows attempted to prevent him from delivering it before the assembly.[46]

Hirai spoke to the Parliament about the unfair treaties foisted by the nations of the West on Japan, an injustice sanctioned by the charge that the Japanese were uncivilized idolaters and heathen. "Is it Christian morality," he asked, "to trample upon the rights and advantages of a non-Christian nation, coloring all their natural happiness with the dark stain of injustice?" "I read in the Bible," he continued, "'Whosoever shall smite thee on the right cheek, turn to him the other also'; but I cannot discover there any passage which says: 'Whosoever shall demand justice of thee smite his right cheek, and when he turns smite the other also.'" Calling attention to anti-Japanese demonstrations in Hawaii and San Francisco, Hirai linked bigotry in the West to racism among missionaries overseas: "If such be Christian ethics—well, we are perfectly satisfied to be heathen." Shintoism, Taoism, Confucianism, and Buddhism were all tolerated in Japan, as was Christianity, but anti-Christian societies had been organized "to protect ourselves from false Christianity and the injustices which we receive from the people of Christendom. . . . We, the forty million souls of Japan . . . await still further manifestations as to the morality of Christianity."[47] The next day the *Herald* reported that "Loud applause followed many of his declarations and a thousand cries of 'Shame!' were heard when he pointed to the wrongs which his countrymen had suffered through the practices of 'false Christianity.'" In Neely's collection of Parliament papers, Walter Houghton reported that "Christian missionaries on the platform contracted and their heads shook in disappointment."[48]

Equally critical comments came from south Asia when Anagarika Dharmapāla, a young lay Buddhist and Theosophist who was to become one of the Parliament's Asian luminaries, pointed out what seemed to him the destructive impact of the missionaries on Asian society. "The missionaries sent to Ceylon, China, or Burmah, as a rule, have not the tolerance we need. The missionary is intolerant; he is selfish. . . . Seeing the selfishness and intolerance of the missionary not an intelligent man will accept Christianity." He was concerned that Christians in Asia were undoing the mild civility of Buddhist civilization. "I warn you," he concluded, "that if you want to establish Christianity in the East it can only be done on the principles of Christ's love and meekness."[49] B. B. Nagarkar, a Hindu reformer, pointed both to the financial power of missionaries and to the unfavorable impression they made on Asians. "Every year you are lavishing—I shall not say wasting—mints of money on your so-called foreign missions and missionaries sent out, as you think, to carry the Bible and its salvation to the 'heathen Hindu,' and thus to save him! Aye, to save him. Your poor peasants, your earnest women, and your generous millionaires raise millions of dollars every year to be spent on foreign missions. Little, how little, do you ever dream that your money is expended in spreading abroad nothing but Christian dogmatism and Christian bigotry, Christian pride, and Christian exclusiveness." He offered missionaries "unqualified, unmodified, earnest pity, and we are ready to ask God to forgive them, for they know not what they say."[50]

Pung Kwang Yu, secretary of the Chinese Legation in Washington D.C., drew attention to the way in which the allegedly civilizing power of the gospel fostered chaos in China. He complained that missionaries confused Christ's spiritual kingdom with the political and economic arrangements of the nations of the West, noting that Jesus "certainly did not hold up the foreign masters that were exercising supreme political control over his own country at the time, as an example worthy of imitation." He admitted that Confucians cared little which Gods were worshipped, be they Buddhist and Taoist genii or Mary and Jesus. But, religion was not to be used to undermine the social relations at the foundation of the Confucian social order. "Chinese converts are still Chinese subjects. The sooner they are made to give up the notion that by turning Christian they can claim exemption from burdens which the rest of the community have to bear, the better it is for their good."[51]

Many Christians were not unmoved by these criticisms, but their sensitivity to the charges neither called into question their religious faith nor dampened their conviction that only Christianity could serve as the basis for a global community. "We have already in this Parliament been rebuked . . . with the charge that Christians do not practice the teachings of Jesus," exclaimed evangelist B. Fay Mills. "We have done something; but with shame and tears I say it . . . we have not been practising the teachings of Jesus as he said them and meant them." Mills maintained, however, that the only hope of Asia, America, Africa, and Europe "is the love of God, and the establishment of his universal kingdom of peace, which must be set up on earth, and which shall have no end. It is of universal application."[52] Dressed in the robes of a mandarin, British Methodist George Candlin presented himself as an outspoken advocate of the need to foster more cordial relations among Christians and Asians. However, his combination of liberality and condescension disguised a particularly insidious understanding of the authority of Christian missionaries in the religious lives of "cultured heathens." Christianity's mission to non-Christian religions, he suggested, "is not one of condemnation, but of interpretation. . . . Each presents a problem the Gospel is bound to solve. It has to explain them to themselves. . . . Every ray of truth, every spark of holy feeling, every feeble impulse of pure desire, every noble deed, every act of sacrifice, every sign of tenderness and love, which is in them and have made them dear to their believers, will be an open door for its [Christianity's] entrance, and its right to supplant will rest finally on its power to comprehend."[53]

Less subtlety characterized the remarks of less liberal supporters of the missionaries. Francis Clark, president of the American Christian

Endeavor Society, spoke to the Parliament about his recently concluded tour around the world. He had learned that "the religion of Christ is the power of God unto salvation" in "the stagnant pool of heathenism." "The greasy bull of Madura and Tangore," he assured his audience, "has little in common with the Lamb of God who taketh away the sins of the world."[54]

The Specter of Comparability

The missionary question was a flashpoint for an important controversy, but a more fundamental contest was waged around questions about which religious party had the authority to define the terms of a common religious discourse and what shape relations among the different religions would take. These questions were the crux of the matter, bearing on issues from the universality of the Columbian myth to the legitimacy of the evolutionary perspective on history, religion, and race, which were primarily addressed on the floor of the assembly in the highly abstract realm of religious ideas. The western contribution to this realm was a range of theological opinions and convictions that alternatively signified a broad, liberal theism or a dogmatically and doctrinally specific Christian or Judeo-Christian God. The eastern contribution, however, was an entirely different range of philosophies and theological ideas, which, with the aid of the science of religion, could be creatively reinterpreted in the interest of the Parliament's goal to forge a common religious discourse for a global society.

The problematic nature of such an undertaking had been foreseen at the outset by no less a person than the Archbishop of Canterbury, who found it necessary to deny the request of leaders of the Department of Religion for a letter of support. In his view, there were several problems with their "scheme." Any presentation of Christianity would entail a public discussion of faith and devotion, topics he considered "too sacred for such treatment." The Department's organizational plan was, moreover, based on the "untenable" proposition that Rome was the Catholic church, which placed both American Episcopalians and British Anglicans outside the pale of Catholicity. More to the point, the Archbishop saw that if Christians were members of the Parliament, it would seem to deny that Christianity "is the one religion" and to imply further "the equality of other intended members and the parity of their position and claims."[55] The Archbishop was pointing to what can be called the specter of comparability. If the claims of Asian religions were assumed to have parity with those of Christianity, and if the authority of western Christendom was itself divided by the competing claims of Catholic churches, might not Christian theology lose its focus, clarity, authority, and meaning?

The fatherhood of God and the brotherhood of men created in God's image—central features in the Parliamentary ground rules, in traditional Christian theology, and in the more expansive theology of the Protestant liberal movement—served as the theological ground on which the contest between East and West was waged. The western proposition was stated with unusual clarity by Henry Harris Jessup, an American Presbyterian with the Syrian mission, who presented an extraordinarily explicit account of the Anglo-Protestant vision of the theological ground for a common religious discourse in his address, "The Religious Mission of the English-Speaking Nations."[56]

Jessup began at what he considered the beginning—the conversion of the Saxons to Christianity in the seventh century. He then recounted how the hand of God led that "sturdy northern race" for nine centuries, until "the hidden torch of truth was wrested from its hiding-place by Luther, and held aloft for the enlightenment of mankind, just at a time when Columbus discovered the continent of America, and opened the new and final arena for the activity and highest development of man." Jessup asked the audience to imagine a map of the world and to note how Great Britain and America, with their innumerable harbors on many coasts, held all the strategic positions, giving them "the control of the world's future and the keys to its moral and ethical problems." Britain and America were permeated with the principles of the English Bible, he continued. Their poetry, history, science, and philosophy were moral, pure, and religious. Their people believed in God and final retribution; in law and conscience; in the sanctity of home, women, and family. "Such principles as these are destined to mold and control all mankind."

Jessup's vision was shot through with all the parochial arrogance and ethnocentrism at the foundation of the Columbian myth, but, even so, it was based on what he thought to be a generous faith. The preeminence of English-speaking people in particular and Protestant Christians in general derived from their knowledge that they were children of God. "This then is our mission: that we who are made in the image of God, should remember that all men are made in God's image. To this divine knowledge we owe all who we are, all we hope for. We are gradually rising toward that image, and we owe to our fellow men to aid them in returning to it in the glory of God and the beauty of holiness." This was, he concluded, "a celestial privilege and with it comes a high responsibility, from which there is no escape." Some Asians tacitly acknowledged the authority of Christianity to define the basic terms of a common religious discourse. They engaged in the kind of theological discourse articulated by Jessup, with its idea of a God and the importance of living in his image, by creatively adapting the Parliament's bottom-line theology to theological sensibilities informed by their own traditions. In the interest of forging a common religious discourse, they raised one specter of comparability by further attenuating the already ambiguous image of God as father.

Vivekananda, a Hindu reformer, affirmed God's fatherhood, while, at the same time, he declared his devotion to Lord Krishna and the Vedas. Hindus considered the soul divine, but in the thrall of matter, he explained. "The word they use for perfection is *Mukto*—freedom, freedom from the bounds of imperfection, freedom from death and misery." Appealing to Christian scripture, he drew out an important parallel: "this reaching God, seeing God, becoming perfect, even as the Father in Heaven is perfect, constitutes the religion of the Hindus." He also noted that Buddhists, even though they do not believe in a God, seek "to evolve a God out of man." Again making an appeal to Christian scripture, he concluded with the statement that Buddhists "have not seen the Father, but they have seen the Son. And he that hath seen the Son hath seen the Father."[57]

Pung Kwang Yu transposed the idea of the fatherhood of God into categories derived from the Confucian tradition, with reference to the relation between the "unclouded and empty intelligence" of nature and the "pure consciousness" that man is given at birth. He observed that nature and man are so intimately linked that "to call the pure creative power of nature, Father, and the pure consciousness of man, child, is by no means contrary to the principles set forth in the *Book of Changes*." He concluded from this, moreover, that the attainment of perfect mastery by the suppression of the flesh and by living wholly in accord with nature is to attain what the "Buddhists call a Buddha, the Taoists a genius, and Christians a child of God." Buddha, Lao-tze, and Christ, he observed, "have practically the same end in view, though each points out a different road to reach it."[58]

Other Asians affirmed the Christian idea of the fatherhood of God, even while pointing completely beyond the officially-sanctioned norms of western theism. Echoing western delegates Offord and Murdock, B. B. Nagarkar, a member of the Hindu reform group Brāhmo-Samāj, made an eloquent call for a new religious dispensation under the universal motherhood of God. The idea of a divine mother, he explained, supplemented the image of father as creator, protector, and judge and intensified the ideas of both the brotherhood of man and the sisterhood of women. "Our frail and fickle human mother is nothing in comparison with the Divine Mother of the entire humanity, who is the primal source of all love, of all mercy and all purity. . . . Let us approach her footstool in the spirit of her humble and obedient children."[59]

The specter of comparability raised its head in a more radical way when other Asians, seeing the idea of a personal God, be it father, mother, or son, as untenable and ill-conceived, simply rejected Christian norms completely.

Dharmapāla explained to the Parliament that the Buddha had denied the existence of a creator God altogether. "Accepting the doctrine of evolution as the only true one, with its corollary, the law of cause and effect, he [Gautama] condemns the idea of a creator and strictly forbids inquiry into it as being useless." Any God was subject to the laws of evolution and of cause and effect; "There is no difference between the perfect man," he argued, "and this supreme god of the present world-period."[60]

Virchand Gandhi described the Jain tradition as denying a personal God and creator, which was not to say that Jains were atheists. Matter and soul are eternal and cannot be created, he explained. "What is God, then? God, in the sense of an extra cosmic personal creator, has no place in Jain philosophy. It distinctly denies such [a] creator as illogical and irrelevant in the general scheme of the universe." He argued instead for a "subtle essence underlying all substances, conscious as well as unconscious, which become an eternal cause of all modifications, and is termed God."[61]

Hindu philosopher Manilal Dvivedi explained that in the orthodox Advaita Vedanta philosophy of Hinduism, religious aspirations were not expressed in terms of theology at all, but in terms of physics, spiritual ontology, and ethics. "I humbly beg to differ from those who see in Monotheism, in the recognition of a personal God apart from nature, the acme of intellectual development. I believe it only a kind of anthropomorphism which the human mind stumbles upon in its first efforts to understand the unknown. The ultimate satisfaction of human reason and emotion lies in the realization of that universal essence which is the All."[62]

As delegates to the Parliament attempted to forge a global religious discourse on the Parliament floor, theological ambiguities became legion. Paul, who had rebuked Athenian pagans for their love of superstition, might well have blanched at developments in Chicago, when the call sent out by the Department of Religion to discuss the idea of God and the impregnable foundations of theism opened a Pandora's box of issues related to religious and theological parity in the modern ecumene.

The traditional role of Christian missionaries and the rationale for their mission was, moreover, called into question on the missionaries' home turf, in often unequivocal terms, before the public and press, at a convention that many had determined in advance would be an epoch-making assembly.

Vivekananda, in his remarks at the close of the Parliament, stated bluntly that "much has been said of the common ground of religious unity. I am not going just now to venture my own theory. But if anyone here hopes that this unity would come by the triumph of any one of these religions and the destruction of others, to him I say, 'Brother, yours is an impossible hope'. Do I wish that the Christian would become Hindu? God forbid. Do I wish that the Hindu or Buddhist would become Christian? God forbid." He suggested that if the Parliament was to prove anything to the world it would be "that holiness, purity, and charity are not the exclusive possessions of any church in the world, and that every system has produced men and women of the most exalted character. In the face of this evidence, if anybody dreams of the exclusive survival of his own and the destruction of others, I pity him from the bottom of my heart."[63]

Narasima Charya, a Madrasi brahmin, made his point more quietly. A century later his remarks would be understood as elementary insights into the sociology of knowledge. Do not cast aspersion upon missionaries, he requested. Their labor stemmed from noble motives and their work among an unsympathetic people was done only with the hope of a reward from their God. But, Charya also asked that Christians try to understand that "there is the difference between your temperament and ours. We are brought up so differently from you that the things that affect you do not affect us. Those parables in which you see so many beauties, those sayings and doings of the Saviour, which seem to be an all-sufficient guide for you through life, nay, your very belief in the necessity of a vicarious Saviour, which is the corner-stone of your faith, are mere words to us. They convey no impression. They carry no conviction."[64]

Virchand Gandhi became a minor *cause célèbre* by defending Hinduism against the charge of fostering temple prostitution, leveled against it by a British delegate, George Pentecost. The *San Francisco Examiner* did not get Gandhi's religious affiliation right in its report, but its headline conveyed the note of censure that could be turned upon missionaries as a result of the Parliamentary debates:

ATTACKED THE HINDOOS

A Quiet Hindoo Delegate's Cutting Answer to the
Englishman's Vicious Speech Greeted with
Great Applause.[65]

In his response to Pentecost's speech, Gandhi challenged many missionaries' vision of the mythic past and mythic future, while, at the same time, he both ridiculed the traditional rationale for Christianity's mission and called into question its claim to normative authority. The *Chicago Tribune* put an overly nice face on the situation when it characterized Gandhi's cut at the missionaries' tendency to identify themselves with St. Paul as pitting "the soft answer which turneth away wrath" against "muscular Christianity."[66]

"Some men in their ambition think that they are Pauls," Gandhi began, "and what they think they believe, and where should these new Pauls go to vent their platitudes but India? Yes, sir, they go to India to convert the heathen in a mass, but when they find their dreams melting away, as dreams always do, they return back to pass a whole life in abusing the Hindu. Abuses are not arguments against any religion, nor self-adulation the proof of the truth of one's own. For such I have the greatest pity."[67] Mr. Gandhi, the *Tribune* reported, "seemed to have the sympathy of his audience, for they applauded loudly almost every point he scored."[68]

The harnessed horse and yeoman farmer represent "Labor." Daniel Chester French's tribute to liberty is at the right. The Peristyle forms the background. At far left is Music Hall, near where the fire began that destroyed much of the Exposition in January 1894. J. W. Buel, *The Magic City*.

The Palace of Agriculture, at left, abutted the Intramural Railway Station on the South Canal. The obelisk evoked historical continuity with Egypt, Rome, Paris, London, and New York City. This ensemble was considered a particularly well-executed prototype for the ideal twentieth-century American city. J. W. Buel, *The Magic City*.

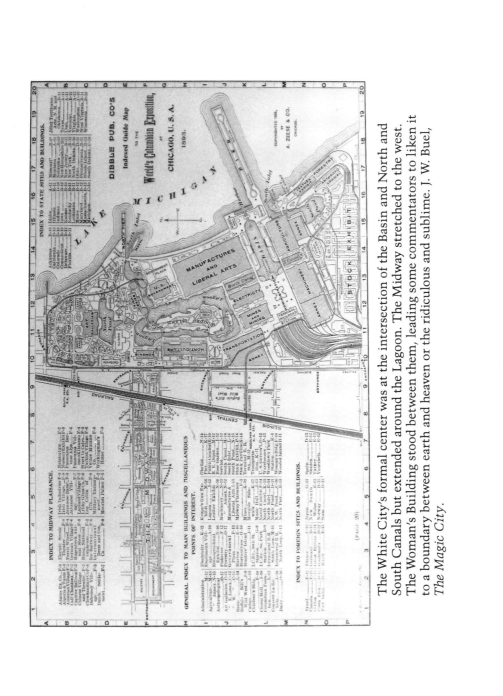

The White City's formal center was at the intersection of the Basin and North and South Canals but extended around the Lagoon. The Midway stretched to the west. The Woman's Building stood between them, leading some commentators to liken it to a boundary between earth and heaven or the ridiculous and sublime. J. W. Buel, *The Magic City*.

This photo's caption read "the several types represented in the above illustrations are: a Persian, Algerian chief and girls; a Hindostanee; a Turk; group of Egyptians; and a girl that danced at the Eiffel Tower Exhibition." Note the background of columned halls suggesting the contrast between the White City and Midway. J. W. Buel, *The Magic City*.

The entryway to the Irish Village was inspired by the St. Lawrence Gate at Drogheda. Beyond it lay reproductions of the ruins of the banqueting hall at Donegal Castle, Castle Blarney, and cromlechs, dolmens, and other pre-Christian Celtic stone-work. J. W. Buel, *The Magic City*.

Cairo Street elicited mixed responses to Islamic civilization. Its mosque, which served both Muslims and Jews, impressed commentators, while dancing girls in the bazaar became the source of folk myths about the origins of the hootchy-kootchy, the authenticity of which is still debated by musicologists. J. W. Buel, *The Magic City*.

In this illustration, Greco-Roman, Judeo-Christian, and patriotic signs are linked to the Exposition in a model for theological unity based on the fatherhood of God and brotherhood of man. The sticks in the fasces are labeled: Episcopal, Reformed, Swedenborgian, Methodist, Quaker, Catholic, Baptist, Unitarian, Presbyterian, Universalist, Congregational, and Synagogue. *Cosmopolitan* 3 (March 1893).

This illustration captures the spirit of the liberal movement in Protestantism that was on the rise in the American mainstream. The scepter with light bulb is labeled "Inspiration," "Religion," "Research," and "Science," which together dispel the bats and owls of chaos, ignorance, and superstition. *Cosmopolitan* 3 (March 1893).

John Keane was the most prominent Roman Catholic delegate to address issues in the East/West encounter. His vision of religious unity rested on a fundamental distinction between East and West, which was grounded in a highly traditional Christian theology of history. Barrows, *World's Parliament of Religions*.

Baptist George Dana Boardman saw the Exposition and Parliament as intrinsically linked, both witnesses to the dawn of a new era of religious unity. His comments implicitly connected the Christian triumph in classical antiquity to the globalization of Christianity in the late nineteenth century. Barrows, *World's Parliament of Religions*.

George Candlin, a British Methodist missionary in China, was an advocate for the religions of Asia. In the last analysis, however, he understood Christianity to be the norm against which all human religiosity was to be measured and the sole foundation for world religious unity. Barrows, *World's Parliament of Religions.*

Protap Chunder Majumdar was among the Asian delegates committed both to their national traditions and to modern and progressive universalistic ideals. His vision of a Hindu Christ played an important role in suggesting that world religious unity might be at hand. Barrows, *World's Parliament of Religions.*

Augusta Chapin was among the twenty-three women to present papers at the Parliament. Most hailed from liberal Protestant traditions, and their advocacy of new roles for women contributed to the sense that a wholly new era was dawning in world religious history. Barrows, *World's Parliament of Religions.*

Jeanne Sorabji, a Zoroastrian convert to Christianity, was the only Asian woman to deliver a paper at the Parliament. The contrast in style and composition between Sorabji's portrait and Augusta Chapin's is suggestive of contrasts often made between the Midway and White City. Barrows, *World's Parliament of Religions.*

Anagarika Dharmapāla is pictured here with a Buddha image he brought to the Parliament. His charming English, his familiarity with the western intellectual tradition, and his vision of Buddhism as resolving the war between science and religion helped to transform the Parliament into a world-class assembly. Barrows, *World's Parliament of Religions.*

Vivekananda was the most celebrated Asian delegate at the Parliament. He presented Hinduism as a modern, progressive religion, and his reputation is closely linked to the event, for he set in motion both the Hindu mission to the West and an important Hindu revitalization movement in India. Barrows, *World's Parliament of Religions.*

This scene of the closing of the Parliament is one of two known photographs of the event. Charles Bonney presides with Ellen Henrotin, vice president of the Woman's Branch of the World's Congress Auxiliary, at his side. Note the statues of Cicero and Demosthenes at the rear. The press is in the foreground. Barrows, *World's Parliament of Religions.*

5

"A RAPT GAZE INTO THE
MILLENNIUM"

Just as the Parliament of Religions gave us not the Christianity of Augustine or Aquinas or Calvin, but of the present hour, so to it gave us not the Hinduism of Gautama's time or the Buddhism of Asoka's, or the Confucianism of Chu Hsi, or the Taoism of Chuang Tzu, but of the men who in the present hour carry the lamp into the unexplored future.

—George Candlin, "Results and Mission of the Parliament"

THE GREAT WORLD's fairs of the nineteenth century, such as London's Crystal Palace Exhibition of 1851, Paris's *Exposition Universelle* of 1889, and Chicago's World's Columbian, were set before the public as markers by which humanity's collective march toward the promise of modernity could be measured. The cultural authority of fairs waned in the twentieth century, however, and commentators began to analyze them with both a new awareness of their complex significations and a degree of suspicion that, in the fairs' heyday, was the possession of scoffers and elitist critics. America's fairs are now seen as having served a variety of functions. They were cultural blueprints used to give a comprehensible shape to the flux created by rapid social and technological change and to forecast future possibilities for the nation. They were triumphant expressions of the hegemonic power of America's capitalist classes, who, through skillfully ordered displays, propagated elitist ideals and values in a showcase designed to elicit the emotional support of the masses. America's fairs also served as pedagogical tools to teach lessons about race; contrasting images of Caucasians and other peoples were used to encourage white racial solidarity and to mask class conflict, by deflecting the public's attention away from issues of class to those of race.[1]

The idea that these fairs may serve as cultural place markers, however, should not be dismissed, even though the issues measured by them today may not be those intended by their contemporaries. This is the case when considering the World's Parliament of Religions as an integral part of the Chicago Exposition. The Parliament was a wholly unique exposition showcase that was meant to display the transcendent truth of religion, or a religion, a fact that does not in any way negate the Exposition's racial and cultural significations. On the contrary, these significations inform the Parliamentary debates. But, as a marker of religion's march into modernity, the Parliament demands as a standard of measurement a kind of sliding historical gauge. For instance, the Parliament was an event in the history of Christian ecumenism and, as such, it points back to the fifteenth-century Council of Florence, the last of the pre-modern church councils attended by Greek, Latin, and Protestant Christians. Its American Protestant, Catholic and Jewish delegations also point to the Parliament as a marker in a long-term national development that culminated only in the 1950s, when a triple melting pot composed of those forces came to dominate the mainstream.[2] The Exposition was also a major event for women, and their prominence on the Parliament floor suggests that the Parliament might also serve as useful marker for gauging the growth of a movement that had been on the rise in America since the antebellum decades.

In this interpretation of the Parliament, however, it is the Asians and the East/West encounter that are at center stage, which suggests a very different sliding historical gauge. With delegates from ten different religions of the world meeting on a single public platform, the assembly was an extraordinary, perhaps wholly unique, event in world history, a fact that did not deter Asians from placing it on Asian historical continua. They likened the Parliament to Akbar's attempt in the sixteenth century to forge a universal religion for the Moghul Empire or, alternatively, to the Emperor Asoka's pan-Buddhist Patiliputra conference in the third century BCE. But, like the Exposition, the Parliament was meant to be a marker of progress into modernity, and given its delegations from around the world, its natural setting is the universal history of the modern period. Several broad developments help to set the East/West encounter in this important perspective.

One is "the onset of global cosmopolitanism," the spread of intellectual, political, and cultural values with European roots to many quarters of the globe.³ This process was irreversible by the mid-nineteenth century, when the traditional societies of Asia proved unable to stave off the West's military and industrial economy. Liberal ideals, democratic values, nationalism, individualism, and the critical spirit followed in the wake of trade and flag and began to transform Asian religions and societies, just as they were transforming the religions and societies of the West, in many ways. The global dissemination of a stock of general ideas and sentiments in the decades before the Parliament meant that a similarity of outlook existed among many delegates, despite the fact that their religious worldviews were formed in very different cultures and their aspirations were often expressed in incompatible theologies and philosophies. Yet, liberal ideals such as egalitarianism, the authority of science, the inspirational qualities of religion, universalistic ambitions and aspirations, and toleration were common property, which helped in ways unexpected by many in the West to level the playing field on which the contest between East and West was played.

A second development specific to the Asians was more problematic in regard to the success of the Parliament's quest for religious unity. It was not the case that western delegates, in a Eurocentric haze, simply misperceived Asians as people from a monolithic East. Many Asian leaders, particularly in India and Japan, thought of themselves as representatives of a single "Oriental" civilization. In contrast to an aggressive, materialistic West, they presented themselves as citizens of a pacific and mystic East,⁴ and the idea that "the East" held a certain primacy, if not finality, in matters of religion had a wide currency at the Parliament. But, even as many of these leaders identified themselves as pacific easterners, they were also engaged in a process that James E. Ketelaar called "strategic occidentalism," the selective and often highly politicized appropriation of western ideas, techniques, and critiques for use in undermining the claims of the West, asserting Asian independence, and negotiating roles in the emerging global society. As a result of this dialectical embrace of both East and West, leading Asians at the Parliament held a position that gave them strategic leverage; they were of the East, and thus untainted by the West, yet able to utilize modern and western concepts, values, and sentiments to serve their own ends. The potential advantages that could be gained by this leverage, as well as the aggressive intent of some Asians in using it, are expressed in the words of Ashitsu Jitsusen, a Japanese Buddhist, as he anticipated the Parliament: "While we promulgate our own teachings we must confound our enemy. We must use that controlled by the enemy in our attack upon the enemy itself."[5]

Thus, the Asian at the Parliament set out to accomplish a number of things—to check Christian missionaries, counter western aggression, assert the integrity of their own religious traditions, and gain public support for their objectives. Leading Asian delegates also answered the call sent out by the Department of Religion to forge a common religious discourse for an emerging global society. Their contribution to the liberal quest for unity was decisive because, as the drive for unity arose on the side of the West, it found complements, albeit cast in alien terms and unauthorized theologies, among delegates from the East. The liberal inclusivism of Howe, Hirsch's vision of a coming religion, and the virtuosi performances by liberals like Rexford and Boardman, with their eclectic, free-form theologies, were mirrored by the equally compelling and dramatic visions of modern Asian inclusivities. The end result was the apparent creation of a global religious discourse forged in the ambiguous realm of religious ideas in the interstices of the great religions of the world. The Parliament, many could reasonably think, had accomplished its stated goals by becoming the harbinger of a global community of religious sentiment for the twentieth century.

"Our Movement"

A total, global vision was clearly glimpsed and enthusiastically embraced on the side of the West by George Candlin, a liberal British Methodist attached to the China mission. In the pages of the *Biblical World* two years after the assembly, he called the Parliament "the Mount Tabor of our experience."[6] His reference was to the account of the glorious change in Jesus' appearance, while in the company of Moses and Elijah, as witnessed by his disciples on Mount Tabor before the crucifixion. By this allusion, Candlin implied that Christ and Christianity had been once again glorified and transformed, this time universalized or globalized, at the Parliament. For Candlin, the drive for unity in a world of religious diversity resolved itself in an essentially romantic vision, and the possibilities for what he called "our movement" were staggering.

Candlin wrote that science, literature, politics, and even a conservative force like religion were rushing forward into a "new era." The harmony of sentiment among all religions was shown at the Parliament to be a demonstrable fact: "The inward and true intent of every faith the world has known has been the worshipful recognition of the divine; that is the sure and sufficient ground on which to rest the claim for union." There remained, however, an "intellectual problem," a fundamentally theological problem, that Candlin considered the greatest stumbling-block to unity. He suggested the remedy was for religion to follow the lead of science and cut itself adrift from metaphysics. Ideas like nirvana and reincarnation and speculative ideas about the nature of Christ and the soul, what he called "mere farrago[es] of metaphysical nonsense," should be abandoned, as should the Bible as an exclusive source of revelation. "What we have to safeguard is the truths of inspiration and of revelation themselves," he wrote, "the Bible being a record of them, but not therefore to the exclusion of revelation elsewhere. Our safe foothold is that inspiration is not a thing packed up in a book, but a divine influence on the human mind and that the Divine Spirit is universal."[7]

In letters to Charles Bonney shortly after the Parliament, Candlin linked his vision of the universal spirit to a plan of action. "Without such stimulation as the Parliament of Religion has afforded me," he wrote, "I should find myself simply unable to believe in the possibility of union. But nothing can shake my confidence that the historic and consecrated gathering in Chicago was the herald of a great spiritual movement, and that the fire it has kindled will not be blown out till the refining and fusing mission is complete." He proposed to advance this mission on a broad front by forging a covenant among the Asians and Christians who had been at the Parliament. Each was to promote brotherhood through teaching and the press and to advance reform, progress, and enlightenment. They must regard their labor for union as "the holiest work on earth" and discourage all nonessential rituals as inimical to religious purity and impediments to world unity. "The result within our own lifetime from a united action of this kind . . . would be incalculable. All over the world man would be crying to his fellow-man in cheery tones of brotherhood, and answering echoes of love and the holy name of religion. . . . I ask you, our noble President, you who have the warm love and unstinted confidence of us all—Why may we not do it?"[8]

Yet, in another letter to Bonney, Candlin revealed the limits to and the fundamentally Christian core of both his mission and vision. Aboard the *S. S. Victoria* in the Arctic circle on his return to China, he waxed eloquent about the significance of the Parliament—it was of the "mountainous order of greatness. It suggested infinitude and eternity." It was, he thought, prophetic of the twentieth century. It had not been a chronicle of old Christian victories, but an open door to future and immeasurably greater ones. "It was a prelude not a finale, a promise not a boast, a prospect not a recollection. Like Christianity itself it was a rapt gaze into the millennium." Candlin was, however, deeply distrustful of conservatives who might balk at his liberal program, for the Parliament, like the gospel, would be taken as a declaration of the greatest religious struggle since the Reformation. He also harbored doubts as to the universality of his vision. "During the Parliament I watched with intense eagerness to see how many of that great assembly were wholly clothed with its spirit, entered into the fulness of its meaning and realized all its bearing upon *the future*. Of all there only two could I be absolutely sure of—yourself and Dr. Barrows."[9]

But in the last analysis, Candlin's plan and his transfigured vision remained little more than a highly enthusiastic form of standard liberal Christian inclusivity, a mystical version of Christ's conquest of the world in the name of global religious unity. "I am absolutely convinced that it [the Parliament] was a sheer necessity," he wrote, "and the spirit it may be expected to create and foster is the indispensable condition, without which the great object of all missionary effort whatever—the conversion of the world—is impossible." That conservatives would find his embrace of streamlined heathen faiths, his abandonment of Biblical exclusivity, and his scuttling of creedal theology a compromise of truth, did not disturb him: "It is not a compromise of truth but the complete triumph of it and of charity. The great work we have only begun. All the promise of the future is in it; it is a bright new dawn of Gospel morning for the world, for all the world." Nor did the cost to Christian supernaturalism seem too high: "Once more the gates of day unlock as the stars pale and the sky flushes with hope unlimited, immortal, and the morn of joy bursts on human hearts. It is the only argument left to us that Christianity is divine."[10]

For Candlin, the Parliament was a harbinger of a rapidly approaching day when all the religions of the world would reveal their essential spirit, the one divine spirit—tolerant, enlightened, progressive, reform-minded, wary of ritualism, holy, and cheery—a spirit remarkably similar to the spirit of liberal Protestantism. Circular reasoning, myopia, an *idée fixe*, or a preferential option for a unitive vision are all ways to understand how an assembly of the great religions of the world could appear in his eyes as the dawn of world religious unity. But more to the point, Candlin's vision was strictly of a piece with the teleological idealism of Protestants in the liberal movement, who saw change and process in both nature and human society as signs of the handiwork of the Christian father and as testimonies to the movement of the Holy Spirit.[11] The logic in the situation was compelling. Liberalism was providentially designed, and as a result, changes, in keeping with liberal values, were Christian. The Parliament, moreover, witnessed to the fact that the hard edges of religious difference could be eliminated by a liberal spirit that was itself the essence of the retransfigured Christ and Christianity. It followed that the rapidly changing world, as glimpsed in the Parliament, seemed likely to be on the verge of going over to what was, in essence, liberal Protestant Christianity.

More Farragoes of Metaphysical Nonsense

For all Candlin's enthusiasm, a very important question remains. What was it that the Asians said on the floor of the Parliament in a constructive, rather than critical vein, that could lead liberals like Candlin to make such extraordinary concessions, to make such extraordinary claims?

To find an answer, one must listen to the words of the Asians in two ways. The first requires an ear alert to religious differences, for Asian delegates often went to great lengths to convey to the audience the specific symbols, complex histories, and theological and philosophical particularities of their respective traditions, as well as the existential conclusions and commitments they drew from them. Thus, one way of interpreting the words of the eastern delegates is to conclude that Asian religions describe so many "mythological universes," to use Northrop Frye's phrase, that had structured the inner life of different civilizations for millennia.[12] In this respect, the Parliament was a quintessentially pluralistic event, where representatives of multiple religious systems from the East and West, all of which had their own internal logics, defensive strategies, and universal pretenses, were cheek by jowl on a single platform, vying with one another over both the ultimacy of their respective codes and the outcome of the assembly.

As importantly, one must also listen to the words of the Asians while keeping in mind the transcendental tenor of the Parliament's goals and spirit. The second way of listening is more oceanic and universalistic, sensitive both to theological analogies and to the pietistic confidence and hope that Candlin and other Christians took for granted as they marshalled evidence from the Asians' remarks that world religious unity was at hand. In this respect, the floor of the Parliament was an open sky for the theological imagination, where ancient symbols, philosophies, and theologies could be swept up into a single fugue worked out around a recurrent theme of world religious unity.

Of the twenty-nine papers presented by Asian non-Christians most can be considered minor—brief papers on the histories, doctrines, rituals, and creeds of various traditions. These were often presented by foreign translators in stilted English, a fact that did not insure the undivided attention of the assembly. They were, moreover, often seemingly contradicted by papers critical of the tradition in question, presented by missionaries or Christian converts from the same religion. These minor presentations also contained a great deal of densely-coded mythological language that a liberal like Candlin could dismiss, as he dismissed nirvana, reincarnation, and questions about the nature of Christ, as more farragoes of metaphysical nonsense.

Of the ten great religions, Islam was the most poorly represented, in part a result of the refusal of Sultan Abdul Hamid II, the Emir of Turkey, to endorse the assembly. The overall picture of Islam, as presented by the Muslim delegates, was highly generalized and idealistic. J. Sanna Abou Naddara of Paris wrote in a brief letter that he would not speak of the holiness of the Quran lest he defame it; besides, he added, "I am not an Imam." He presented instead scriptural quotes to show that Islam taught religious tolerance and humane and moral values.[13] An equally streamlined view was presented by Alexander Russell (Mohammed) Webb, a former American diplomat in Smyrna and a convert to the religion of the prophet. Webb attempted to correct western misconceptions about Muslims by arguing that their social ethics were comparable to those of Christians. In the process, he created a stir by pointing out that the Quran supported neither polygamy nor purdah, the seclusion of women, and by announcing the opening of an American Islamic mission in New York City.[14]

The most comprehensive discussion of Islam came from George Washburn, a missionary and the president of Robert College in Constantinople. He presented an extended contrast and comparison of Islam and Christianity, observing that although the two faiths shared "a common Father" and are "brethren," the two were "mutually exclusive and irreconcilable." "We are one in our hatred of evil and in our desire for the triumph of the kingdom of God, but we are only partially agreed as to what Truth is, or under what banner the triumph of God's kingdom is to be won." He also portrayed Islam as standing in the path of the progress-driven millennial destiny of the Christian West. "Mohammedanism has been identified with a stationary civilization," he wrote, "and Christianity with a progressive one.... If progress is to continue to be the watchword of civilization, the faith which is to dominate this civilization must also be progressive."[15]

The presentations on Taoism suggested the tradition was degenerate and in need of a savior. An anonymous paper on the *Tao* contained a brief, unsympathetic account of the "corruption" of the quiet virtue of the philosophy of Lao-Tzu and the *Tao Teh King* into "a genii religion" of charms, incantations, alchemy, and magic. One wonders why the Department of Religion deemed this paper "a prize essay"; perhaps it was its suggestive and plaintive conclusion: "Oh! that one would arise to restore our religion, save it from errors, help its weakness, expose untruth with truth, explain the mysteries, understand it profoundly and set it forth clearly.... Would not that be fortunate for our religion?"[16]

The overall view of Shintoism portrayed the ancient Japanese tradition as about to be engulfed by Christianity. Reuchi Shibata, the hereditary leader of the Zhikko sect, brought a brief paper, delivered by Barrows, which was a rich description of Shinto mythology and cultus.[17] A second presentation by P. Goro Kaburagi was frankly Christian and apologetic: Shintoism "is dying, not because of its own weakness, but because a better religion has appeared—the teaching of Jesus. Christianity is the rising sun of Japan."[18] A third speaker, Takayoshi Matsugama, described the emergence of Shinto out of the indigenous tradition of Japan, but concluded: "Christianity alone can satisfy our every demand. All Shinto sects hate Christianity, but Japan's primitive religion does not oppose it, and is ready to transfer to it its power and influence."[19]

The Jain, Nichiren Buddhist, and Vaisnava Hindu traditions were presented in densely-coded papers by their respective adherents. Virchand Gandhi presented a concise account of the Jain canon, sects, doctrines, ethics, and metaphysics.[20] Yoshigiro Kawai presented an outline of the popular Nichiren sect of Japan in which he gave particular attention to *Daimoku* (scripture), *Honzon*, (the mandala of the enlightened Buddha body), and *Na-Mu-Myo-Ho-Ren-Ge-Kyo*, the chant used to induce enlightenment.[21] S. Parthasarathy Aiyangar presented an equally brief but comprehensive presentation of the Tenkalai S'ri Vaishnava tradition of South India, in which he touched upon the five worshipful manifestations of Vishnu and his consort Laksmi and the five ways of attaining salvation—good works, knowledge, love, faith, and the grace bestowed by the guru. Aiyangar explained that Vaishnavas consider the Vedas to be revelation and to have binding authority, but that the great Indian epics such as the *Mahabharata* and the *Ramayana*, as well as commentaries such as the *Krishna Yajur-Veda* and the works of the theologian Ramanuja, remained authoritative.[22]

The Asian delegates who made minor presentations displayed neither the charismatic, visionary qualities nor the self-conscious concern for public relations that was one important element in the outcome of the Parliament. Two Muslims presented Islam as having ideals similar to Christianity, while a Christian presented Islam as quite different and likely to be superseded by the modern, progressive values of liberal Christianity. Taoism and Shintoism seemed about to be engulfed by Christianity. A liberal like Candlin could dismiss the codes of the Jains, Nichiren Buddhists, and Vaishnavas as nonsense. As a result, the field might well have seemed open for a transfigured Protestant Christianity.

"Brains in Their Theology"

There was, however, more to the Asian presentations than just these minor papers. Herant Kiretchijian, a young Armenian from Constantinople, delivered what amounted to a manifesto for a rising tide of the new men in the East. "BRETHREN FROM THE SUN-RISING OF ALL LANDS," he began, "I stand here to represent the young men of the Orient . . . from the land of the pyramids to the ice-fields of Siberia . . . from the shores of the Aegean to the waters of Japan." He proceeded to discuss the confluence of western and eastern forces that had been transforming Asian thought over the course of the century and displayed one rudimentary version of the occidentalist strategy. On the one hand, he evoked the concept of a single oriental civilization, arguing that science, philosophy, theology, religion, poetry, and music all had their origins in the East, and as a result, it was to the East that the West owed a massive debt. On the other, he praised the liberal currents of western thought spreading out across Asia from Paris, Hiedelberg, Berlin, and other European capitals and from Asian outposts of western civilization such as Constantinople's Imperial Lyceum. "There is a new race of men that have risen up out of all the great past whose influence will undoubtedly be a most important factor in the work of humanity in the coming century. . . . I mean the young men of the Orient; they who are preparing to take possession of the earth with their brothers of the great West."[23]

As Kiretchijian's manifesto suggests, the most powerful accounts of the religions of the East would come from those Asians who were both conversant with the modern West and steeped in their own traditions. Methodist theologian Charles Little later remarked that "there was at Chicago a surprise at the intellectual power and subtly insinuating eloquence of the speakers from the Orient. The people expected pagans. And pagans, they thought were ignorant and impotent of mind, with no reasons for their worship and no brains in their theology. To them the Parliament was a stunning revelation."[24] A small cadre of Asian scholars were in part responsible for this revelation. As did Christian missionaries, these scholars applied the science of religion to draw parallels between their own religion and Christianity to further their apologetic aims, while interpreting them to fit within the framework of a global religious discourse. As importantly, they were able to communicate effectively with the American public by connecting the relatively unknown mythological universes of the East to more familiar western ideas. In doing so, they conveyed both the intelligibility and distinctiveness of their religions, creating in the process the impression, if one was inclined to be so impressed, that unity was a definite, perhaps an imminent, possibility.

Pung Kwang Yu, the First Secretary of the Chinese legation in Washington, D.C., delivered a lengthy and learned paper on orthodox Confucianism and its heterodox sects. A Confucian official-scholar, Pung openly displayed his lack of interest in what the West called theology. Missionaries in China, he pointed out, had in the past used *Shangti* (the Ruler of the Upper Regions), *Shen*, (Spirit), *Chan Shen*, (True Spirit), and *Tuh-i-chi-Shen*, (the Only Spirit) to signify the Christian idea of God. He also noted that religion was, according to Webster's dictionary, "the recognition of God as an object of worship, love, and obedience" and that Confucianism was not, in those terms, a religion at all, but a system of social ethics. Pung also explained that Confucianism was based on three ideas—*Ti*, the dispenser of heaven, and *yin* (passive) and *yang* (active) forces, all of which were in constant interplay in nature and society. To him, this was a philosophy that seemed to be in substantial agreement with "what the Buddhists say concerning 'One in Union and Three in Division,' what the Taoists say concerning the 'Three Pure Ones in Unity' and what Christians say concerning the 'Trinity in Unity' and the 'Godhead of the Three Persons.'"[25]

Pung Kwang Yu's applications of the science of religion contributed to the Parliament's many ambiguities. He likened the biblical account of the loaves and fishes to the tale of a Buddhist queen who, while sitting high in her castle, fed an army of a thousand men with milk from her breasts. He compared Jesus' miracles to the healing arts of Chinese alchemy. But more importantly, by flinging open China's door to liberal missionaries, he seemed to suggest that a brilliant future lay in store for Christianity. "If the Pope and the Propaganda, on the one hand, and the Protestant Missionary Societies on the other," he observed, "really desire to confer some lasting benefits on the people of China, as well as show the love they bear to Christ, I beg to suggest that such men be selected for missionary work in China as shall combine with their religious qualifications a proficiency in . . . sociology, philosophy, political economy, natural science, chemistry, international law, astronomy, geology, [and] mathematics." He noted that "the result from such a change in missionary methods will doubtless be immediate and satisfactory. . . . Missionaries as a class will doubtless be held in higher esteem than the Buddhist and Taoist priests."[26]

Jinanji Jamshedi Modi of the Bombay Parsi community drew upon the scholarship of F. Max Müller, James Darmesteter, and Martin Haug to create a surprisingly modern piece of interpretation, conveying a clear sense of both the uniqueness of Zoroastrianism and its essential compatibility with Christianity. Modi reviewed the history, scripture, and theology of Zoroastrians, but a main thrust of his presentation was to describe the Parsi community as bound together by the theological symbol of fire. The community "believes in the existence of one God," he began, "whom it knows under the name of Mazda, Ahura, and Ahura Mazda." He told his audience that, contrary to popular western misconceptions, Parsis did not worship fire, but considered it "an emblem of refulgence, glory, and light" and "the most perfect symbol of divinity." They gathered fire from lightning because nature was the temple of God and the surest evidence of his existence; purification rituals in the fire temple were not heathen rites, but were meant to signify that mortal man, like the most natural and refined symbol of God, must be purified. Fire was also used to bind the Parsi community. It was collected from braziers in the houses of all classes and brought to the temple for purification as a symbol of the equality of all people before God. "In short," he concluded, "the sacred fire burning in a temple serves as a perpetual monitor to a Parsee (sic) standing before it, to preserve piety, purity, humility, and brotherhood."[27]

Modi drew parallels between Parsi and Christian practice, comparing the application of ash from the sacred fire to the forehead in the course of daily prayer to the Catholic use of holy water when entering a church. He also drew a parallel between Parsi initiation and Christian confirmation. Young boys received a sacred shirt and thread to wear as "symbols of his being a Zoroastrian"; they acted as "perpetual monitors advising the wearer to lead a life of . . . physical and spiritual purity." He also emphasized traditional Parsi values that mirrored those of many in his American audience, such as temperance, marriage, and education, and he noted that the Bombay community valued tolerance and mixed freely with members of other faiths. Modi concluded his address with the words of the orientalist and feminist Frances Power Cobbe in order to remind the West of the debt it owed to "the first spiritual patriarch," the Bactrian sage. "'We might hardly conceive what human belief would be had Zoroaster never existed.'"[28]

Manilal Dvivedi, a philosopher and scholar, in his detailed presentation of Hinduism, combined a history of the development of the Hindu tradition with a critique of the bias of western orientalists, a defense of Hindu ritualism and theism, and a characteristically Hindu model for religious unity. He complained that western scholars and theologians formulated theories of Indian nature-worship and polytheism, which they then contrasted unfavorably with the Christian idea of a single God, refusing to acknowledge that, in addition to the many deities in Hinduism, the Vedas and Upanishads taught that unity existed within divine multiplicity. He explained, moreover, that the philosophical tradition of the *Vedanta* "is a system of absolute idealism in which subject and object are welded into one unique consciousness, the realization whereof is the end and aim of existence, the highest bliss—*moks'a.*" Other philosophical systems paled "before the blaze of unity and love lighted at the altar of the Vedas by this sublime philosophy, the shelter of minds like Plato, Pythagoras, Bruno, Spinoza, Hegel, and Schopenauer in the West and Krs'na, Vyasa, S'ankara, and others in the East."[29]

He also mounted a defense of the popular religions of India, a frequent target for the scorn of both scholars and missionaries, by explaining that the *Puranas* of folk Hinduism were commentaries on the ancient teaching of the Vedas in a popular form to appeal to the masses. Failing to comprehend this was why scholars and missionaries completely misunderstood the Hindu use of idols: "It may be said, without the least fear of contradiction, that no Indian idolater, as such, believes the piece of stone, metal, or wood, before his eyes as his god, in any sense of the word. He takes it as a symbol of the all-pervading, and uses it as a convenient object for the purposes of concentration, which being accomplished, he does not grudge to throw away." The use of images by Hindus found "an exact parallel in the worship of the Tau in Egypt, of the cross in Christendom, of fire in Zoroastrianism, and of the *Kaba* in Mohammedanism."[30]

Dvivedi concluded his address with a Hindu model for religious inclusivity that complemented, even as it differed, from western inclusivities. "I would ask you, gentlemen of the august Parliament, whether there is not in Hinduism material sufficient to allow of its being brought into contact with the other great religions of the world, by subsuming them all under one common genus." He thought it was possible "to enunciate a few principles of universal religion which every man who professes to be religious must accept apart from his being a Hindu, or a Buddhist, a Mohammedan or a Parsee, a Christian or a Jew." He suggested that these were "belief in the existence of an ultra-material principle in nature and in the unity of the All" and "belief in reincarnation and salvation by action." In them, "I see the salvation of man and the possibility of that universal love which the world is so much in need of at the present moment."[31]

The remarks of Asian scholars like Yu, Modi, and Dvivedi, though formal and, as some commentators noted, somewhat dull and a bit too long, suggested both differences and similarities among the religions of the world in a way that contributed to the ambiguities that multiplied on the floor of the Parliament. It required no great stretch of the imagination for a liberal Christian to see in the Confucian *Shangti,*

Shen, or *Ti*; in the Zoroastrian Ahura Mazda; and in the Hindu unity of the All, heathen extensions of the roughly synonymous theological terms of the modern Christian West—father, deity, divine spirit, infinite self, and extrahuman power in the universe. It was both logical and pious for some liberal Christians to draw the conclusion that the triune, spirit-filled God revealed most fully in Jesus had not left himself without a witness in the other religions of the world. The mythological universes described by the great codes of Asia could all be seen as pointing toward a new theological synthesis—a higher, modern, if most likely liberal, Protestant Christian synthesis—and a universal religious discourse for all the world.

"Something Like a Panic"

The Asian contribution to forging a common religious discourse would not have drawn the enthusiastic attention of the West had only concise papers on doctrines and creeds and scholarly briefs on the history of religion been delivered on the floor. The Asian delegation, however, included highly politicized individuals who had a keen sense of both the epochal nature of the event and the advantages that might accrue to them as a result of successful performances. Among them, moreover, were charismatic visionaries who, like Rexford and Boardman, had the capacity to strike a responsive chord in the American public: men like Anagarika Dharmapāla, Vivekananda, B. B. Nagarkar, and Protap Chandra Majumdar, who, in effect, carried the public-relations burden for all the Asians at the assembly.[32]

These were the men who fit most fully Kiretchijian's description of the rising men of the East—inspired by liberal ideals and conversant with western ways, but also deeply convinced of the validity of their traditions and determined to carve out a place for them in the emerging global ecumene. To paraphrase William Hutchison, they represented the "modernist impulse" in Asia rising within Hinduism and Buddhism. As the leaders behind the drive for religious unity on the side of the East, their charismatic performances, as Charles Little later noted, "might well startle an occidental audience to something like a panic."[33] Given the momentum of western expansion, the tenor of the Columbiad, and the skewed playing field of the Parliament, the Asian delegates entered the contest between East and West as underdogs, but these charismatic individuals emerged from the theological fracas on the floor as darkhorse candidates.

The modern Asian forces represented in Chicago were, moreover, allied, sharing a broad religious and political agenda for the modernization and revitalization of the East. Chandadat Chudatdahr, a Buddhist prince of Siam, and the Theravadin high priest Sumangala Nayaka Maha Thera (both of whom had papers delivered by proxies), together with Dharmapāla of Ceylon and Shaku Sōen of Japan, were members of the Maha Bodhi Society, a modern reform group working to unite northern and southern Buddhists to check Christian advances in the East.[34] A strong link between them and America already existed; Dharmapāla was the founder of the Maha Bodhi Society but was also a member of the Theosophical Society founded in New York in 1875 by Helena Blavatsky and Henry Olcott, who, after their move to India in 1878, joined the modernizing forces in the East.[35] Nagarkar and Majumdar were members of the Brāhmo-Samāj, a Hindu reform group in Bengal, which had throughout the nineteenth century been the religious avant-garde of India. For several decades, the Brāhmo-Samāj had forged links to an international network of Unitarians and scholars in the science of religion in both Europe and the United States. It had also served as Vivekananda's inspiration in the 1880s, and in 1892, the year before the Parliament, the Brahmos warmly welcomed Dharmapāla and the Maha Bodhi Society into the Asian modernizer ranks.[36]

The Japanese Buddhist delegation was made up of Shaku Sōen, Yatsubuchi Banryū, Toki Horyū, Ashitsu Jitsunen, and Hirai Kinzō, and they came to Chicago prepared to engage the West in both a common quest for religious unity and a duel. With the exception of Hirai's, their papers were largely philosophical, but due to their poor skills in English and mistranslations, the delegates' attempts to fashion a discourse that met the Parliament's ground rules while serving Buddhist ends were not readily apparent. But, they did bring with them English translations of short Buddhist essays, which they distributed throughout Chicago. "These five have journeyed to the Parliament," one Japanese press account noted, "to present Mahayana Buddhism, to stand amidst heterodox and barbarian teachings and to learn the subtle aspects of each." The goal of their trip to Chicago was to place "the brilliant light of Mahayana in the heavens over the Occident."[37]

Although English was never formally declared the official language of the Parliament, delegates who spoke English had a natural advantage at an assembly skewed toward the values and ideals of Anglo-Americans. It is, moreover, hardly an accident that the most successful of the Asian delegates hailed from nations and cultures under the direct influence of the British Empire. Anagarika Dharmapāla, a Sinhalese who spoke English with an accent that recalled to many an Irish brogue, was the most popular and charismatic representative of Buddhism. "With his black curly locks thrown back from his broad brow, his keen, clear eyes fixed upon the audience, his long brown fingers emphasizing the utterances in his vibrant voice," the *St. Louis Observer* noted, he "looked the very image of a propagandist, and one trembled to know that such a figure stood at the head of the movement to consolidate all the disciples of Buddha and to spread 'the light of Asia' throughout the civilized world."[38] Standing before the assembly with an image of the Buddha, he made a plea that Bodh-gaya, the site of the Buddha's enlightenment, be restored to Buddhist hands, and he presented a progressive form of Buddhism cast in terms drawn from the nineteenth century's intellectual mainstream. Destined to lead a Buddhist revival in South Asia in subsequent decades, Dharmapāla presented a form of Buddhism that could resonate with Candlin's liberal Christianity, except that it was neither Christian nor theistic.

"History is repeating itself," he declared. "Twenty-five centuries ago India witnessed an intellectual revolution. . . . Six centuries before Jesus Christ walked over the plains of Galilee preaching a life of holiness and purity, the Tathagatha Buddha, the enlightened Messiah of the World . . . traversed the whole peninsula of India with the message of peace and holiness to the sin-burdened world." Dharmapāla pointed out that during the nineteenth century William Jones, James Prinsep, Eugene Burnouf, Thomas Rhys Davids, and other European scholars had reopened the long-hidden archives of Buddhist thought. As a result, the world now faced "the dawn of a new era."[39] Citing Ernest Haeckel and Thomas Huxley, Dharmapāla also noted how the rise of evolutionary science and idealistic philosophies had prepared the way for the modern resurgence of Buddhism; "The tendency of enlightened thought of the day all over the world is not towards theology, but philosophy and psychology. The bark of theological dualism is drifting into danger." Western scholars might debate the message of the Buddha in western terms: did he teach agnosticism, monotheism, pantheism, idealism, or monism? No, Dharmapāla argued, Buddhism was "a comprehensive system of ethics and a transcendental metaphysic embracing a sublime psychology." Its goal was to realize nirvana—eternal peace in the "vortex of evolution," a transcendent state in which the "eternal changefulness in evolution becomes eternal rest."[40]

Vivekananda was a second charismatic Asian with great influence and appeal. At the time of the Parliament, he was still an obscure Bengali ascetic but shortly thereafter became the founder of the American Vedanta Society and the Indian Ramakrishna Math. Like other western-educated and politicized Asians, he combined elements of East and West in order to forge a strategy to further an Asian agenda. His Neo-Vedanta theology was to play a significant role in the "New Hindu Movement," in which nationalism, Hindu theism, and the quest for spiritual illumination were linked to a vision of *Bharatavarsa*, a mythic vision of ancient India.[41] Vivekananda was a favorite of the press and crowds, and Barrows recalled that when Vivekananda appeared in his ochre robes and turban, greeting the audience as his sisters and brothers in America, he received several minutes of tumultuous applause.[42] To his American audience, Vivekananda's physical presence evoked a sense of both familiarity and difference, like Dharmapāla's Sinhala-Irish brogue. The *Daily Inter-Ocean* noted that "great crowds of people, the most of whom were women, pressed around the doors leading to the Hall of Columbus . . . for it had been announced that Swami Vivekananda, the popular Hindoo (*sic*) monk who looks so much like McCullough's Othello, was to speak." More substantially, Merwin Marie-Snell, Bishop John Keane's secretary, was quoted as saying Vivekananda was "beyond question the most popular and influential man in the Parliament."[43]

Vivekananda's Hindu theism was the basis for an inclusivist theological vision that made a major contribution to the Parliament's protean ambiguities. The Vedas, he told the Parliament, were divine revelation which, unlike the Bible, were not confined to a single book but formed a beginningless and endless "accumulated treasury of spiritual laws." Like natural laws revealed by modern science, these spiritual laws had existed from eternity, but at various times they had been discovered by seers or *rishis*, some of the best of whom, he was quick to point out, had been women. The universe was also eternal. Thus, there was no creator God, because God and the universe ran together in a parallel track. But "at the head of all these laws, in and through every particle of matter and force, stands one through whose command the wind blows, the fire burns, the clouds rain, and death stalks upon the earth." For Hindus, he explained, God was the everywhere pure and formless one who may be called father, mother, and friend, but whose greatest incarnation was the dark lord Krishna, whose grace and mercy revealed itself to the pure of heart to release them from the bondage of *karma*.[44]

Vivekananda presented Hinduism in a progressive mode. It did not consist of dogmas, doctrines, or creeds, but "in being and becoming"; its goal was to unite the soul with the universal consciousness of God. "The whole religion of the Hindu is centered in realization," he noted. "Man is to become divine, realizing the divine, and, therefore, idol or temple or church or books, are only the supports, the helps of his spiritual childhood, but on and on he must progress." Vivekananda observed that to Hindus, "all religions from the lowest fetichism to the highest absolutism mean so many attempts of the human soul to grasp and realize the Infinite, determined by the conditions of its birth and association. . . . The Lord has declared to the Hindu in his incarnation as Krishna, 'I am in every religion as the thread through a string of pearls. And wherever thou seest extraordinary holiness and extraordinary power raising and purifying humanity, know ye I am there.' "[45]

The brightest and most progressive lights of modern Asia were members of the Brāhmo-Samāj, which had been founded by Rammohun Roy in 1828 on theistic principles drawn from the Vedas, the Quran, and the European Enlightenment. Throughout the century, the political, religious, and cultural crosscurrents of modernization in India had buffeted the Brahmos. After an alliance with Unitarians early in the century, they veered, under the leadership of Keshub Chandra Sen, in the direction of an ecstatic Hindu Christianity. Then, in the mid 1870s, they began to experiment with the disciplines of all the world's great faiths and philosophies, and many Brahmos enlisted in Sen's eclectic Brahmo splinter group, the Nava Vidhan, the Church of the New Dispensation of God. Sen died in 1884 leaving behind a weakened church and a faction-ridden membership, but his example, as well as his theology, informed the words of both B. B. Nagarkar and Protap Chandra Majumdar, when they spoke before the assembly.[46]

Consider the way in which Sen's theology, both visionary and highly concrete, could complement, perhaps overwhelm is the better word, the free-form and inclusivist theologies of western liberals. In "God-Vision in the Nineteenth Century," one of Sen's widely noted lectures, he likened nineteenth-century men to "apostles of nature and votaries of science" with a commission to "interpret the soul's vision of Heaven." What occult force, he asked, "nourishes and quickens all the known and undiscovered forces in nature. . . . This mysterious primary force, underlying all secondary force, I unhesitatingly call God-force." Sen wrote that this "Living Deity in everything," "Personal First Cause," "Parent of the universe," or "Supreme Mother" is manifest in all the prophets of the world. "Every prophet who came down from heaven, as an emanation of spirit-force from the Almighty, went back to him, as Christ did, after fulfilling his mission," as did "all the Jewish prophets of olden times, and Paul and all the apostles. And Chaitanya too, the blessed prophet of India, and the immortal Sakya Muni and Confucius and Zoroaster too. All our masters are there assembled. Seated on smaller thrones, they surround the throne of the Great Spirit, whose glory is in them and in whose glory they dwell."[47]

Sen's ecstatic theology, reiterated by his disciples and linked to the critical, aggressive, and prophetic spirit of a colonialized nation, was the ultimate driving force behind the Parliamentary quest for unity from the side of the East. Their occidentalist strategy amounted to nothing less than a wholesale adoption of the liberal spirit and a selective appropriation of Christianity, only to place it at the service of chastening the West, describing a vision of rising Asia, and generating universalistic religious discourses rooted in the traditions of the East.

Unlike Dharmapāla and Vivekananda, B. B. Nagarkar did not cut an exotic profile in Chicago, rather one that was distinguished and familiar. As the *Daily Inter-Ocean* noted, he was "a polished scholar and gentleman, whose hair is tinged with silver. He has a strongly intellectual face, and but for his complexion, might be taken for Marshall Field."[48] Nagarkar presented two papers, the first being a kind of cost-benefit analysis of British colonial rule in India. "Your English cousins," he told the assembly, deprived Hindus of their liberty, stole their wealth, and plundered their art, but they also gave in exchange an "inestimable boon of knowledge." The European Enlightenment had awakened India to its once forgotten past. Hindus, led by the example of the Brahmos, were now working to revive India's ancient learning, abolish caste, prevent infant marriage, outlaw the burning of widows, and elevate the position of women. Of the rise of the English from petty shopkeepers to imperial rulers, he exclaimed, in this "there was the hand of God."[49]

In his second address, Nagarkar laid out the spiritual principles of the Brahmo movement. First of all, God was a stern reality that must be realized in daily life, a capacity apparently lost in the West due to the artificiality of its commercial civilization. He also noted that truth was born in time, but not in place, and that no nation or religion could claim a monopoly on it. He also explained that the Brahmos were committed to the harmonization of all the prophets—Vyas, Buddha, Moses, Mohammed, Jesus, and Zoroaster; "it is the duty of us who live in these advanced times to put these messages together and thereby harmonize and unify the distinctive teaching of the prophets of the world." This was a "dispensation for the age," he noted. "Let us seek the guidance of the spirit, and interpret the message of the Supreme Spirit by the help of his Holy Spirit."[50] Nagarkar also explained that, above all, Bramos were devoted to the Motherhood of God. "Oh what a world of thought and feeling is centered in that one monosyllabic word *ma*, which in my language is indicative of the English word mother!" he exclaimed. "Once we see and feel that God is our Mother, all the intricate problems of theology, all the puzzling quibbles of church government, all the quarrels and wranglings of the so-called religious world will be solved and settled. We of the Brahmo-Samaj family firmly hold that a vivid realization of the Motherhood of God is the only solution of the intricate problems and differences in the religious world."[51]

A second of Sen's disciples, P. C. Majumdar, was the only Asian at the Parliament to have visited America before the Parliament. In 1883, in his widely noted *Oriental Christ*, he had outlined Sen's views of Jesus. Majumdar's argument was that because Jesus was a Palestinian, he was an Asian, and Asians therefore most clearly understood the message of his gospel. He proposed, for example, that the baptism of Jesus in the Jordan reflected the Hindus' love of ritual purifications and holy rivers, such as the Ganges.[52] In one of his two addresses as a speaker at the Parliament, Majumdar reiterated the social ideals of the Brahmos in much the same fashion as Nagarkar, and he reviewed the life and work of Rammohun Roy in the early part of the century.[53] In a second address, "The World's Religious Debt to Asia," he negotiated what amounted to a reversal of current by sending the impulse toward unity built upon western signs and sent heading East by western delegates, back to the West but built on signs from the East. Charles Little later remarked that "the words of Mozoomdar (*sic*) fell upon the startled listeners like flakes of biting flame."[54]

Majumdar's extemporaneous address was the Parliament's most comprehensive defense of Asia. It was a version of the occidentalist strategy in which he selectively appropriated elements normally understood to be a part of the western, Jewish-Christian historical continuum and linked them to comparable elements in Asian traditions, while criticizing many modern western attitudes in the light of the ancient spirit of the East. Majumdar's main line of argument was that Asians had repeatedly conferred spiritual gifts on the entire world. They first discovered that nature was more than a stimulus for romantic verse, but was, rather, an object of religious contemplation as "God's abode." King David of ancient Israel, Nanak, Yogavasista, Arjuna, and the ancient Vedic seers all testified that God lives in every particle of nature as its immanent spirit. Asia, he exclaimed, "calls upon the world to once more enthrone God in his creation." Introspection was also a gift of Asia; it had long taught that "on the framework of your own soul the warp and woof of all the worlds are woven, the universe of light and order is to be seen within. There is no glory without which the soul did not put there from within." A third gift was the knowledge that it was through natural instincts, not logic, observation, or scripture, that God was most fully revealed to the world: "Asia has the seeing of God within her spirit. . . . The progress of true religion is not in the conversion of the so-called heathen, but in the conception, the inspiration and realization of the ideal of the man or spirit."[55]

Asia had also taught the world to worship. Majumdar explained that India was "a land of impulse," where religion meant joyousness, exaltation, excitement; "there is a force that draws every drop of dew into the sea, a spark into the conflagration, a planet to the sun. They feel in the East a similar force of impulse drawing them into the depths of God. That is worship." For the Asian, he continued, love of God is "a growing passion," a "wine that inebriates," a "madness of spirit," a "tearful and fervid love," an "ecstasy of trust." It is the dance of Moses' sister Miriam, the fit of the prophet Mohammed, the madness of Hafiz, and the devotional chant of Vaishnavas. It is also devotional silence and ritual form—flowers, incense, sacrificial fires, sacramental foods, symbolic postures, fasting, and vigils. "Ceremonies without spirit are indeed dangerous," he noted, "but when words fail before God symbols become indispensable."[56]

Above all else, Asia had taught the world the ideal of renunciation. "We Orientals," he reflected, are "all descendents of John the Baptist."

Buddha fled the palace at Kapilavastu with an alms-bowl; Mohammed lived in a cave; the fakir of the Muslims and the *saddhu* of the Hindus were regarded by all the devout in India with awe. "This great law of self-effacement, poverty, suffering, death, is symbolized in the mystic cross so dear to you and dear to me. Christians, will you ever repudiate Calvary? Oneness of will and character is the sublimest and most difficult unity with God. And that lesson of unity Asia has repeatedly taught the world." Roman Catholic contemplatives, he added, had made a great impression upon Asians and it seemed "a sign of the times that even Protestant orders are reverting to the monastic principles of Asia."[57]

Majumdar closed with a comparison of the respective virtues of West and East, suggesting that, when the Parliament achieved its work, the two "might combine to support each other's strengths and supply each other's deficiencies." The West observed, watched, and then acted, he noted. In comparison, the East contemplated, communed, and was carried away by the spirit of the universe. The West wrested secrets from nature, enslaved it, and conquered it to become rich, but the East saw nature as the sanctuary of the soul. Westerners loved equality, justice, and the rights of man, but people in the East found the ecstatic love of God in loving human beings. The West emphasized morality, proper conduct, and public opinion, while the East aspired after absolute self-conquest whose only model was God. The West worked incessantly—"your work is your worship"—but in the East, "we meditate and worship for long hours; worship is our work."

Before surrendering the floor, Majumdar flung down a gauntlet before the imperial pretenses of the West. "In the East we are the subject race, we are talked of with contumely. The Asiatic is looked upon as the incarnation of every meanness and untruth. . . . Yet in the midst of the sadness, the loneliness, the prostration of the present, it is some consolation to think that we still retain some of our spirituality, and to reflect upon the prophecy of Ezekial: 'Behold the glory of the Lord cometh from the way of the East.' "[58]

All Things Made New

It was a species of pious common sense that led Candlin to conclude from the Asians' remarks that the world was about to go over to liberal

Protestantism. He had discarded traditional creeds and theologies, both Christian and non-Christian, discounted the importance of ritualism, abandoned the finality of all scriptures, and thoroughly naturalized faith and religion. If he listened carefully to the Asians, Candlin probably selectively focused on the theological and religious analogies they made before the assembly, while neglecting to attend to the distinctive theological, philosophical, and mythological universes they also described while on the floor. The theological subtleties in Majumdar's occidentalist strategy might well have been misread by Candlin as evidence that the Brahmo was, more or less, a deeply pious, liberal Protestant. Candlin had, moreover, placed his faith in what he called the Divine Spirit, be this, under close examination, the Confucian dispenser of heaven, the progressive spirit of the age, or the Holy Ghost of traditional Christianity. As a result of all this, Candlin made a logical, if mistaken, move when he concluded that the Parliament was a rapt gaze into an approaching Christian millennium, and he was not alone in making it.

The Parliament, however, presented to many American observers further ambiguities. In the minds of its organizers, the assembly was officially sanctioned by a theology derived from, alternatively, the Protestant, Christian, or Judeo-Christian traditions, which dovetailed neatly with a generic form of western, modern, liberal theism. Along with the classical and Christian signs, this theology also served as the foundation for America's Columbian myth and as the divine sanction for the White City. But like Jamal Effendi on the Midway Fourth, the Asian delegates at the Parliament confounded the taxomic logic in this situation by utilizing what amounted to another form of occidentalist strategy. They introduced Asian theologies and cultural ideals onto the floor of the assembly in full parity with those of the West, while, at the same time, they selectively appropriated American patriotic ideals and placed them at the service of the Asian cause.

Dharmapāla appealed to Americans' high regard for religious tolerance and their mistrust of creeds. "My brothers and sisters, born in this land of freedom, you have learned from your brothers of the far East their presentations of the respective systems they follow. You have listened with commendable patience to the teachings of the all-merciful Buddha through his humble followers. . . . Learn to think without prejudice, love all beings for love's sake. . . . If theology and dogma stand in your way in the search for truth, put them aside. Be earnest and work out your own salvation; and the fruits of holiness will be yours."[59]

Hirai appealed to America's revolutionary heritage. "You, citizens of this glorious free United States, who, when the right time came, struck for 'Liberty or Death'; you who waded through blood that you might fasten to the mast your banner of the stripes and stars upon the land and sea; you, who enjoy the fruition of liberty through your struggle for it; you, I say, may understand somewhat our position, and as you asked for justice from your mother country, we too, ask justice from these foreign powers."[60]

Shibata praised Americans for their intelligence, politeness, kindness, and sympathy, and he urged them to continue their struggle to achieve true universality. "What I wish to do is assist you in carrying out the plan of forming the universal brotherhood under the one roof of truth. . . . So long as the sun and moon continue to shine, all friends of truth must be willing to fight courageously for this great principle. . . . Now I pray that the eight million deities protecting the beautiful cherry tree country of Japan may protect you and your Government forever, and with this I bid you good bye."[61]

Vivekananda praised America's effort to realize the universality of the Vedantist vision. "It was reserved for America to call, to proclaim to all quarters of the globe that the Lord is in every religion. May he who is the Brahma of the Hindus, the Ahura Mazda of the Zoroastrians, the Buddha of the Buddhist, the Jehovah of the Jews, the Father in Heaven of the Christians, give strength to you to carry out your noble idea. . . . Hail Columbia, mother-land of liberty! . . . It has been given to thee to march at the vanguard of civilization with the flag of harmony."[62]

Nagarkar linked the progressive goals of New India to Americans' sense of their millennial destiny and mission. "My brethren and sisters in America, God has made you a free people. Liberty, equality and fraternity are the guiding words that you pinned on your banner of progress and advancement. . . . Give us your earnest advice and active cooperation in the realization of the social, political and religious aspirations of young India. God has given you a mission. Even now he is enacting through your instrumentality most marvelous events. Read his holy will through these events, and extend to young India the right hand of holy fellowship and universal brotherhood."[63]

Majumdar challenged Americans to see both the Brahmo and the Columbian theological platforms through to their final completion. "In the fullness of time you have called the august Parliament of Religion, and the message that we could not propagate you have taken into your hands to propagate. . . . May the spread of the New Dispensation rest with you and make you our brothers and sisters. Representatives of all religions, may all your religions merge into the Fatherhood of God and in the Brotherhood of Man, that Christ's prophecy may be fulfilled, the world's hope may be fulfilled and mankind may become one kingdom with God our Father."[64]

In the Parliament's concluding moments on its ceremonial closing day, the delegates from the West called back to those from the East as Chicago's Apollo Choir sang Mendelssohn's "Judge Me, O God" and Handel's "Hallelujah Chorus."

George Dana Boardman parted saying, "Fathers of the contemplative East, sons of the executive West, behold how good and how pleasant it is for brethren to dwell together in unity. The New Jerusalem, the City of God, is descending, heaven and earth chanting the eternal hallelujah chorus." Emil Hirsch saw the Parliament as "a portal to a new life, for all of us a life of greater love for and a greater trust in one another." The assembly had "kindled the cheering fires telling the whole world that a new period of time has been consecrated." Noting the important role played at the Parliament by delegates from "the darker races," AME bishop B. W. Arnett, the highest ranking African-American delegate, hoped the assembly would "teach the American people that color is not the standard of excellency or of degradation" and that "not only the Fatherhood of God be acknowledged, but the Brotherhood of Man." John Keane noted: "Friends, will we not look back to this scene of union, and weep because separation continues? But will we not pray that there may have been planted a seed that will grow to union wide and perfect? O, friends, let us pray for this. It is better for us to be one." John Henry Barrows bid farewell by noting that "the last words which I speak to this Parliament shall be the name to Him I owe life and truth and hope and all things, who reconciles all contradictions, pacifies all antagonisms . . . Jesus Christ, the Saviour of the world."[65]

Charles Bonney, chairman of the entire World's Congress Auxiliary, closed the assembly with the words, "WORSHIPERS OF GOD AND LOVERS OF MAN, the closing words of this great event must now be spoken. With inexpressible joy and gratitude I give them utterance. . . . What many men deemed impossible God had finally wrought. . . . This Congress of the World's Religions is the most marvelous evidence yet given of the approaching fulfillment of the apocalyptic prophecy. 'Behold! I make all things new!' "[66]

For seventeen days, a search for a common religious discourse for a single global community of sentiment had been underway on the floor of the Parliament. Currents of faith and brilliant rhetoric from around the globe crested in a great flood of inspired visions, grand possibilities, and theological ambiguities. The father seemed to be above it, Jesus to be written all over it, the human and Holy Spirit to be moving throughout it, together with the *kami*, the Divine Mother, Krishna, Confucius, and the Buddha too. The nineteenth century seemed to have found a fulfillment in the Columbian ingathering of nations and tribes, the first in the history of the world, on the threshold of the twentieth century, when the promise of modernity might be fulfilled and when all things might be made new.

III.

FURTHER AND FRACTIOUS MISSIONS

6

ACTS OF APOSTLES

The two-thousand-year failure of Christianity roared upward
from Broadway, and no Constantine the Great was in sight.

—Henry Adams, *The Education of Henry Adams*

AFTER THE PARLIAMENT, all things were not made new, and modernity, while remaining very promising for quite some time, did not present the world with a global religious discourse and a common community of religious sentiment, even as the process of globalization that
had made the Parliament possible proceeded apace. The Christian century that many had foreseen was eventually revisioned as the American century, but the nation grew less and less to be the America of the
Columbian myth and White City. The question of what shape relations among the different religions was to take, both in the global community and at home, was never quite resolved, and although ingenious
formulas, contests, and fractious debates multiplied, in many quarters
indifference to the question and resignation to the unlikelihood of ever
finding a satisfactory answer eventually reigned supreme. Likewise,
the question of which religious party could finally discern truth from
superstition for either the global or domestic communities remained a
topic to be avoided, forgotten, or ceaselessly debated as consensus on
religious authority, be it Constantine, scripture, the Spirit, or human
instinct, seemed increasingly to evaporate.

The Peristyle Goes Back to Heaven

Assuming that an American world's fair might possibly reveal the
will of God, what transpired in the White City soon after the Parliament closed did not suggest that classical, Christian, and patriotic
signs and millennial energy could remain the building blocks of a

mainstream American myth indefinitely. Just a month after the Parliament, mayors of major American cities gathered at the Exposition for Cities Reunion Day, hosted by Carter H. Harrison, the mayor of Chicago. "I have stood upon the seven hills of Rome. . . . I have been in Athens," he mused, but they could not begin to compare with the White City. The day seemed "propitious"; Harrison's hopes ran high that Congress would authorize the Exposition to remain open for another year. But later that night, on returning from the White City to his home on fashionable Ashland Avenue, Harrison was shot by a young Catholic assassin, an activist in his mayoral campaign, in an apparent act of political revenge.[1]

Two days later, on October 30, the Columbian Exposition was scheduled to close. The elaborate ceremonies—the reenactment of the landing of Columbus, the presentation of awards to foreign exhibitors, the ringing of chimes, and the firework spectaculars at noon and dusk—were cancelled. Flags in the White City hung at half-mast, where a small crowd gathered in Festival Hall for a solemn benediction. Thomas Palmer, the Exposition President, noted that what ought to have been a "day of jubilee" had become a day of mourning.[2] On Sunday morning, Chicago's mainstream Protestant preachers expressed their shock and horror: John Henry Barrows at the First Presbyterian—"a great shadow has come over our pride and our rejoicing"; P. S. Henson at the First Baptist—"a dreadful finale was this to the great Exposition of which we were all so justly proud"; O. P. Gifford at Immanuel Baptist—"Carter Harrison is dead. The World's Fair is ended, the life of the World's Fair has gone out. . . . Like a white lily touched by frost it blackens and withers"; Joseph Cook at the First Congregational—"Red floats across the American sun. Only the breath of the Holy Ghost filling the canopy of our civilization can dispel the ghastly portent of storm.[3]

But things got worse. The Exposition had served Chicago as a local dike against a failing national economy, but with its close, the ranks of the city's unemployed rose to an estimated 200,000.[4] By January, the empty palaces in the White City were, according to the *Tribune*, "fairly swarming" with "tramps." At 5:30, on the night of January 8, fire broke out among the packing crates and excelsior on the second floor of the Casino, then quickly spread to Music Hall. Sparks blew onto the roofs of the Palaces of Agriculture and of Manufactures and Liberal Arts.[5]

Stoked by a steady northeasterly wind, flames ignited the Triumphal Arch and Peristyle. "One after another the great columns fell with a terrific crash that sent up great clouds of sparks," the *Tribune* reported. A crowd of 20,000 looked on "as one after another the statues toppled and pitched head foremost into the flames." The scene from the Administration Building "was grand and terrible beyond description"; the Goddess of Liberty stood "like a gigantic silhouette, with uplifted arms as if appealing for help." For a moment, the "mute faces on the triumphal chariot were lighted as though a search light had been turned upon them," until a thundering crash signaled the destruction of Columbus and his steeds. Young boys cheered, women wept, and "men of mature years were grieved and thoughtful." Clara Burnham, in her Columbian novella *Sweet Clover*, expressed appropriate sentiments through her heroine Mildred. The Peristyle, Mildred "exclaimed chokingly, 'the Peristyle has gone!—gone back—to heaven!'"[6]

By spring, Chicago was in the grip of what Alan Trachtenberg called the "epic insurgence" of the Pullman Palace Car Company boycott and strike.[7]

Meanwhile, American delegates had begun to mount missions to further what they took to be the spirit of the Parliament. The glow of global fraternalism and a heightened sense of expectation lingered longest among the most liberal of delegates, but even as they attempted to perpetuate the quest for a common religious discourse, centrifugal forces emerged among them quickly. At the same time, highly visible fractures appeared in the invisible church that Philip Schaff had praised on the Parliament floor, and criticism from wary Protestants pointed to a process of fragmentation in the old Anglo-Protestant mainstream.

Sectarian Universalists

Hope for unity ran highest in those quarters where the optimistic mood in which the Exposition was originally conceived maintained a strong head of steam. A headline in the *San Francisco Examiner* on September 28, 1893, read:

A GRAND WORK PERFORMED
GREAT PROGRESS MADE BY THE RELIGIOUS PARLIAMENT
SPREAD OF UNIVERSAL GOSPEL

The *Examiner* reported that at the morning session on the closing day, people overflowed the Hall of Columbus, leaving hundreds outside in the streets. By evening, a line wound halfway around the block and scalpers charged three and four dollars for tickets that were ordinarily free. The evening's proceedings were repeated twice. First in the Hall of Columbus and then in the Hall of Washington, three thousand people at a time leapt to their feet, waving handkerchiefs and cheering. Julia Ward Howe "kissed her hand in benediction of the Parliament, and the Jewish rabbi and the Catholic Bishop asked God's blessing upon its work which is now a part of history." The delegates all called for "a spirit of religious amity and . . . for the breaking down of the barriers of creeds and the spread of a universal gospel that shall embrace all faiths in one glorious whole for the glory and honor of God." Christians, Jews, Buddhists, and Muslims, the *Examiner* continued, all "spoke for a universal religion, advocated it in fact, and fervently hoped for some such, to them, happy consummation as the outcome of this great and historic gathering."[8]

Encouraging words also came from a wholly different quarter, from Shaku Sōen, the Zen Buddhist delegate from Japan. After returning from Chicago to his homeland, Sōen sent a poem to the delegate Paul Carus, the scientific naturalist of La Salle, Illinois, a transliteration of which appeared in Carus's *Monist*.[9]

Men | are | red | yellow | also | black | (and) white.

But the path (of righteousness) | (has) not |
   south | north | west | (or) east.

(If any one) does not | believe (this) | (let him)
   look | (in the) heavens | above | (at the) moon.

(Her) clear | light | fills entirely | (and)
   penetrates | (the) grand | vault | (of the) firmament.

News of the Parliament also traveled to Europe and the remarks of F. Max Müller at Oxford contributed to the sense of wonder. "Who would have thought," Müller wrote, "that what was announced as simply an auxiliary branch of an exhibition could have developed into what it was, could have become the most important part of that immense undertaking, could have become the greatest success of the past year." The Parliament should "take its place as one of the most memorable events in the history of the world." There are "few things which

I so truly regret having missed as the great Parliament of Religions held in Chicago."[10]

Optimism ran particularly high in Chicago where a handful of delegates attempted to keep up the momentum generated by the Parliament, by making calls for religious unity and proclaiming the dawning of a new age in human history. Unfortunately, the grandiosity intrinsic to the Columbian spirit was a conspicuous problem, and the varied agendas of the delegates thwarted their attempts to forge a common religious point of view. Each delegate's universal vision had a highly particular foundation, which only meant that the fact that their religious discourses were multiple and often at crossed purposes kept pushing into view. The happy coincidence of patriotism, classicism, Christianity, and millennial enthusiasm, moreover, seemed to be wearing thin.

In May of 1894, the First American Congress of Liberal Religious Societies was convened in Emil Hirsch's Sinai Temple in Chicago. Parliamentary delegates such as Hirsch, Jenkin Lloyd Jones, E. L. Rexford, Hirai Kinzō, and six hundred others signed a call for "a nearer and more helpful fellowship in the social, educational, industrial, moral, and religious thought and work of the world." As reported by the *Chicago Herald*, one goal of the movement was to form bridges between religious liberals in the churches and the numerous supporters of the liberal cause among the unchurched. D. H. Thomas, the presider, was quoted as saying, "We want no more denominations: there are too many now. . . . But if we could have a union of all these liberal elements it would, to say the least, be a great economy."[11]

But, Jenkin Lloyd Jones proceeded to sketch out a platform for yet another church, one he called the "great prophetic Free Church of America." "Believing as we do that the Parliament was more than . . . a spiritual sensation, we must take to heart the prophecy we find in it," he wrote. "We think it pointed to the possibility to unite men of diverse races and faiths in an actual fellowship, in working organizations, potent, inspiring, in short the Parliament of Religions predicted a movement that will undertake a new church in the world." But, in the last analysis, Jones's vision of a new church was little more than a latter-day restatement of the transcendentalists' critique of Unitarian orthodoxy first made earlier in the century: "the Unitarian denomination that has been hesitating and halting along the cool and ragged edge of Christianity, missing the fervor of its dogmatic heart, but dreading to trust to the splendid inspiration of natural religion . . . will die in order that its spirit of individual responsibility and free inquiry may live."[12]

Jones envisioned Chicago as "the cathedral city of the world" for a universal church standing on the emerging sciences of anthropology and sociology, foundations he thought richer than scripture, more relevant than Greek and Hebrew etymologies, and deeper than theology. It would be a church where the soul might "kiss the hem of the inevitable" and find "to its delight that the inevitable is also the ineffable." The "glimmering lights of the future guide us. We go to build the church of the twentieth century—open temples of reason, holy shrines of helpfulness, confessionals where the soul will not be afraid to confess its ignorance."[13]

Emil Hirsch, even as he played host to the Congress, had reservations. He noted in an interview that "the theory of bringing all liberal churches together meets my hearty approbation, but sometimes I fear that an effort to put it into practice will end only in a dream."[14] More to the point, he had returned from the Parliament asking himself, "How did my own little jewel casket and its contents compare with the displays of others? What perhaps might I find in this vast collection . . . to add to my own spiritual store . . . to render the light of my own lamp more intense?"[15]

The Columbiad had convinced Hirsch of the need for a religion to meet the demands of a wholly new age: "Today I am a man; with me history begins. Neither Jew nor Gentile am I; neither Greek nor Barbarian! The past be dammed back, let now begin a new, the first era." Hirsch understood the man of the new era as seeking self-consciousness, activity, energy, and opportunity. His place was not in another world that could well take of itself but in this world with its constant exertions and relentless activities. Yet, the religion of this new age could not be Buddhism. He thought it condemned self-consciousness as a curse, saw life as a burden, and confused wretchedness with sympathy. Nor could it be Christianity. Traditional Christians taught "that this earth is doomed; that the prince of darkness reigns; that it is not natural man but the mysteriously regenerated man that enters the Kingdom." Among liberals, the situation was little better: "All vigor is held to be evil; certainly all virility. Aesthetics replaces ethical robustness, and vague intellectualism quenches the moral fire. . . . With such method, this present world cannot be leavened."[16]

For Hirsch, the religion of the new era had to be Judaism. The world waits for the presentation of our view on life, he concluded. "Here is the chance for our religion. The Parliament has shown that religion like ours will receive allegiance by the millions. . . . As Jonah was sent to Nineveh, so the Jews must go out and conquer. This duty the Parliament has taught me."[17]

Paul Carus led a second attempt to perpetuate the Parliament quest for unity, when he announced the founding of the World's Religious Parliament Extension in 1895. He saw the goal of the Extension as stimulating friendly relations among religions, awakening worldwide interest in religious problems, and uniting the world in one faith that would prepare the way for the establishment of a "church universal." America, he noted, "is like a new dispensation with new possibilities for a higher, nobler, and grander covenant. What was left undone in Benares, the centre of an old civilization, in Jerusalem, a city sacred to three religions, in Rome, the venerable see of the Popes, and in London, the home of modern science and industry, has been accomplished by the bold spirit of Chicago enterprise."[18]

Carus wanted the Extension to serve the needs of the orthodox and radical, Jew and Christian, both East and West, but he offered very little of interest to traditionalists and conservatives. The leading idea of the Extension was that the religious aspirations of the day were more comprehensive, more liberal, "more cosmic", and in more conscious cooperation with science than ever before, and its leading theological premise amounted to a new, syncretistic faith. One element in this faith was liberal Christianity; the Extension, he wrote, "is decidedly a child of the old religions and Christianity is undoubtedly still the leading star. . . . The dross is discarded, but the gold will remain." A second was religious science; "science is divine, and the truth of science is a revelation of God. Through science God speaks to us; by science he shows us the glory of his works; in science he teaches us his will." A third element was vaguely Buddhist; "self is an illusion," he concluded, "there is no wrong in this world, no vice, no sin except what flows from the assertion of self. . . . The ultimate aim of religion is to eliminate self and let man become an embodiment of truth, an incarnation of God."[19]

Fundamental tensions, however, were also apparent among Carus and his Extension allies. Catholic delegate Merwin-Marie Snell was also an advocate for a liberal religious science, and at the time of the Parliament, he argued in Carus's *Open Court* that such a science, by critically examining all metaphysical religious concepts, had furnished, for the first time in history, a practical basis for a universal religious fellowship. All "alleged invisible entities supposed to lie behind or beyond the cosmic activities," he wrote, were "inessential to religion," advocating in their stead a subjectivist syncretism: "Universal subjectivity may be equally the object of love and devotion and obedience, whether it be called Osiris-Ra-Tum, Assur-Il, Ahura-Mazda, Tien, Atma-Brahma, Karma, Mahadevi, Adonai-Elohim, or the World-All. . . . Elysium, Valhalla, Devachan, Tushita-world, Spirit Land, Happy Hunting Ground—what do these signify but the joyous outcome of duty accomplished?"[20]

But, for all his talk of universal religious fellowship, Snell's universal religion of science only thinly disguised a Roman ecclesiology. At about the same time, he wrote to a Catholic colleague that "my studies of all religions and philosophies, ancient and modern, Christian and non-Christian, in the fullest light of the most rationalistic modern science, have only served to day by day strengthen my conviction that . . . the Catholic Church is not only the grandest possible confederation of human energies, but the Supreme Organon of the Divine Spirit, and the veritable Kingdom of God upon earth." He saw the world undergoing "the throes of a sublime parturition" from which it would emerge with a church for a new era—"one, holy and apostolic in her essential nature, and Roman, more and more dutifully and unswervingly Roman, in her allegiance." He noted how "the world-wide structure of the Divine Hierarchy is now firmly established; Christian influence is now dominant throughout the planet. . . . By the irresistible efficacy of light and love, will all nations turn to the Incarnate Truth, accept the ministry of the Eternal Priesthood, and become united to the visible center of the world's unity, the radiating focus of all celestial influences, the Holy Roman Church, the See of Blessed Peter, the triple-crowned Pontiff of a Redeemed humanity."[21]

Charles Bonney remained an Extension associate, even as he grew concerned that liberal speculation was getting out of line. "In a certain high and representative sense, the Parliament was an exemplification of monism in religion," he wrote in Carus's *Monist*, but it was "not a scheme to form a new religion." He also expressed dismay at a mounting chorus of conservative critics: "It is remarkable that most of the criticisms have come from persons assuming to speak in the name of Christianity." He was perplexed and curious to know "how it is that a great religious assembly, which for seventeen successive days was opened with the prayer that Jesus taught to his disciples, the representatives of all the religions of the world reverently joining in its devout recital, has been or can be a subject of censure from persons who claim to be his followers. Evidently there is some mistake in regard to the matter."[22]

Bonney attempted to clarify the situation by reiterating his own conviction that Jesus, as the light of the world, was the light in every man, that salvation was for all persons, and that God had not left himself without a witness among any people in the world. But, it was a Swedenborgian doctrine, more clearly stated on the floor of the New Church Congress by a colleague, L. P. Mercer, which enabled Bonney to see the assembly as exemplifying an irenic and stable, if essentially unequal, relationship between other religions and Christianity. Mercer had explained that for Swedenborgians the Parliament was a direct result of the Last Judgement, an event that occurred in the spiritual world, as witnessed by Emanuel Swedenborg in a vision in 1757. All religions had been revealed at that time to have their origins "in the same Word or mind of God which wrote itself in the Hebrew lawgivers and prophets and became incarnate in Jesus Christ." He understood the Parliament to be a witness to the fact that the millennium was already in the process of unfolding and that, quoting Dante, all religions were being drawn to Jesus Christ, through "the organic course of events in that Providence which works on, silent but mighty, like the forces that poise planets and gravitate among the stars."[23]

Visible Fractures in the Invisible Church

While the quest for unity among the Chicago liberals splintered into a multiplicity of competing universal visions, observers closer to the mainstream churches attempted to clarify the meaning of the Parliament for their respective constituencies. It soon became clear that the Christian consensus ecumenists had hoped for was not going to gel. The plurality of the Christian churches, not their unity, was more the order of the day, and ominous signs appeared that spelled trouble ahead for the custodians of American culture in the old Protestant mainstream.

Roman Catholic participation at the Parliament was part of a liberal movement in the American church, one that would be quashed by the Pope within a decade, a development aided in part by Catholic critics of the assembly.[24] Yet, even before censure from Rome, liberal prelates showed little inclination to compromise the claims of their church or to loosen their moorings to the papacy. Delegate John Keane, in an interview in the *Boston Pilot* immediately after the Parliament, noted that some people saw the assembly as a great injury to Christianity, while others viewed it as the ushering in of the millennium. According to Keane, both views were "extreme, and therefore erroneous." The Parliament had been an exercise in comparative religious history, he noted; "the study of stages of arrested progression in the religious life of mankind has only served to show more clearly that the Christian religion contains the fulness of all that is good and true in all." He noted as well that "the same is true of the Catholic Church in comparison with the other Christian denominations. The more they are studied in comparison with one another the clearer it becomes that she is the one universal church as her name, Catholic, implies." Keane concluded that the archbishops who had accepted the invitation to the Parliament had anticipated this outcome, and that "things have turned out, I think, quite in conformity with the reasonable expectations of sensible people."[25]

Signals coming from Catholics who were observing the reactions to the Parliament were mixed, displaying the contradictory responses Keane had observed. Immediately after the event, the *Catholic World* was both amused and laudatory. "It was a unique sight, one that, mayhap, will not occur again this side of the brig of doom, to see marching into the hall the procession led by C. C. Bonney, the bearded patriarch of the Cosmic religions. . . . One need not dip into the future even as far as the eye can see to behold in this vision of the religious world the signs of a coming millennium."[26] But a year later, the *American Catholic Quarterly*, in a review of Barrow's official history, raised a caustic voice at the other extreme. "The effect produced by the parliament upon Dr. Barrows himself is . . . too enthusiastic and poetical for comprehension by the dull mind of ordinary readers. 'Striking the noble chord of universal human brotherhood,' he says, 'the promoters of the World's First Parliament of Religions have evoked a starry music which will yet drown the miserable discords of earth.' Beautifully said, could one but understand what it means." As far as the *Quarterly* was concerned, there were in "cold reality" only two alternatives— "Christ's Holy Catholic Church" or "the abyss of universal negation."[27]

In August of 1894, German-American delegates to the *Katholikentag* in Cologne condemned the liberal tendencies of Catholicism in the United States, citing as a prime example the "unholy memory" of the Parliament. In September 1895, a letter from Pope Leo XIII to Archbishop Satolli, the Apostolic Delegate to the United States, arrived with the pronouncement: no more "promiscuous conventions." In 1896, John Keane was dismissed from the rectorship of Catholic University.[28]

Delegate Augustine Hewitt, rector of the liberal Paulist order, wrote the most comprehensive Catholic response to the Parliament, and for him, the entire Columbian spectacle seemed to have taken a turn for the worse. The East/West encounter, however, was not for him a complex affair: the Parliament made it abundantly clear that Christianity alone had "any reasonable claim to be a supernatural, revealed, universal religion, demanding the homage of all mankind." His real concern lay elsewhere, with the question of Christian unity. He thought Schaff's suggestion that the Pope infallibly declare his fallibility in matters pertaining to other churches was "one of the most extraordinary sentences ever penned." If the Pope "is willing to accept the arbitration of Dr. Schaff as an unerring interpreter of history, he gives up his supremacy and with it all the ecumenical councils except the first seven recognized by the Greeks." He considered Schaff's proposal for reunion no more than a "grand Evangelical Alliance by the way of compromise and a visionary scheme." Christian unity, he concluded, "has never existed except in the form a great circle or sphere having its center in the Roman See of St. Peter. All schisms and divisions have arisen by centrifugal movements away from this center. Catholics believe that this sphere with its center was established by Jesus Christ, to endure until the end of the world."[29]

As importantly, Hewitt was also deeply troubled by the apparent meaning of the White City, and when reflecting on the nation's destiny, he veered in the direction of the premillennialists' jeremiad. "I shall not be understood as condemning the Chicago Exposition," he wrote, "nor do I condemn the grand achievements in every kind of material science and art of our modern civilization, the world of the present age, as evil and wicked. . . . My contention is this: not that there is evil, but that there is a total shortcoming in all this grand and splendid civilization." The Columbian year ended in financial panic, labor uprisings, anarchist rebellions, and the calling up of the military to quell riots in Chicago's streets, all of which raised for him grave questions about America's commitment to human welfare, rights, and liberty. "Is there anything wrong in this civilization?" he asked. "Is it in any way a cause provoking this deadly hostility?[30] Hewitt concluded that America's commercial society lacked moral fiber and religious vision. Its democratic ideals were leading not to a greater commonweal, but to a perpetual state of anarchy in which the citizens of the republic were continually excited to rivalry over the material prizes of life. "Our great republic must find its vital force and strength in morality. The only sufficient basis of morality is in religion, the only possible religion for America is Christianity, and the only pure and perfect embodiment of Christianity is the Catholic Church. . . . Hereafter it must be the Pope and the People." America could have the reign of Christ if it wanted it; "otherwise, there is nothing to be awaited but the triumph of the Antichrist and the final conflagration of which the burning of 'The White City' is a type."[31]

Meanwhile, leaders in the liberal theology movement in mainstream Protestantism remained serene. The *Biblical World* saw Christendom as united at the Parliament; the Asians had, moreover, demonstrated that "God was working in them; that they were not left to themselves; that their religions were not 'false' in contradiction to the one 'true' gospel." As a result, the ideal of Christian conquest could give way to Christian fulfillment, incorporation, and assimilation of the other religions of humankind. The *Biblical World* concluded that the ultimate religion was "that one which has the greatest capacity of growth manward and Godward. . . . For man ultimateness must be in a living person. In this sense not Christianity but Christ is the ultimate religion. Such was the deepest voice of the Parliament."[32]

Lyman Abbott wrote that through his participation at the Parliament he had learned that the East and West were complementary; the West could instruct the East in practical affairs, while Asian mystical tendencies "can teach us how to be still and know that God is God." But, he drew from this no radical conclusions. Some might "applaud more generously the unexpected utterances of religious feeling by the apostles of curious face, figure, and attire than the more familiar, if soberer, utterances of Anglo-Saxon Christians," he wrote. The final result of the Parliament, however, would be "at once to broaden our conception of Christianity and to make its acceptance both a logical and a spiritual necessity."[33] Washington Gladden concurred. Recalling his participation at the Parliament, he wrote in his memoirs twenty years later that the Parliament had been a witness to "the likelihood that Christianity will be the solvent and unifier of mankind."[34]

David Swing had not been a Parliamentary delegate, but he displayed a confidence in the liberal Protestant position that rested on a letter-perfect version of the Columbian logic of history. In a post-Parliament sermon, Swing surveyed western history from Greece and Rome through the Renaissance to the Reformation, seeing in the progress of literature, art, philosophy, and the "simple religion of Jesus" a witness to the fact that the West possessed "a mind which surpasses the East in breadth and utility." He praised the "charming picture" of the contemplative life painted by Asians such as Majumdar, but concluded that "the pagan creeds omit too much. Their survey of man is not as broad as that taken in Christianity." Swing understood America to be building up a religion "under whose flag men will live as Christ lived, with all rights sacred, all men as brothers, with life divine, and with death not a defeat but a triumph," and he thought the Asians had come to the Parliament to help America achieve this. During the Parliament, he wrote, "this lake shore, where the wild Indians gave their war whoop within living memory, grew almost roseate with the passing of the chariot of the Infinite. . . . The old Orient came to help inspire the West. The morning of piety came to pour its glow and colors into the sunset of magnificence. No such scene has been witnessed since the coming of Jesus Christ."[35]

If Protestant liberals remained confident, however, skeptical observers just to the right saw the assembly as a danger signal both for America and for the old Protestant mainstream. Charles Little, a Methodist evangelical at Garrett Bible Institute who had not attended the assembly, wrote that "the Court of Honor is in ruins, the Midway is silent, and the Parliament is dumb. Let no one wince at the association; for the Midway had its serious and pathetic aspects, while the gathering of priests and preachers oscillated sometimes to the edge of the fantastic and absurd." He did not condemn the Parliament. On the contrary, he called it a "beautiful display of charity, courtesy, and culture," and he saw in it the leaven of Christianity at work in the world. Yet, he considered the declarations of a new era at hand to be "sweet delusions" and compared the euphoria in many quarters to the joy of the French at the Feast of the Federation on the eve of the Terror.[36]

In Little's view, the problem with the Parliament rested not with the admittedly stunning performances of the Asians. On the one hand, he simply dismissed all that was unfamiliar in their remarks. Of Dharmapāla's address, he wrote, "here we have an exposition by a powerful oriental mind . . . here, too, we have the grandeur of a desperate faith." On the other, he attributed all that was familiar in them to Christ and the Holy Spirit. Little thought a Christian could reflect on the words of Majumdar with joy because this was a voice, not of the old, but of a new orient; "He sees the Mediterranean miracles of the second and third centuries repeated before his eyes." The Brahmos' remarks displayed "the intellectual reaction by which we can measure the stupendous influence that Jesus Christ is already exercising in the Hindoo (sic) mind. And what is true of Mozoomdar (sic) is true of all the representatives of the Orient." Like Candlin, Little saw the best of the Asians as displaying a kind of incipient Christianity; they were men "driven to an answer by the imperative energy of the Holy Ghost. . . . It was through such gateways as Manichaeism and neo-Platonism that Augustine found his way to Jesus Christ."[37]

The Parliament did, however, raise a serious set of problems in regard to what it seemed to suggest about the nation's religious destiny. First of all, there was the fact that Jews and Catholics made successful presentations. "That the Jew would gladly avail himself of the opportunity for social and intellectual recognition was expected by all who have studied Israel," Little wrote. "Those who knew the power of the Hebrew pulpit were not surprised at the magnificent exhibition of Moses and the law. From both camps, liberal and orthodox, arose the voice of exultation. For had not Jehovah triumphed in the Western world?" For their part, Catholics "marched through the Parliament like a Macedonian phalanx. A common purpose animated the utterances of all her speakers, and their bearing was the perfection of tact. Never bating one jot of their claim to religious supremacy, they pushed themselves forward quietly as the intellectual synthesis of all philosophies, the spiritual synthesis of all creeds, and the ethical synthesis of all moralities." Little was deeply troubled because "these prelates and divines made the utmost of an opportunity the like of which they have never had in American history."[38]

At the same time, Protestantism displayed neither coherence nor unity. Little noted that the Protestant churches were abundantly represented in well over a hundred papers, "but lights frequently quenched each other." No one had made "a clear, definite, and powerful statement of the fundamental positions of Protestantism. . . . Was there no one in England or in Germany or in America to state the Protestant case . . . or is Protestantism after all without a common basis and a sure ground of existence." He concluded on the hopeful note that the twentieth century would see the consolidation of a Protestant orthodoxy but added, "freedom is indeed a costly privilege, and Protestants are paying for it a tremendous price. And there are moments when the outlook is neither comforting nor inspiring."[39]

The most comprehensive Protestant critic of the Parliament was A. T. Pierson, a leading exponent of the conservative resurgence then gaining ground, who had not attended the assembly.[40] His comments in the *Missionary Review of the World* witness to a growing sense of displacement among conservatives and to the wholesale unraveling of the coherence of the Columbian myth of America among traditionalists in the old Anglo-Protestant mainstream.

Pierson thought the Exposition, with its radiant beauty, grand symmetries, and sculptural allegories, might well suggest to visitors that the dream of Paradise had become a reality and that the White City was at least a forecast of the City of God. He was, however, extremely wary about the popular perception that the meaning of the Exposition and Parliament were in some way intimately connected, and he sought to plumb the significance of the assembly in light of two other conventions convened in the Department of Religion, the Congress of Missions and the World's Evangelical Alliance. To him, it then became clear that the fundamentally liberal platform of the Parliament was a rebuke to Christian supernaturalism; it called into question both Christianity's "sublime monopoly" and its missionary enterprise. It seemed to suggest that Americans had exchanged the national ideals of liberty, equality, and fraternity for laxity, apathy, and compromise. The Parliament, moreover, suggested a shift away from evangelicalism to a form of syncretism as the dominant force in the nation's mainstream: "On the whole, Humanitarianism, Unitarianism, Universalism, and Romanism triumphed at the Parliament, or we do not read the signs of the times," he wrote. "The creed that emphasizes universal brotherhood, human charity, alms deeds and culture . . . can of course clasp hands with heathen priests, rationalists, free thinkers, and idolaters. Why not? But such a creed means a surrender of every vital doctrine, or a vague, misty faith fit only for a new sect that might well be called, *Confusionists*." Pierson also detected the beginnings of "a new era of propagandism" for Asian religions and asked, "Are we in no danger lest the new god of this age, *Civilization*, may be another colossal image of gold, which all men are now called on to worship, and may not another firm protest be the duty of God's holy children"[41]

A year later, Pierson charted the Parliament's ripple effect on the mission fields, where the spectacle of Asians triumphantly returning from Chicago drew alarmed commentary. He noted that the *Madras Mail* dismissed the Hindus' remarks in Chicago as nothing but "a mere echo of the usual cheap tirade against Christianity heard in India from the lips of every university undergraduate, at every street preaching, in every lecture-room." But, the *Indian Standard* called the assembly "a colossal mistake" and the *Christian Patriot* observed that the returning Hindus were treated as celebrities; "every sentence uttered, whether containing sense or not, seems to have been greeted with vociferous applause." The *Japan Weekly Mail* reported that "Christianity gained little and lost much in the World's Congress." The Parliament "opened ways of intercommunication between all religions. It showed to the world much religious worth hitherto unknown in civilized lands. It was instrumental in breaking through the obstinate isolation of sects. . . . It took away from proud Christianity its religious sovereignty, compelling Christianity to share this sovereignty with others. It laid the foundation for a future religious unity."[42]

Pierson also published letters from missionaries, among them William Ashmore, a veteran in China, who described how the Asians were turning the Parliament to their advantage. "Hindu pundits, Mohammedan apostles, Buddhist priests, and Shinto 'right reverends' . . . have come back to flaunt their garlands in the faces of Christian converts and boast of the triumph they achieved at the expense of missionary teachers." It made a wonderful story that would be "exaggerated immensely in repetition. They will tell what the newspapers said, they will tell how they were applauded . . . how the spirit of Buddha was represented as hovering over the place equally with the Spirit of Christ,

and how they themselves, one and all, Buddhists, Hindus, Mohammedans, agnostics alike, were hailed as envoys extraordinary and ministers plenipotentiary in the kingdom of God." Ashmore saw that
Asian interpretations of the Parliament could have devastating consequences into the next century: "For years to come it will be slowly
percolating through the three to four hundred millions who are under
the influence of Buddhism, and working mischief that the good Christian men who got up that kind of a Parliament of Religions could never
have foreseen."[43]

Pierson summed up conservatives' charges against the Parliament.
It misrepresented evangelicalism, created the impression that all religions stood on a natural plane, and propagated false faiths. More to the
point, he saw that it established a precedent for the next century. He
reported that at Long Beach, California, a small Parliament had already
been held and that a Kyoto interfaith assembly was soon to be convened. Majumdar had issued a call for a permanent council of the religions of the world. Nor did Pierson miss the ferment among liberals
in Chicago: "The original parliament had scarcely adjourned when the
air was full of rumors of the new religious brotherhood, whose platform
was to be broad enough for Christians, Hebrews, Agnostics, Confucians, and Pagans to stand in loving fellowship." The Christians, he
complained "were to include Universalists and Unitarians, all sects
and no sects, Hicksite Quakers, Swedenborgians, and disciples of Ethical Culture!" He also quoted an Associated Press release that made it
sound as if the new religion was a *fait accompli*: "The constitution
upon which the organization will be built will say that religion is natural, progress a necessity; true religion is a matter of life, not doctrine,
character, not creed." He closed by banishing the Parliament from the
pages of the *Missionary Review*, "praying God that such a gathering
may never again give occasion to the enemies of the Lord to blas-
pheme."[44]

The American Asoka

The Parliament's quest for unity resulted in the revelation of the
plurality of religious forces on the American scene. The public theology of the Columbian myth and the Parliament's ground rules, whether
civil, broadly-theist, Jewish, Christian, or Judeo-Christian, lacked sufficient weight to sustain a sense of national unity, much less a global

convergence. The way in which the myopia involved in such theological over-extension could be compounded by cultural biases and ethnocentrism is intimately revealed in the post-Parliamentary experiences of John Henry Barrows, who Dharmapāla had praised on the Parliament floor as "an American Asoka," a man that could spread harmony and peace in the emergent global community.[45]

Barrows undertook his own mission—a lecture tour through south and east Asia—in the spring of 1896, after Caroline Haskell, a parishioner at his First Presbyterian church, endowed the Barrows Lectureship in Asia through the University of Chicago. In Haskell's words, the goal of the lectureship was to promote "friendly, temperate, and conciliatory" relations among the religions of the world and to encourage the "fraternal spirit" that had been evident at the Parliament. Barrows was not the first choice for the job. The University offered one thousand pounds to William Gladstone, former prime minister of Great Britain, and then to Charles Gore, a prominent Anglican cleric at Oxford. Only when both men declined did Barrows undertake the assignment to preach what he later called "the larger Christ."[46]

Barrows presented his lectures as the science of religion, but they were also an apology for Christianity as the universal religion for all the world. He based his argument on an evolutionary theory that saw every "lower" religion absorbed into "higher" forms, with all forms eventually assimilated to the religion of Christ. He presented himself as a representative of "Jesus Christ, the greatest cosmopolitan, the greatest humanitarian of all history." He taught what he considered to be neither a Protestant, nor a Catholic, nor a Greek Christianity, but "a common, catholic, historic Christianity." It was the "faith delivered once and for all in apostolic times unto the Christian saints," a timeless, efficacious truth in the form of a "celestial seed capable of indefinite expansion and wide variation." Christianity was the "universal religion," the Bible the "universal book," and Jesus Christ "the one magnetic center in the world of thought and religion today" and the "universal man and savior."[47]

Barrows lectured in China, Japan, and Ceylon, but his longest stay was in India, where he revealed in a number of letters to the *Chicago Record* and *Interior* the thoroughly conventional limitations to his cosmopolitanism. The reality of India shocked him into a realization of "how tame and commonplace was the Midway Plaisance." Benares, the holy city of the Hindus, was "an endless succession of scenes weird, beautiful, and disgusting." The movement of the throngs on the burning ghats looked like "insanity"; it was a spectacle comparable to "opium dreams." He longed to take charge of one of the many *saddhus* on the banks of the Ganges: "A barber's shop, a Turkish bath, a tailor's establishment, a Christian dinner-table might in a week transform him into a respectable if not useful member of society." Barrows also became preoccupied by Indians' legs: "Brown legs, slim legs, black legs, hairy legs . . . legs of boys and young men and old men, of little girls with sweet faces and dark, fawn-like eyes"—these were all so many "objects which the non-Christian population of India thrust before the eyes of travelers." He concluded that if India were converted to Christianity overnight, "the demand for pantaloons would enrich hundreds of wholesale clothiers" in London and New York.[48]

By his own record, Barrows was warmly received wherever he traveled, even when he ran afoul of representatives of the Hindu revival and Indian nationalist movements, and he praised the Hindus for "their general gentleness of spirit and fineness of mind." He could not contain, however, his sense of outrage over their religion, particularly their use of *murti* or images. Before a group of Madrasi lawyers, he commented that "even granting, which I do not, that idolatry is fitted to national infancy, granting, which I do not, that this is the kindergarten of true worship, why should the Indian populations have been kept in this kindergarten for more than three thousand years?"[49] When speaking to the students of Vishuddthanand Swami, one of the leading philosophic lights of Benares, he learned that they had not read the Bible because they had not yet plumbed the depths of their own scriptural traditions. He could only "smile at such provincialism, narrowness and conceit." With all their knowledge, he wrote, "they did not realize that their minds were dwelling in a hideous past" and that "their lives were girt by a grotesque, wretched, and pitiable present."[50]

Once back in the United States, Barrows delivered a series of lectures that he published as *The Christian Conquest of Asia*, a work he called "the literary completion of my connection with the Parliament of Religions." He made little attempt in these lectures to disguise his contempt for Hinduism. Even a sympathetic observer felt "the hopelessness of raising the people out of the bottomless depths of moral rottenness." Hinduism taught "false morality, false history, false science, and false philosophy." Benares was a place where a Christian was forced to ask: "Is this the nineteenth century? Where is our boasted civilization? Are all men maniacs? Is insanity the natural condition of some portions of the human race?" He loathed what he considered a peculiarity of the Hindu mind—its tendency to Hinduize truth and thereby degrade it. He complained that Hindus turned the Bible into an idol, put it to sleep at night, and worshipped it in the morning. They used modern maps and knew modern science, but continued to believe in the geographies and cosmologies of the *Puranas*. They turned Jesus into a Palestinian incarnation of the Hindu God Vishnu.[51]

Even while Barrows criticized Hindus for Hinduizing truth, his own conviction that Christianity was a superior religion was a kind of *idée fixe* that knew no limit in its drive toward the assimilation of all things sacred. Barrows went so far as to liken Hinduism to the Dead Sea in Palestine; it was an "acrid expanse, above which hangs the mist of restless discontent, while along its shores the driftwood of many a weary and bitter century has been tossed." Then, in the same breath, he compared Christianity to the sacred Ganges and its great tributaries: "Coming down to earth from the highest heights, feeding the thirsty grasses along its banks . . . giving a cup of water to the Pariah and the Prince," Christianity "rolls like the Ganges through a hundred channels into the Indian sea."[52]

7

BEYOND THE WHITE CITY

On the Midway,
On the Midway,
They do such things
And they say such things
On the Midway.

—Barker's Cry on the Midway Plaisance

Marcus Braybrooke observed that the Parliament was "something of a seventeen-day wonder," the memory of which soon dropped from the scene.[1] Barrows, however, was of another opinion. In an 1894 assessment of the assembly's significance, he noted that "the world appears to be determined to regard the parliament of religions as vastly significant."[2] In 1895, as criticism of the event mounted, he collected favorable commentary from ministers, missionaries, bishops, priests, and professors in the United States, England, and the continent and notices of the event from a wide range of papers and journals including the *Baltimore Sun*, the *New York Tribune*, the *Daily Chronicle* and *Daily News* in London, Paris's *Le Temps* and *Revue des Deux Mondes*, and the *Journal de Geneve*.[3] For a time, the Parliament drew widespread attention, but by 1898, and certainly by the turn of the century, interest in it seemed to vanish. Almost a century later, Joseph Kitagawa observed that the Parliament, while warmly remembered in many quarters overseas, "has been all but forgotten in Chicago."[4]

Given this fact, the Parliament might stand accused of having been a particularly exotic example of what Daniel J. Boorstin called the "psuedo-event" in American history. It could be dismissed as a well-planned illusion with no basis in social reality, as transient as the plaster palaces of the White City and built on extravagant expectations and publicized by news-hungry media for a public becoming accustomed to drama and celebrity.[5] There is an element of truth to this charge and it might well be that Chicagoans let the Parliament slip from memory because its grandiosity, naiveté, and left-handed liberalism became not only passé, but embarrassing, by the early decades of the twentieth century.

But, the fact remains that the Parliament was an assembly unprecedented in history, and part of its importance rests simply in the many things it represents—the religious dimensions to imperialism, the ongoing process of globalization, and both the problematic and creative aspects to the increasingly frequent and intimate contacts between West and East. As importantly, it also serves as a marker from which to gauge concrete transformations that have occurred as a result of the assembly on the American scene. In the immediate wake of the Parliament, two things stand out as quite distinct from others, both prescient of important, subsequent developments later in the next century. The first was a type of commentary on the importance of the assembly, which struck a significantly different note than all others, a note in which a hint of the new idea of religious pluralism could be discerned. The second was more concrete—the Asian delegates to the Parliament began missions of their own, to propagate in the West the once alien religions, philosophies, and theologies of the East.

The Hint of a New Idea

A century later, the controversies surrounding the 1992 Columbiad indicate the high degree to which the implications of the protean concept of "pluralism" have entered into the American mainstream. For many people, a repeat of the triumphalism explicit in an Anglo-American Columbus in a Roman chariot on the shores of Lake Michigan would have been despicable, pathetic, or, at very least, embarrassingly out-of-date. Many ideas embedded in the White City, with its mystique suggesting canonicity, universality, and authority, have not disappeared from the American scene, but an important seachange in the national temperament dictated that 1992 could not remotely resemble the Columbiad of 1892–93.

A pluralistic myth of America is quite new, and the implications to be drawn from it are hotly debated. There is, moreover, little consensus as to what the concept "pluralism" means, a result of both its different political uses and its origins in a variety of theories. "Cultural pluralism" was coined and put into currency by Horace Kallen, who in 1915 wrote "Democracy Versus the Melting-pot," arguing that the maintenance of the languages and traditions of non-Anglo immigrants was essential to democracy in a highly conformist society. "Pluralism" is also used to describe American political culture with its numerous, competing interest groups, a use originating with Robert Dahl in 1961, but gaining a wider audience with *Beyond the Melting Pot* by Daniel Moynihan and Nathan Glazer. Both cultural and political ideas about pluralism were central to the civil rights, feminist, and ethnic revival movements of the 1960s, and have since been linked to more strictly philosophical, theological, and religious debates. Philosophical pluralism is most closely associated with the religion-friendly pragmatism of William James, whose influence in the 1960s was marked in the pluriform theology of such Protestant radicals as Paul M. Van Buren and Langdon Gilkey.[6] Pluralistic ideas about religion and theology also owe a great deal to comparative studies in the history of religion and anthropology, which, while not necessarily addressing the American situation directly, have drawn attention to the fundamentally different ways groups structure and experience ultimate reality.

Culture, philosophy, religion, and theology, all mediated by political group processes and informed by gender, ethnicity, and race, are at issue in the debate over a pluralistic myth of America today, much as they were at the Parliament, when a more universalistic and assimilationist myth of America was at stake. But, in the wake of the Parliament, the suggestion of a pluralistic option could be heard in the words of a few commentators, even if they only engaged with the religious and theological elements in the total debate. With a skepticism more typical of the next century, they questioned both the realism and the necessity of quests for religious unity and brought the distinctly different claims of the religions of the world into sharp relief.

Matthew Trumbull, a labor organizer in Chicago, criticized what he called "the phantom of unity which the Parliament had been chasing for three weeks." He wrote that the assembly had been "a genial transmutation of religious animosities into social friendships, but it was neither Pentecost nor Babel." His main point was that, while Christian delegates had talked a great deal about God, he seemed to remain illusory. They had appealed to God as a demonstrable fact, a hope, a sentiment, an intuition, a natural instinct, a supernatural revelation, and a "giant omnipotent." To Buddhists, the God of Christians must have appeared to be a "creation of spiritual hasheesh," while to Hindus, a childish conception to be treated compassionately. The idea of the fatherhood of God had been inflated into a universal creed, but it turned out that there had not been "enough of that manna and quail for the wants of the world."[7]

Trumbull observed that if it had been the Christians' intention to display their superiority to Asians and Jews, they failed: "The heathen carried away the prizes of most value, while the agnostics and unbelievers cheered." If it had been their intention to legislate religious unity, they also failed because the Parliament had not been a parliament at all, but "a World's Fair of theological exhibits with a sort of Midway Plaisance for the bric a brac of creeds." It was simply a case that common courtesy had been mistaken for religious harmony and unity at the assembly, because religions "are, from the nature of their separate claims, irreconcilable." The Parliament had, however, been a sign of progress and a promise of greater tolerance in the future, because it served as an "intellectual crucible" in which people showed themselves willing to submit their beliefs to the refining furnace of each other's scrutiny.[8]

Commentaries with a similarly skeptical tone came from two east coast Unitarians, both of whom were religious liberals, but displayed little enthusiasm for the visionary excesses of Jenkin Lloyd Jones, their Chicago colleague. The first of these was Joseph Henry Allen, former editor of the *Unitarian Review*, who likened the Parliament to the medieval truce of God. Over the course of the seventeen days of the assembly, he noted that Muslims and Hindus battled in Burma; Christians and Muslims killed one another in North Africa; Catholics killed Protestants and Protestants, Catholics in north Ireland; and Russians and Turks persecuted Jews and Armenians. American liberals may have grown weary of religious disputes and thus they may have preferred to see in the Parliament a revelation of unity, but the world was "not quite ready yet to proclaim the advent of a new reign of peace."[9]

In Allen's view, the flourishing of contradictory truth claims and theological disputes were signs of religious vitality. He argued that religions grow from a single seed with a distinct "trade mark" due to race, climate, and history, but tend to branch spontaneously into new, independent forms. The evolution of the Puritan tradition in New England was a case in point. The Unitarian controversy had been one among many disputes over the Puritan legacy. No sooner had that controversy waned, than Emerson and the transcendentalists gave it new life. Phrenology, Spiritualism, Christian Science, and Theosophy followed quickly on the transcendentalists' heels, as did Saint Simonianism, Owenism, Fourierism, and Icarianism. Such a process of mutation occurred in all the religions of the world, and in every case, each mutation appeared to its adherents as a new, stunning, and absolute revelation.[10]

Given such vitality and diversity, Allen thought it made little sense to press for unity. "It is quite possible, no doubt, by the powerful solvent of metaphysics, to reduce the intellectual elements of these warring faiths into some colorless compromise which we might call a 'universal' or 'absolute' religion. . . . But history tells us much of the conflicts of religions, little of their sympathy." In this light, the Parliament was best understood as an example of a cooperative spirit. "The great success of our Parliament is not to be had by merging the great faiths of humanity in what at best would only be a flavorless neutral compound; but rather in showing how they may best flourish, independently, side by side." Religious unity belonged purely to the realm of the ideal and was likely to remain so for at least another thousand years.[11]

Joining Allen in skeptical commentary was Unitarian John W. Chadwick, a self-described mystic and religious radical, who also hinted at a pluralistic perspective on religion. His understanding of the significance of the Parliament was essentially a restatement of Thomas Higginson's idea of sympathy among religions sharpened by criticism of the reductive and assimilative schemes for religious unity presented on the floor of the assembly.

Chadwick pointed to Hebrew scripture as the source of the mystical triumphalism implicit in most of these unitative schemes—"Who is this that cometh from Edom, with dyed garments from Bozrah, this that is glorious in his apparel, marching in the greatness of his strength." The Christian element in them was little more than a latter-day reflection of the ancient church's claim to be the only true religion in antiquity. Modern Christians now based their visions of unity on a variety of strategies—conquest, assimilation, fulfillment, incorporation, and absorption. Still others hoped to forge a universal religion based on moralism or ethicism or electicism. But "we have been far afield in quest of a universal religion," Chadwick wrote, "and we have come back with empty hands."[12]

Chadwick was personally convinced of the superiority of Christian revelation, but he did not draw from this the conclusion that others ought to become Christians. "Would Christianity be better for the Mohammedan, the Brahman, the Buddhist than the religions to which they adhere?" On the contrary. Appealing to biological theory and to the idea of relativity only then gaining currency, Chadwick argued that religions are like any other organisms that gradually develop in harmony with particular environments. "It is not a question of whether the elephant's amusing trunk and baggy trousers are better than the outfit of the lion or the horse. . . . They are better for him because he is used to them, because they are correlated with his general anatomy and physiology." So it was with religions: "Let their absolute values be what they may, relatively, to the peoples who acknowledge them and believe in them, they are doubtless the best religions possible because they have come into existence in answer to their special needs."[13]

Onward Asian Soldiers

The Asian delegates at the Parliament overcame at least one challenge presented to them by the logic of the Columbian myth: few commentators could easily dismiss Vivekananda, Majumdar, and others as semi-civilized heathens. The enthusiasm of Jones, the syncretisms of Carus and Snell, the qualified affirmations of Abbott and Little, Pierson's bitterness, and the discomfort of Barrows all attest to the fact that the peoples and religions of the Midway Plaisance had done more than simply amuse those of the White City. The Asians, moreover, fanned out across America immediately after the Parliament. Some continued to further an Asian agenda by making pointed, public criticisms of Christian missionaries and by calling into question the legitimacy of Christianity's claim to normativity. Others began missions of their own to America and other western nations. The success of these missions—little at first, but increasingly substantial in subsequent decades—helped to create a new religious climate in the next century, as eastern religions began to sink roots in the West. In the United States, Asians brought their philosophies and theologies to a nation that would in time find itself shedding the Columbian myth and abandoning the classical formalities of the White City. It would, moreover, find its center of gravity continually shifting westward, until a century later, when it would begin to rethink its priorities and its destiny in terms of the growing importance of "the Pacific rim." Perhaps most importantly, the Asian delegates returned home from the Parliament with renewed confidence and zeal to preach national self-determination and the revitalization of tradition, two significant contributions to the major realignments that would alter the international scene in the twentieth century.

In America, Purushotam Rao Telang, a Brahmin, took up the missionary question in the pages of the *Forum*, where he contributed his own comments, riddled with sarcasm and invective, on an issue important to many American Protestants: Have the missions failed? "How can an enterprise fail," he asked, when every year fourteen million dollars are added to the capital invested in the missions? How could a missionary be seen as a failure when he lives better than the average gentlemen at home, has "four or five servants, a good house, free of cost to him, and a horse and carriage—at a cost less than a hundred dollars a month?" Telang reported that in the course of a day a missionary took his breakfast, made his reports, strolled in the church yard and tended his garden, sat in an armchair on the veranda reading his Bible, ate a hearty lunch, took a nap while a servant pulled a fan, and then, finally, stood on a street corner with a convert doing the preaching. "The missionaries have not failed," he concluded, "and will not so long as Christians have money to waste in this useless way."

Telang admitted to admiring western civilization for its material achievements, "but as a Hindu reads Christian history it is full of cruelty such as shock the Hindu mind and cause doubt of Christian morality." Shootings, bank robberies, and the lynching of blacks filled American papers. How has America treated the Indian and the buffalo? he asked. "What became of the aborigines of Australia? How was India conquered and by whom? Who snatched the kingdom of Hawaii from the Queen of those islands? Who were the Crusaders? Who burned people at the stake and invented torturing machines?" Telang knew Christian history to be full of such episodes and thought that "Christian nations are the most aggressive and most intolerant people." If Americans wished truly to improve the conditions of India's poor, he suggested that they aid them with modern education and let them select any religion they like. It was, however, "a sheer waste of money to spend [it] on the missionaries."[14]

The same issue was raised nearer the corridors of power when Virchand Gandhi, the Jain from Bombay, together with Bishop J. M. Thoburn and Paul Carus, debated the missionary question before the

Nineteenth Century Club in New York. "There is nothing personal in my remarks at all," Gandhi began, but there is the old English saying— "the fool of the family goes into the Church." He claimed to have studied Christianity in America and he was compelled to admit that for missionaries he had nothing but pity. Granted they were good husbands and fathers of large families, "but they are generally ignorant." His main complaint was that missionaries taught things in India that they dare not teach in American public schools, and they expected Hindus to permit it. "Brothers and sisters of America," he concluded, "there is not the least shadow of a hope that India can ever be Christianized." In India, even the "street-sweeper is frequently more profoundly versed in subtle metaphysics and divine wisdom than the missionary sent to convert him."[15]

More substantial accomplishments were being made by Majumdar, Vivekananda, Dharmapāla, and Shaku Sōen, a little-noticed Japanese Buddhist delegate to the Parliament, all of whom fostered in different ways a familiarity with Asian religious movements and sensibilities in the United States. Daniel Walker Howe has discussed an English-speaking trans-Atlantic network that functioned as a kind of international reference group during the Victorian heyday. It would seem the Asians were moving through, perhaps were a central part of, a similar, somewhat later, and more truly global reference group around the turn of the century. From their diary entries and letters, and from the dinner parties and receptions they attended, it is clear they moved through an international network of religious radicals and liberals, which ran along the ligaments of the western empires, directly through the United States. As a result, the Parliament was a kind of relay station, linking London, New York, Cambridge, Washington, and San Francisco to Paris, Yokohama, Colombo, Calcutta, and Bombay.[16]

Immediately after the Parliament adjourned, Majumdar headed to Boston, with stays in Indianapolis and Buffalo. Once in Boston, he visited with friends from his 1883 visit, delivered two series of lectures at the Lowell Institute on the races, religions, and societies of India (both times to overflowing crowds), and preached at the morning and evening services in Appleton chapel at Harvard. He made side trips from Boston to lecture in Washington and New York City. His biographer estimates that in the course of his three months in America Majumdar delivered two hundred addresses, sermons, and after-dinner speeches. A highlight of his stay in Boston was the warm reception he received at the Unitarian Club, where Samuel J. Barrows read a poem dedicated to "our mystic Mozoomdar (*sic*)."

> Sweet heathen of another race,
> Our fathers damned thy sires.
> A gentler flood of Christian grace
> Has quenched those hellish fires,
> Too good to damn, but not to burn
> With Pentecostal flame,
> No more thy message we shall spurn,
> But kindle at the name.[17]

Majumdar delivered his farewell address at Boston's Arlington Street Church, on December 5, 1893. The gist of his speech was a plea for the liberal movement, largely a product of the intellect, to present itself to the world in a way that would "stir our deepest feeling, enter into our consciences, and influence our daily life." He paid tribute to all the great prophets of the world, but elaborated on his own special devotion to Jesus. "Christ is the type," he proclaimed, "the summing up of all those great good men who have blessed the various nations of earth." He went on to warn Christians, however, that their creeds and churches "confine you within an iron wall that you cannot break through." These creeds and churches formed "so many stones under which your spirit lies." He urged that all such barriers be broken down by people of universal faith. He saw Christian liberals as having a "higher calling" to reconcile truly universal principles with personal conviction.[18]

Majumdar's experience as both a Hindu and a devotee of Christ epitomized the mutual distrust and suspicion that hampered the attempts of even the most liberal religious leaders to establish a common basis for religious unity. Toward the end of his life, F. Max Müller wrote a series of final messages to the Brāhmo-Samāj through Majumdar. Like many other Protestant liberals, Müller had watched the Brahmos closely, with the hope that they would serve as the vanguard for the Christianization of India. His letters were lengthy pleas to Majumdar to lead the Brāhmo-Samāj to identify itself formally as a Christian church. He reviewed in one letter the many traditions that Brahmos had surrendered in the past—polytheism, the use of images, sacrificial worship, and the uniquely divine inspiration of the Vedas. He also reviewed what he knew to be the standard Hindu objections to Christianity—the aggressiveness of its missionaries and the anthropomorphic and apparently quixotic character of its God. Over these objections, Müller urged Majumdar to "form your own Church, be in unity with all other Christian Churches. . . . However you may differ from them, or they from you, the treasure of truth, shared by you and by them, will be infinitely greater and more valuable than the miserable differences that separate the followers of Christ on earth."[19]

Sometime later Majumdar responded to Müller. "A wholesale acceptance of the Christian name by the Brāhmo-Samāj is neither possible nor desirable, within measurable time." It would lead to misconceptions and bring undue harm. Christian liberals would have to be content with what Majumdar called "the Christ spirit" among Hindus.[20]

Müller wrote back the following year and suggested that Majumdar, in his reluctance to bear the Christian name, was being ungrateful. "Your very movement would not exist without Christianity. . . . I thought that truth and gratitude would [have you] declare in favour of Christian Brahmos, or Christian Aryas.[21]

Majumdar made his sentiments clear in a rejoinder to Müller, which was published in many Indian papers. "What disconcerts me is the half-expressed contempt which Christian leaders, even the leaders of the most liberal school, seem to have of the Hindu ideal and spirituality. . . . The moment I say that Christ and his religion will have to be interpreted in India through Indian antecedents and the Indian medium of thought," he complained, "I am suspected of trying to bend Christianity down to heathenism." Majumdar saw three options for Hindu devotees of Christ—to renounce the Indian temperament, to renounce Jesus, or to "re-embody our faith and aspiration under a new name, and form, and spirit. We have taken the third course."[22]

Majumdar maintained this independent stance for the rest of his life. He persisted as a Hindu devotee of Christ, even as the Brāhmo-Samāj declined and other Hindus more aggressively linked nationalism to the revitalization of their traditional faiths. In Boston in 1900 for the seventy-fifth anniversary of the founding of Unitarianism, he once again declined to become a Unitarian because he regarded the group as a sect, not a true platform for universal faith.[23]

In many respects, Majumdar epitomized the best in the liberal spirit of the late nineteenth century, but he never failed, it seems, to maintain a vital link between that spirit and the traditions of Asia. In 1905, Majumdar fell ill and he retired to his sickroom at Peace Cottage in Calcutta, where he received numerous guests and spent his days in prayer and silent meditation. He died on the twenty-first of May in the company of his wife. That evening, two hundred mourners carried his body, wrapped in the traditional ochre robe of the *sannyasin*, strewn with jasmine and roses, to the Nimtollah cremation ghat on the Ganges. Hindu *shradda* rites were performed a week later and, with due solemnity, his ashes were deposited beneath a white marble obelisk in the garden at Peace Cottage. The inscription on the monument was taken from his last book, *Ashis* or *Benedictions*: "I have gained thee with very little spiritual culture while living this lowly life on earth. Now I start on my way to gain Thee in a degree beyond all measure."[24]

Vivekananda's reputation is now more closely linked to the Parliament than that of any other Asian.[25] When he arrived in Chicago he was unknown in America and little known in reformist circles in India, but he returned home from his American tour as a highly visible, celebrated, but controversial figure and subsequently became an inspiration to generations of Hindu religious nationalists. Vivekananda made two tours of America, but his Parliamentary tour has taken on legendary proportions among his followers. His original motive for the tour was to raise funds for his work in India and to educate Americans about Hinduism, but it soon developed into a full-blown mission to teach Vedanta to America and the West.[26]

Vivekananda remained in Chicago for several months as a guest in the homes of various prominent people, including Thomas Palmer, the President of the Columbian Exposition, and he lectured on the Indian tradition in Chicago and in surrounding cities and towns. He eventually signed a contract with a lyceum lecture bureau and began a series of wide-ranging tours throughout the United States, speaking in Congregational churches, women's clubs, Reform synagogues, academies, theaters, and opera houses. Wherever he went, Vivekananda received largely favorable attention in the press, but drew criticism from conservatives and supporters of the Protestant missionaries.[27]

A brief review of his press notices indicates the aggressive style Vivekananda developed in the United States, one reason why he became known among his devotees as "the Lion of Vedanta." The *Min-*

neapolis Journal of November 27, 1893, did not get his title right, but
its headline conveys a sense of the controversy he generated, which was
a significant element in his popularity:

AN ORIENTAL VIEW
—
LIVAMI VIVEKANANDA ADDRESSES A MINNEAPOLIS AUDIENCE
MERCENARIES IN RELIGION
—
IN THIS WAY HE CHARACTERIZES THE WESTERN NATIONS.

The *Des Moines News* of November 28th emphasized the metaphysical theories that he was publicizing in his tours:

> 'Reincarnation' will be the subject of Swami Vivekananda's lecture at
> the Central Christian Church tonight. . . . Do not fail to go.

Similar notices, with attention to the wide audiences he was seeking,
were printed in the *Memphis Commercial* of January 21, 1894:

HE'LL SPEAK TO ALL CLASSES

SWAMI VIVEKANANDA WILL LECTURE ON
COMPARATIVE THEOLOGY

> The conditions of the arrangements are such that the
> man would secure a large audience of all classes of
> people, as he no doubt will.[28]

Vivekananda made a particularly lengthy stay in Detroit, where he
was toasted by society but ran afoul of participants in the Second International Convention of the Student Volunteer Movement. As was
his style, he seemed to thrive on adversity. The *Detroit Journal* of February 16,1894, reported:

SCORED CHRISTIANITY
—
Vivekananda Tells About The Troubles It Has
Caused In India

The week after the convention adjourned, fiercer headlines ran in the
Detroit Tribune:

KANANDA, THE PAGAN

—

Attacked Christian Mission in Last Night's Lectures

—

And His Words Were Warmly Applauded
By the Audience

—

Christians Nations Kill and Murder, He Said, and Import
Disease into Foreign Countries, then Add Insult to
Injury by Preaching a Crucified Christ.[29]

In the spring of 1894, Vivekananda traveled to Massachusetts where he lectured at Northampton City Hall, the North Shore Women's Club in Lynn, and Harvard University. He then went to New York, where he spoke at the Waldorf Hotel, lunched with Lyman Abbott, and spoke in numerous gatherings in private homes. His success was, however, beginning to draw criticism. The quest for unity in Chicago had a discordant ripple effect back home, displaying the fractures in the pan-Asian front presented on the floor of the assembly. Orthodox Hindus began to challenge Vivekananda's credentials; Theosophists expressed resentment over his success with the public. Majumdar, moreover, was reported to be spreading slanderous rumors about his behavior in the United States—eating beef, smoking cigars, and attending parties with American women.

After further lecture tours to Baltimore, Washington, and Philadelphia, Vivekananda returned to New York where he began to offer classes on *jnana*, *bhakti*, and *raja* yoga. He went to England in April of 1896, but left behind the kernel of the Vedanta movement in America in the form of two initiates, Swami Abhayananda (Marie Louise) and Swami Kripananda (Leon Landsberg), and a larger, loosely-organized group of followers who had been introduced to the philosophy and spiritual disciplines of Vedanta.[30]

Back in south Asia, Vivekananda was greeted with great popular acclaim in Colombo, Madras, and Calcutta. He began to preach what he called an "aggressive Hinduism," designed both to go on the offensive against Christian missionaries and to link his modernist form of Hinduism to the revitalization of Indian national traditions. In May of 1897, he formally inaugurated the Ramakrishna Mission Association in order to spread Vedanta in the West. During the final months of his life, Vivekananda meditated on his *guru* Ramakrishna and the Divine

Mother in preparation for his death. He died on July 4, 1902, and was laid in state in the traditional robes of a world-renouncing monk at the Ramakrishna Belur Math in Calcutta. *Arati* services with the traditional waving of lights were performed. *Mantras* were chanted and conch shells blown, and then his body was cremated under a sacred Vilva tree in the temple compound. A temple was eventually built upon the spot and his relics were placed in a receptacle on the altar of his guru Ramakrishna.[31]

A few days after the Parliament, Dharmapāla initiated C. T. Strauss, a Jewish haberdasher from New York, into Buddhism in a well-attended public ceremony under the auspices of the Chicago Theosophical Society. He then headed West to California where he lectured before Unitarians and Theosophists in Oakland and San Francisco. He also journeyed to Santa Cruz to meet Philangi Dasa, a self-described Swedenborgian-Buddhist and Theosophist, who was the American representative of Dharmapāla's Maha Bodhi Society and the editor of America's first Buddhist journal, the *Buddhist Ray*. Returning to Ceylon by way of Japan, he was met in Yokohama by one hundred Buddhist priests, including members of the Japanese delegation to the Parliament. When he arrived in Ceylon in January of 1894, a great crowd greeted him at the dock and carried him in a triumphal procession to his preceptor, Sumangala Nayaka Maha Thera.[32]

Dharmapāla made two subsequent trips to the United States, the longest in 1896–1897 at the invitation of Paul Carus. En route to the United States, he stopped in London where he renewed his acquaintance with the poet Sir Edwin Arnold, the Buddhist scholar T. W. Rhys Davids, and F. Max Müller, all of whom he had met in the course of his 1893 tour, and lectured before the Theosophical Society in Hyde Park. Once in the United States, he undertook an extensive lecture tour stopping in New York, Boston, Providence, Chicago, Grand Rapids, Cincinnati, Duluth, Minneapolis, Iowa City, Des Moines, Fargo, and San Francisco. He lectured in Chicago on "The Dawn of the New Era: the Union of East and West" before an audience that included Jenkin Lloyd Jones and Charles Bonney. He dined with Mrs. Potter Palmer, the chair of the Board of Lady Managers of the World's Columbian Exposition and president of the Women's Branch of the World's Congress Auxilary.

Dharmapāla lectured in Boston on the Buddhist no-self doctrine on the thirtieth anniversary of the founding of the Free Religious Association, spoke before a variety of women's clubs, and led the Procopeia Club of Harvard in Buddhist chanting during a picnic in Salem. In San Jose, Alameda, and San Francisco, he preached Buddhism before several congregations of Theosophists and Unitarians. In May of 1897, he officiated at what is reputed to be the first American *Wesak* ceremony, a Buddhist feast commemorating the birth of the Buddha, before a crowd of four hundred in San Francisco, using a censer borrowed from a sympathetic Roman Catholic priest. Returning to Ceylon by way of Paris, he attended the Congress of Orientalists in September and offici-ated at the Buddhist Peace Celebration at Paris's oriental museum, the Museé Guimet.[33]

As was the case with Vivekananda, Dharmapāla's career displayed the kind of fracturing among Asian allies that was conspicuous in the wake of the Parliament. Since the mid-1880s, he had been a member of the Theosophical Society, a Buddhist modernizer, and a co-worker with others who sought self-determination for Asian nations and faiths. But by the late 1890s, tensions became apparent in the pan-Asian cause. Sectarian splits divided the Theosophical Society into Buddhist, neo-Brahman, and Christian camps, and Vivekananda, along with others, was accusing the Theosophists of fraud.

Dharmapāla also grew disenchanted with the mystical fascinations of many enthusiasts in America and grew concerned about the way in which Christians were eagerly embracing Hindu theism. "The people are going from one extreme to the other," he wrote in his diary. "At one time it was 'depraved sinners' now it is 'you are gods.' Well," he added, "people are glad to live in stupidity." He also became increas-ingly skeptical about the capacity of Americans to realize the ethics and spirituality of Jesus, much less the rigorous disciplines of Bud-dhism. "Slaves of passion, controlled by the lower senses, wallowing in sensuality," he wrote. "These so-called Christians live in killing each other, hating each other, swindling each other, introducing liquor and vice where they hadn't existed."[34]

In subsequent years, Dharmapāla maintained his missionary work both in America and in England, while he pursued his great passion to restore Bodh Gaya. His labor for Buddhist rights, although primarily religious and educational, was also highly political, and he was in-terned in Bombay for five years during the nationalist upheavals in In-dia during and after World War I. Always a Buddhist layman, in 1931

Dharmapāla took first ordination to the priesthood. As a heart ailment progressed, he took higher ordination vows in January of 1933. In April, he proclaimed his wish to die quickly in order to be reborn again to continue spreading the Buddhist *dharma*. He took a solemn vow on his deathbed to be reborn in a Brahmin family of Benares to further his goal of regaining Bodh Gaya from the Hindus. In 1948, in an article in the journal of the Maha Bodhi Society, it was noted that he had been without doubt "the greatest Buddhist missionary after Asoka the Great" and a modern *boddhisattva*.[35]

Shaku Sōen spent the week after the Parliament at the home of Paul Carus in LaSalle, Illinois, and then returned to Japan with the rest of the Japanese Buddhist delegation, who were hailed as *bukkyo no chapionra*, champions of Buddhism, immediately upon landing. Confirming the fears of old-lines Christian missionaries such as William Ashmore, press releases in Japan presented them as having triumphed in Chicago and as setting in motion an unstoppable religious revolution on the world stage. "These globally minded priests are the true pioneers of Buddhism's international movement," the journal *Kokkyo* noted. They "have returned singing the songs of victory and their speeches have profoundly moved the religious world of Japan. They have in fact come to embody the ideal hopes of religious revolutionaries throughout the land."[36]

It was not until 1905 that Sōen returned to the United States, a full seven years after the first band of Japanese Buddhist missionaries arrived in the country. "Sea stretches out into sea," he wrote on board the steamer *Cleveland* as he left for the United States,

> Mountains join into mountains.
> Where is the center of water?
> Where is the destination of clouds?
> I do not know!
> My heart tells me there is a happy field
>   in the American land.
> I presume myself as a follower of old Columbus.[37]

On his American tour, Sōen stayed with the Alexander Russells of San Francisco, reputed to be the first Zen Buddhists in America, in their Pacific coast compound, the House of Silent Light. He lectured and taught in Fresno, Sacramento, San Jose, Oakland, and San Francisco to both Americans and Japanese immigrants. In March of 1906, he headed to the east coast by way of Carus's home near Chicago to speak at the Greenacre Fellowship in Washington, D.C., the National Geographic Society, and Washington University.[38]

Little is known about Sōen in western scholarship, but he seems to have been well-versed in western culture and Christianity, and he taught a modern Buddhism that displayed syncretistic tendencies.[39] He was particularly sensitive to Americans' difficulties with the Buddhist doctrine of the non-existence of the soul or self. "The arrogance of the flesh," he wrote, was based on the belief in the "ultimate reality of the ego-soul." The "impertinence of the 'old man'" comes from the secret thought that the self is real and abiding; " 'Crucify him,' therefore says Buddhism, as the first work in your religious discipline; destroy this chimerical, illusory notion of self." In lectures on Mahayana Buddhism, he drew out the meaning of Buddhist doctrine with reference to the gospel of John. He taught that the "I" existed only in a social relationship to another "I." To understand this was to take the first step towards realizing the spirituality of John—"all mine are thine, and thine are mine; and I am glorified in them." Love thine enemy was for Sōen more than a Biblical injunction, it was also an expression of the Buddhist doctrine that the self and other selves are ultimately all one in each other in the "*dharmakaya*" or "essence-body" of the Buddha.[40]

Shaku Sōen's trip to the Parliament also resulted in an event of great importance for the subsequent history of American Buddhism—the journey of one of his young students at Engakuji monastery, D. T. Suzuki, to the United States. Sōen sent Suzuki to America in 1897, where he took up residence in Paul Carus's home. He worked there with Carus to produce a translation of the *Tao Te Ching* and Ashvaghosha's *Awakening of Faith in the Mahayana*, while he worked as Carus's handyman and houseboy. At this time, Suzuki also began to work on his first major English publication, *Outlines of Mahayana Buddhism*. Suzuki would later become one of the most influential mid-twentieth-century Buddhist teachers in the United States, and his lengthy career linked the Parliament of 1893 to another major watershed in the history of Asian religions in the United States, the 1960s. Later in his career, he taught at Columbia University, participated in the dialogue between psychoanalysis and Zen, and influenced the Beat-Hip generation of the late 50s and early 60s in their explorations of Asian religions.[41]

Wells of Truth Outside and In

There was no single World's Parliament of Religions, but many—
that of the Chicago radicals with their aborted plans for unity; the Roman Catholics, for which it served in the short run to strengthen the
American church's ties to the papacy; the Protestant liberals, for whom
it confirmed a new tolerance in missionary strategies; the Protestant
conservatives, for whom it was an assault on evangelical Christianity.
There was also the Parliament of the Asians. It was for them, above all
others, an event of great importance, which helped both to bring Asian
religions to American shores and to catapult overseas Asians forward
into uncharted territory. All these Parliaments were, at the same time,
America's Parliaments, and the event deserves a central place in a pluralistic account of American religious history.

But the Parliament, launched as it was as a search for a common
religious discourse for a single global society, was a classic case of a
center that could not hold. Yet, a new perspective on issues began to
emerge in a few quarters that, like the Parliament itself, was prescient
of developments that would become more pronounced in the next century. Only a week into the Parliament, the *Chicago Tribune* announced to its readers:

IT POINTS TO UNITY

PARLIAMENT OF RELIGION WILL
BEAR GOOD FRUIT

They Say It Has Opened The Eyes
Of The Christian World

WELLS OF TRUTH OUTSIDE[42]

The unity to which the Parliament seemed to point turned out to be
chimerical, but for the *Tribune*, the assembly symbolized a broad development that, while in retrospect seems obvious to many people today, was really a new discovery—the enduring value to be found in
"wells of truth outside." At the time, this was not a superficial discovery, but one that struck at the roots of the long-standing claims of
Christianity in particular, the West in general, and the inner coherence

of the patriotic, classical, and Christian signs at the core of the Columbian myth.

At this juncture, it makes sense to return to the beginning—to the flag, the Goddess of Liberty, and the resurrected Jesus, three signs which together formed the core of the Columbian myth. Recall the "unknown gods and rites" and "tiger passions" that Aldrich saw lurking as threats to the republic in nineteenth-century immigrant communities; Bushnell's praise for Greek art, Roman law, and Christian faith, the three forces he understood to be both indestructible and at work in all human history; and Hurlbutt's likening of the Chautauqua curriculum for cultured Christians to a Greco-Roman, Anglo-American railway. It was the finished quality and confident finality of this essentially Anglo-American Protestant myth and canon that was called into question by the Parliament. Progressive Hindus experiencing bliss in *moksa* and Lord Krishna; soul-less and self-less Buddhists at rest in *nirvana* within the world-vortex described by modern evolutionary sciences; Confucian bureaucrats living in accord with the balanced forces of *yin* and *yang*; devotees sitting lovingly at the feet of the great Mother of India: these insights and others struck to the quick of the Columbian myth.

Having the luxury of no doctrinal axes to grind, the *Tribune* could more easily generalize about the lasting significance of the Parliament than could many Christian churchmen. In an unusually perceptive editorial, "Outcome of the Parliament," the *Tribune* observed that the importance of the Parliament rested with the fact that clear statements had been made about the world's religions and that "those whom we have been accustomed to call heathens are not so much heathen as we imagined." People would now better understand that morality is found in every religion and that "all are searching for the truth, though in different ways." The Parliament "may and should bring these followers of various creeds so near each other that Christians shall recognize there are no longer pagans and heathens."[43]

The idea that deep-seated, long-standing distinctions such as Christian and heathen had become obsolete, at least to the editors of an influential representative of the secular press, must be considered another important result of the Parliament. Yet another is more difficult to assess. It is clear that the highly-publicized discovery of wells of truth outside was, at that same time, being compounded by the fact that water from those wells was seeping inside America, even inside

America's Christian churches, as a result of the Asians' performances and post-Parliament activities. The syncretistic visions of the Chicago radicals, the increased popularity of the comparative study of religion, the piety of those people—many of them undoubtedly loyal Christians—who professed a sincere interest in Majumdar, Vivekananda, Dharmapāla, Shaku Sōen, and others, all acted as conduits for the infiltration of Asian ideas into the United States.

The Parliament, along with urbanism, industrialism, immigration, Darwinism, naturalism, and all the other challenges to old America, was undoubtedly an element in the nation's transformation in the Gilded Age. There is irony in the fact that the Christian idea of the universal fatherhood of God masked deep fractures that were revealed at an assembly convened for the purpose of displaying its universal utility. Once noted, these fractures also point to an on-going process of realignment of religious forces on the domestic scene. As evidenced by the responses of representative parties to the Parliament, crosscurrents and undercurrents both within and without the churches made it increasingly difficult to chart a main shipping channel in America's nineteenth-century mainstream. Much of the religious and cultural pluralism that would be so conspicuous a century later was there all along, even if masked by the Columbian myth of America and the world and the mystique of the White City, with its suggestion of authority, universality, and canonicity.

The World's Parliament of Religions did not cause the breakup of the nineteenth-century mainstream. That development had and would continue to have a long and complex history. But, as an unprecedented ingathering of nations and tribes, the Parliament did force many different parties to survey together the broad contours of the nation's religious landscape. As it turned out, all parties were in motion but heading in different directions, even as they all drifted together into the new dawn of an often difficult century.

AFTERWORD

Wall—I'm glad enough I'm hum agin—kin rest my weary
brain. For I've seen an' heered so much *too* much, I guess I've
heered in vain. I thought th' Fair was mixin' an th' Midway
made me crawl, But th' Parl'ment of Religions was th'
mixin'est of all.

> —Minnie Andrews Snell, "Aunt Hannah on the Parliament of
> Religions"

THE PARLIAMENT WAS a major event in American religious history and
it deserves a place of honor as a marker on the cusp between the nineteenth and twentieth centuries. It was also a classic event in the sense
of the term as used by David Tracy, meaning that it deserves repeated
and varied interpretations to plumb the depths of its significances.[1] A
great deal more study is required to assess adequately its total
significance. Scholars with an interest in the Christian churches ought
to bring mainstream/non-mainstream questions to the Parliament,
and other conventions held under the auspices of the Department of
Religion, to unearth in greater detail the shifting alliances and misal-
liances among a wide variety of constituencies that are all too often
studied in isolation. The assembly might well be used as a convenient
marker in the on-going process of revisioning a pluralistic American
religious history. The Parliament points backward to the revolutionary era, when major realignments occurred in the relations between
religion and the culture; to the "great migrations" and the changing
demographics of the nation; and to the Emancipation Proclamation
and the struggles of African-Americans to gain a foothold in the mainstream. It also points forward to the rise of the Protestant, Catholic,
and Jewish triple-melting pot idea of America at mid-century and to
the complex interplay of religious pluralization, secularization, and
the new migrations of the late twentieth century. The Parliament was
sufficiently representative and important that it can serve as a gauge
for standards of inclusion and exclusion at a mid-point and turning-
point in the nation's history.

The Parliament also stands at the apex of the vast body of historical information in the papers of the World's Congress Auxiliary, waiting to reward an intrepid and imaginative scholar with what must be an unparalleled historical view of a culture-specific, yet globalizing, system of modern knowledge in the making. These papers would undoubtedly present extraordinary insights into a universe of American and modern thought, generated precisely at the moment when the nation was announcing its intention to join, if not yet to overtake, Britain, France, and Germany as leaders of the modern industrial society. Spain and the "black legend" also figure very significantly into the Columbiad as well, a fact not taken into consideration in this account, but one of no small interest given that only five years after the Exposition and Parliament the United States would go to war in Cuba and undertake the conquest of the Philippines.

The Parliament and all that it represents also demand the attention of historians trained in the women's history and the interpretation of gender issues as they are refracted in culture and religion. The Parliament was hailed as a breakthrough for women, but that is only a small part of the story about women that might be told. The twenty-three women at the Parliament and the issues they raised in their papers need to be read against a wide variety of Columbian sources—the Jewish Women's Congress, the Congress of Representative Women and other papers, be they from the temperance, moral reform, or finance and banking congresses—to chart more fully the terrain of women's concerns, whether voiced by evangelicals or liberals, Jews, Catholics, or African-Americans, sectarians or post-Christians. There are also the complex stories, now only partially told, about the Board of Lady Managers, an official, national structure within the World's Columbian Commission, led by nationally prominent women. There are important gender issues to be explored through a better understanding of the political struggles over the Exposition's important Woman's Building, in the fact that Froebel's kindergarten was introduced in the Children's Building, and through an interpretation of the omnipresent hieratic statues of women in the White City—Stanford White's "Diana," Harriet Hosmer's "Queen Isabella," Columbia, herself, and of course, the Goddess of Liberty. Topics related to women at the Parliament and Exposition are so deeply embedded in a complex Gilded-Age gender discourse that without specialized training one is at a serious disadvantage and can only intuit the rich possibilities for study and interpretation.[2]

My primary concerns have been with the East/West encounter, but this foray into the Parliament has raised many questions that require further study. To assess adequately its specific impact on the American scene, one still needs to ask a variety of finely-honed questions about the early decades of the twentieth century: Which intellectuals and religious leaders continued to pursue an interest in Asian religious ideas? Who was in the next generation of Asian missionaries and to whom were they speaking? Thomas Tweed has suggested that an optimistic form of Victorian Buddhism functioned for some Americans as an alternative to individualism and theism,[3] but the question of how a broader shift occurred from the confident assumption of the superiority and finality of western and Christian norms that was so conspicuous at the Parliament to the more egalitarian or indifferentist attitudes that are prevalent in many quarters today, remains open to question.

It has been suggested that the erosion of specific religious convictions was well underway in America and the West at the time of the Parliament, largely a product of the proliferation of existential options and the increasing absence of a definitive authority.[4] From thinking about the Exposition and Parliament, I would also suggest that there is a way in which the evolutionary perspective that was so prevalent in liberal thought a century ago, with its unified, if hierarchical, perspective on a common humanity, provided a kind of transitional ideology. Once the peoples of the entire world had been included in a single, global model, it only required a change in sensibilities due to the rise of anthropological disciplines and comparative studies, the erosion of western confidence in the finality of its own traditions, and the politicization of culture both domestically and overseas, to create the more even ideological playing field that is, comparatively speaking, conspicuous today.

The Parliament is also a window onto a world less formally preoccupied with theological issues and the rise and demise of ideologies, a world of dinner parties and gala receptions, weekend stays in the country, afternoon teas in women's clubs, and whistle stop tours across the Great Plains by ascetics and swamis. One wonders about the Parliament's impact on those Americans who were not actively engaged in debating the outcome of the proceedings, for whom the uses of religion did not include intercontinental strategizing and highly politicized theological posturing.

Some evidence suggests that the Parliament elicited odd, if fervid, responses in many different quarters. After the assembly, Barrows was deluged with mail, some from populists in Utah and Colorado who sent an immense petition asking him to bring the free-silver question before another world's parliament. A Hindu Christian wrote him to announce that the end of the world was at hand, for was it not prophesied in the Bible that once the gospel had been preached to all nations, Christ would make his triumphant return? He also received a "Proclamation of Ezra" said to be from an ancient cuneiform tablet, which called for a parliament among the worshippers of Jehovah, Baal, Moloch, Dagon, and the other gods of the 120 provinces of Babylonia. Letters of support for the idea were signed by Haggai the prophet; Zerubbabal, the Architect of the Temple; and Edowin-ben-Arnol, the poet laureate of Baal.[5] Barrows also conveys a sense that the popular reception accorded the Parliament began to plague him. During a California vacation after the assembly, he wrote to his daughter that the Parliament "is like a shirt of Nessus—something that sticks rather tight to your poor father. The mail is full of it. The people at the hotel talk of it." Thirty-five Los Angeles ministers petitioned him to preach on the Parliament; he declined. He and his wife hiked into the Sierra Nevada mountains to worship at a secluded Congregational church, only to find the minister preaching an upbeat sermon on the Parliament, the first in a series on the religions of the world.[6]

It is difficult to assess what the press notices, which, as James Ketelaar noted, were "almost painfully enthusiastic," say about the responses of the average American to the East/West encounter at the Parliament. Some of the notices reveal the excitement the Parliament generated, but do not convey a clear sense of peoples' religious responses. For instance, the *Daily Inter Ocean* and other papers reported on the stir caused by the appearance of Reuchi Shibata, the Shinto priest, whose paper, at least as evidenced in the published record, was somewhat lackluster. Standing before an oil painting of sacred Mount Fuji in what was reported to be a "statue-like attitude with his eyes fixed on the floor," he received wave and after wave of applause. "Women from the audience climbed over chairs and tables to pay their compliments to the distinguished oriental. He was almost swept off his feet in a whirlwind of enthusiasm. Then a loud cheer rent the air and there was a mad rush for the platform. The surging mass was kept back only be the strong lungs of Secretary [William] Pipe, who said the stage would break down." Shibata was "the hero of the moment."[7] Whether this reception was because of his complimentary remarks about Americans, the audience's exoticist fascination with the orient, or a by-product of their forbidden desires projected onto non-white peoples,[8] it seems likely that the crowd was not motivated only by the sudden wish to convert to Shintoism and become devotees of *kami*. But, the possible religious implications of this kind of response were not missed by beleaguered conservatives like A. T. Pierson, who considered it a sign of the times that Christian "women, wild with delight, scramble over chairs and benches to get near Dr. Barrows's 'right reverend' Shinto, who had been throwing mud at Christianity, and were, some of them, *kissed* by him."[9]

Occasionally one gets a glimpse of the way in which the ambiguous theological messages conveyed by the Parliament were perpetuated among average people after the assembly. At the Greenacre Religious Conference in Eliot, Maine, Vivekananda told his assembled students that "I do not come to convert you to a new belief." I want you "to keep your own belief; I want to make a Methodist a better Methodist; the Presbyterian a better Presbyterian. . . . I want to teach you to live the truth, to reveal the light within your own soul." But, one student responded to a reporter's inquiry about her religious goal by noting, "We are not giving up the religion of our forefathers, nor the Christ of Nazareth." Vedanta is "a delving to the roots of all religion leaving us free to worship in whatever form we choose." Mary Phillips, a New York philanthropist and seeker added: "there have been many Christs. . . . All represent the fundamental principles of the Vedanta."[10]

As evidenced in published accounts, the range of possible reactions by people of faith to the Asians in Chicago was fairly limited, with Jenkin Lloyd Jones and A. T. Pierson standing at the extremes, but most taking an appreciative, if somewhat facile, view of the proceedings, informed throughout by sentiments and ideas wholly Christian in origin. Florence Winslow's somewhat perplexed assessment in her impressionistic "Pen Picture of the Parliament" was probably typical of many thoughtful and religiously concerned observers who did not grasp the interconnection between religion and geo-politics. She praised the assembly as a lesson in brotherly love and as a tribute to a "common Father," and she showed great respect for the "strong personalities" of the delegates from the "ethnic religions" who were "no men of straw." But, "strange as it seems," she noted, Vivekananda, Majumdar, and others could express both their love for Christ and their contempt for Christianity.[11]

The Parliament also directs attention to a whole range of questions on the international scene. In the larger scheme of things, it remains an open question as to how important a role the Parliament played in the rise of Asian religious nationalism in a half-dozen countries in the Far East. Recent scholarship has explored the way in which a few Asian delegates used the event to advance their modernizing agendas at home and to develop further their criticism of the Christian West, even as they continued to appropriate and integrate selected western elements into their own societies.[12] But, as in the case of the average American, it is unclear what direct impact the Parliament may have had on people in the broader reaches of Asian societies. The Parliament also directs attention to what appear to be far-flung religious networks among liberals, East and West, that ran through a dozen different countries, but without systematic explorations of biographies with an eye to religious questions, it is difficult to assess the way in which personal sentiments and political and religious commitments operated among these liberals in the transmission of ideas. As a discrete event in the history of the East/West encounter, the Parliament also suggests comparative studies of related assemblies, such as the missionary conferences of the Protestant churches and the Paris Congress of the History of Religions of 1900. In a more formal vein, the Parliament also points out the degree to which the long history of the East/West encounter, while touched upon in numerous monographs, is far from being a coherent field of study.

As an historian working in the American field, I have been repeatedly made aware of the way in which the story of the Parliament might be told and evaluated quite differently by a fundamentalist, an African-American, a Unitarian, a Mormon, or an Anglo-Protestant woman. As a consequence, we need a more layered historiography about the event if we are to have a fuller understanding of its significance. Even a small portion of the attention directed to perennial figures in the American field such as Jonathan Edwards or Charles Finney, if directed to the Parliament and related assemblies, would undoubtedly reveal new sides to it. As a marker of religion in American history, the Parliament will also constantly appear in different lights as the nation continues to change. This account was prompted by my interest in the Orientalist vogue of the 1960s, reason enough to trace out a thin line from Shaku Sōen's mission in 1905 to D. T. Suzuki. Yet, by the centennial of the event, the religious landscape of America had shifted as Asian immigrant communities burgeoned and Asian-Americans from a wide range of traditions began making their own selective appropriation of America's prodigious myths, much as did the leading Asians at the assembly. The Asian dimensions of the Parliament now have a kind of relevance to American religious history that was not apparent to me at the outset. For instance, Alexander Russell (Mohammed) Webb, a heretofore obscure Protestant convert to the religion of the prophet, is only now being hailed by American Muslims as a pioneer who helped to lay the foundations for an Americanized Islam.

It seems most appropriate to begin to conclude, however, not by suggesting what yet needs to be done, but by reiterating some of the concrete accomplishments of the assembly. First, the Parliament undoubtedly contributed a significant measure of leaven to an early-twentieth-century discourse about religious pluralism, both on the domestic scene and overseas. The diverse reactions of many Americans to the assembly speak for themselves. On a more formal note, Marcus Braybrooke began his 1980 history of the interfaith movements of the twentieth century with an account of the Parliament, noting that "no subsequent interfaith gathering has come near to it in size or complexity." The range of theological positions articulated in the subsequent decades of dialogue and debate were "nearly all foreshadowed at the Parliament."[13] Second, the Parliament was a large-scale, public forum that served as a formal debut for the Asian mission to the West. East and West were at that time already deeply engaged in the process of meeting, but the Parliament served as a launching pad for the pioneering efforts of figures like Anagarika Dharmapāla, Shaku Sōen, and Vivekananda to carry to the West the religions of the East. The Parliament must also be credited with encouraging revitalization and modernizing movements in Asia and the rise of religious nationalism in Ceylon, India, and Japan. To what degree it played a role in those highly complex developments remains unclear. Joseph Kitagawa may have pointed to its importance, when in 1983 he pondered the question of why it was that the Parliament "remained so vivid in the memories of many religious people in other parts of the world," but was "all but forgotten" in Chicago.[14] In a very different vein, the Parliament also seems to have contributed to an on-going process of realignment among domestic religious forces in the late-nineteenth-century American mainstream.

Quite aside from these concrete developments, the Parliament also serves as a convenient marker against which to gauge a whole range of more diffuse concerns. Standing as it did in the midst of the ocean of American idealism generated by the Columbian quadricentennial, it is a reminder of how, in the long term, certain deeply-running preoccupations of American civilization persist, even as the emphasis changes. The United States was constitutionally unable and unwilling in 1992 to expend the vast amount of energy and material lavished upon an extraordinarily grand act of self-celebration like that held in Chicago in 1892–93. This may or may not have pointed to a fundamental chastening of the nation's often exaggerated ideas about itself, but it certainly suggested changed priorities. Despite the revival of traditional or conservative Christianity that marked the 1980s, 1992 did not see a ground swell of popular enthusiasm for Columbus's role in the Christianization of the continent. On the contrary, the wide-spread realignment of sentiments in light of the fate of Native American peoples, the history of slavery, and the mixed blessing resulting from the conquest of the continent by industrialization, technology, and other elements of modernity that were widely hailed as millennial breakthroughs a century ago, suggested a seismic shift in our collective understanding of what the nation had become and what it might yet be. But still, the often aggressive, ethnocentric tone of some voices in the revival of the 1980s and the breadth of their influence pointed up the perennial nature of a desire on the part of selected businessmen, philanthropists, well-placed political figures, and their constituencies to assert the primacy of a traditional brand of mainstream American Christianity.

The World's Parliament of Religions, that crowing glory of the World's Congress Auxiliary and the World's Columbian Exposition, also directs our attention to how much our concept of "world" has changed over the course of a century. Quite aside from nuclear issues, environmental problems, and the prospect of advertising in outer space, the idea of the world has lost a certain luster that it had for many people at the end of last century. The Parliament, with its grand hopes to forge a common religious discourse for a global community of sentiment, reminds us that "one worldism" or the "global village" was then a new, fresh vista just opening up for all to see, pregnant with heady possibilities. The open day statement by Augusta Chapin, a Universalist minister and one among the new breed of religious women moving into positions of authority, ably caught the mood of expectation shared by so many others at the assembly. "The world's first Parliament of Religions could not have been called sooner and have gathered the religionists of all these lands together. We had to wait for the hour to strike, until the steamship, the railway and the telegraph had brought men together . . . until the scholar had broken the way through the pathless wilderness of ignorance, superstition, and falsehood. . . . A hundred years ago the world was not ready for this Parliament. Fifty years ago it could not have been convened."[15] The sense that the world had been made ready through the ripening of technology and the dissemination of knowledge, and that one could now strike while the iron was hot to accomplish glorious and high-minded things—be it uniting the world on a single platform in Chicago or evangelizing it in a single generation on mission fields overseas—would by the end of the twentieth century seem to many people quaint or grandiose, if not hostile or alien.

The Parliament also provides an occasion to reflect upon what it is that we mean by "modern," an activity all the more important with the current vogue for the "post-modern" in popular journalism and academic debates. While modern denotes only that which is contemporary, a more common usage has come to imply either a particular spirit, such as modernism in art, or a historical period, which is various dated. In either case, the idea of the modern has been deeply embedded in a nexus of western aesthetics, ideas, values and can be used to refer to anything from the Seagram Building in New York to the White City, from the eighteenth-century *philosophes* to the nineteenth-century advocates of liberal Protestant theology. The Parliament is, however, a powerful reminder that modern in its largest sense refers to both a spirit and a period, which had their origins in the renaissance and in the scientific revolution of the sixteenth century and then radiated geographically outward from Europe and forward through time, gaining in scope and complexity.[16]

The leading Asians at the Parliament were already moderns when they arrived in Chicago. They had already been reacting to the onset of modernity in their societies and dislodging from it what they took to be extraneous, western, and Christian elements, while retailoring it to suit the needs of their own religious traditions and societies. The

Parliament challenges historians of religion to understand in a more synoptic and comparative vein the emergence of modernity as both spirit and period at home, in Europe, and overseas, to grasp the different timetables for its arrival in different places, to understand its different religious contents, and to chart its different social and political trajectories. The displacement of the modern from its strictly western origins and associations has over the course of this century moved forward with a speed that would have astonished, and most likely have troubled, the conveners of the original Parliament, for whom modernity often seemed to be more or less synonymous with liberal Christianity. Perhaps the many hybrid modernities resulting from this near-universal process of radiation, displacement, and adaptation are underlying factors in the discovery of post-modernity. The Parliament itself can usefully be conceived as an event that was meant to be quintessentially modern, but turned out in the end to point to the fracturing process and the collapse of meta-narratives that many see as a hallmark of post-modernity.

The failure of the Parliament to carry off its quest for unity may also tell us something about the fate of classical liberalism. To most people in 1993, it was probably no great surprise that an assembly whose goal was to attempt to forge a common religious discourse among representatives of both the religions of America and the world could not succeed. The more interesting question is, why was such a scheme hatched in 1893? While it is today axiomatic, at least in the political world, that "liberal" and "conservative" have become problematic categories, this was not the case in the nineteenth century, when liberalism was a powerful and protean concept that implied a nexus of "enlightened" values such as progressivism, tolerance, freedom of speech, freedom of opinion, and free trade. Many people had a keen sense of still living in the shadow of an older, hierarchical order with roots in the medieval period, but were experiencing at the same time the rapid expansion of science, technology, industry, and commerce and the burgeoning of cites. Liberalism in this context meant a preference for the expansion of new alternatives over the conventional and customary. For some, this expansion was seen as a great opportunity and a vision, while for others it was understood to be more a strategic necessity.[17]

In this sense, the Parliament was most definitely a liberal event and the majority of its delegates were in some very real sense liberals. But for Barrows, liberalism meant the necessary relaxation of creeds based on the Westminster Confession to better universalize the conversion experience and to maximize mission opportunities. For Gibbons, it meant attempting to bring the Tridentine Roman church more fully into play with the progressive spirit of the age on the American scene. For Jenkin Lloyd Jones, it was the steering of religion in the direction of a broadly theistic, ethical humanism, while for Vivekananda it was the fusion of both popular Puranic religion and Vedantic philosophies with the leading social and intellectual attitudes of the day. The failure of the Parliament's quest for unity is a reminder that "liberal" signified more an approach to the world rather than an ideology, a process more than a goal, and a strategy rather than a specific value content. In the end, liberalism held out no guarantee that the many different parties walking down the broad, liberal road dreaming their own dreams and tailoring their own strategies would ever arrive in the same city.

Finally, in reflecting on the Columbiad of 1892–93, one faces the problem of having to square the fact of pluralism and multiculturalism with the perennial idea that America has a mainstream. The Columbian myth and the White City discourse about America and the world reflect a nexus of values that helped to define a national mainstream in the past. These values continue to play important roles in the present, even though they rarely receive such an august expression as they did at the Exposition and the bald-faced triumphalism associated with them in Chicago has waned. The Columbiad, however, remains a powerful reminder as to why the politics of identity that have played an enormous role in reshaping the American landscape since the civil-rights, ethnic-revival, and cultural-liberation movements of the 1960s are of vital importance to people in many different groups. The Columbiad also points to an important aspect of American history that is somewhat obscured when race-based categories of analysis take primacy over those derived from religion or ethnicity. The mystique of the White City rested on the self-evident quality of its claims to authority, canonicity, and universality. The power of this mystique was such that it tended to disguise the fact that the Exposition epitomized values and ideals—some admirable, others definitely not—that had their origins in an Anglo-American or Anglo-Protestant ethnic group that, more than any other, defined the national mainstream in the nineteenth century. Whether issues are now cast in terms of European versus indigenous, Anglo versus Hispanic, White versus Black, Caucasian versus Asian,

Liberal versus Fundamentalist, Man versus Woman, or in other polarities, the tendency for identity to be worked out in sets and subsets of racial, ethnic, religious, and gender categories reflects the degree to which the taken-for-grantedness of the public authority of that older American mainstream has eroded over the course of the twentieth century.

This erosion has provided many different Americans with the opportunity for public self-expression, even as it has forced others to retrench or to reconstruct new identities on inherited footings. The absence of a single, clear center to the nation has had many consequences for American society, but the loss seems more than offset by the gains that have accrued through the rise of those once consigned to the periphery, even if at times we seem to be challenged by what approaches the status of an oxymoron—the need to create a new, national, mainstream consensus based on a wide range of hyphenated American identities. One religious and theological consequence of this for our understanding of pluralism and multiculturalism is perhaps obvious but needs to be restated—America can no longer convincingly present itself to the world as a Protestant or a Christian or a Judeo-Christian nation.

If a new consensus must appeal to a public religion and theology, they will of necessity have to be inclusive of a wide variety of American identities and, as a marker of religious and cultural change, the Parliament can serve, with many serious qualifications to be sure, as a positive precedent. The Parliament was a single platform upon which many different religious people could stand, be they convinced evangelical Protestant Christians or committed modernist Hindus. One legacy of the assembly rests with the delegates' inability to forge a common religious discourse, insofar as this failure underscores both the perennial need to acknowledge difference or otherness and the importance of attempting to sustain conversation over deep institutional, religious, and cultural divides. A second legacy is more related to the attempt on the part of charismatic delegates from both East and West to articulate visions of transcendental unity. In this regard, the Parliament seems to be cut from the cloth of the free-form mysticism, sometimes Christian, sometimes most certainly not, that has been seen as characteristic of the American religious milieu in the late twentieth century.[18] This dimension of the Parliament is a reminder that the construction of identity in the United States is a process that often defies convenient labels, be they indicative of church affiliation, religion, gender, or ethnic and racial heritage. Both legacies point to the fact that the challenges involved in building a pluralistic nation, which is now one of the central tasks being undertaken in a new, emerging national mainstream, were hinted at by events at the Parliament in 1893.

This suggests a third legacy of the Parliament, one related to how historians of American religion might use the assembly to revision the nation's past. The Parliament tells historians little about religious demographics, church affiliation, or congregational practices at the grassroots. Yet, on the more formal level of public religion and theology, the historian can look back at the Parliament and be confirmed in his or her knowledge that in the Gilded Age one could stand within an expanding American mainstream by expressing a deep faith in the Judeo-Christian tradition in a wide variety of distinctly different ways. But, one can also look back and see that even a century ago American civil religion could accommodate itself to the idea that one might be refined into an incarnation of God through the fires of modern science, become realized in the love of the Divine Mother, grow in the bliss of the dark lord Krishna, or be self-emptied in the Buddhist *dharmakaya*. In many different if often incompatible ways, the Parliament also seems to have confirmed America's sense of its extravagant destiny, even if after the assembly the nation would begin to trundle forward through time under an increasingly flexible but officially sanctioned theology, which is to say under a pluralistic if highly ambiguous concept of God. Krishna, the *kami*, the Buddha (technically not a God), and the Divine Mother had all been tucked into the nation's "sacred canopy,"[19] where they joined the Christian Father, Son, and Spirit; Jehovah; the extra-human power in the universe; Apollo and his Muses; and the Goddess of Liberty, too. The United States had built the Exposition and convened the Parliament with the intentions of changing the world. And it had. There was no turning back.

NOTES

Introduction

1. In the absence of interpretive literature on the 1993 centennial, The Parliament of the World's Religions, see the introductory essays in Beversluis, *Sourcebook for the Community of Religions*, pp. 1–21 and the extensive program published by the Council for the Parliament, *Parliament of the World's Religions*.

2. The Research Committee of the Council for a Parliament of the World's Religions, a committee of the Chicago Parliament centennial group, undertook a search for original manuscripts of selected speeches in connection with the Open Court Press publication of Seager, *The Dawn of Religious Pluralism*. The differences between the two published sources are in a few cases extreme. More typically, they differ on stylistic points or as a result of editing. Relatively few original manuscripts are readily available, but those that are indicate the essential integrity of the two published accounts of the event. The fact that the papers of the two most important organizers, Barrows and Charles Carroll Bonney, were either lost or destroyed in the early part of this century, complicates difficulties with the basic texts.

3. Bonney, "Genesis of the World's Religious Congresses," pp. 82–83, 87–89.

4. Persons, *Free Religion*, p. 97; Graham, "Jenkin Lloyd Jones," pp. 62–81. Spencer Lavan mistook John Henry Barrows for Samuel J. Barrows, the editor of the Unitarian *Christian Register* in Lavan, *Unitarians in India*, p. 139.

5. *Programme of the World's Religious Congresses* p. 20.

6. Marty, *Modern American Religion*, 1: 17–31.

7. I have developed this perspective in Seager, "Pluralism and the American Mainstream: The View from the World's Parliament of Religions."

8. *Report of the President*, "Appendix A," p. 326.

9. Ibid., pp. 329–33.

10. Ibid., p, 332.

11. For an introductory discussion of these congresses, see Burg, *Chicago's White City of 1893*, pp. 235–85. The best source for papers is in Dybwad, *Annotated Bibliography*.

12. Hutchison, *American Protestant Thought*, pp. 1–14 and *Modernist Impulse*, pp. 1–11.

13. Jones, *Age of Energy*, pp. 251–65; Horowitz, *Culture and the City*, p. 1–26; Manieri-Elia, "Toward an 'Imperial City," pp. 1–142; Brooklyn Museum, *The American Renaissance, 1876–1979*, pp. 27–51.

14. The most comprehensive selection of Exposition sources and commentaries is in Dybwad, *Annotated Bibliography*.

15. Sources helpful in this regard are Albanese, *Sons of the Fathers*, pp. 46–80; Jones, *O Strange New World*, pp. 251–72; McClung, "American Image" and "From Indian Princess"; Kennedy, *Greek Revival America*, pp. 3–24, 59–61, 387–95; Craig, *Federal Presence*, pp. 2–15.

16. Tuveson describes two mythic strands—America as the New Rome and as the new Promised Land for a chosen people—which underwent a kind of "chemical

combination" during the fervor for expansion and manifest destiny during the Mexican War. See Tuveson, *Redeemer Nation*, pp. 96, 125.

17. Rydell, *All the World's a Fair*, pp. 2–8, 38–71, 235–37.

18. McRae, "Oriental Verities, pp. 7–36; Ketelaar, "Strategic Occidentalism," pp. 37–56.

19. Eliade, *Sacred and the Profane*, pp. 58–62.

20. Victor Turner, *Image and Pilgrimage*, pp. 249–50, *From Ritual to Theatre*, pp. 68–73, *Dramas, Fields, and Metaphors*, pp. 17, 23–58.

21. Lincoln, *Discourse and the Construction of Society*, pp. 3–11.

22. Marty, *Pilgrims in Their Own Land*, pp. 154–64, 406, 425–26. For a parallel but distinct discussion, see Wilson, *Public Religion*.

23. I use the term Gilded Age throughout, but my argument is also informed by the idea of the *fin de siècle* as a period of the dissolution and transformation of older, unitary cultures due to the various forces of modernity. See May, *End of American Innocence*; Persons, *Decline of Gentility*; Schorske, *Fin de Siècle Vienna*; Weber, *France, Fin de Siècle*.

24. *Chicago Tribune*, 9 September 1893.

1. The Columbian Myth of America

1. Kirkland, *Story of Chicago*, 2: 38–40.

2. The importance of the classical sign in the American imagination has been underexploited by historians of religion. For the evolution of the eighteenth-century image of the Goddess of Liberty from a sixteenth-century Indian Princess, see McClung, "The American Image" and "From Indian Princess." The connection between neoclassicism, the American Enlightenment, and the White City is most explicit in Jones, *O Strange New World*, pp. 271–72. See also Kennedy, *Greek Revival America*, pp. 3–24, 59–61, 387–95.

3. The millennialist theme is well known in American religious history. Hutchison defines it in its moderate phase as "a belief that human society is moving toward realization (even though it may never attain the reality) of the Kingdom of God" (Hutchison, *Modernist Impulse*, p. 2). Energy and progress as important Gilded Age motives, particularly as they bear upon the Exposition, are discussed in Jones, *Age of Energy*, pp. 100–37, 241–58. The most extended discussion of the theological, mythical, and cultural elements in American millennialism is in Tuveson, *Redeemer Nation*.

4. In Tuveson's words, America could be either the "New Rome" or "a New Promised Land for a chosen people." Tuveson. *Redeemer Nation*, pp. 96, 125.

5. Studies of Christianity in America are too numerous to cite. The passing of the importance of the traditional role of the classics is indicated in Persons, *Decline of Gentility*, pp. 179–202. Recent treatments of the classical element include Reinhold, *Classica Americana* and Kennedy, *Greek Revival America*. One recent work that brings Christian and classical elements together and is primarily concerned with literary and artistic figures is Vance, *America's Rome*.

6. May, "Religion of the Republic," pp. 171—73.

7. Handy, *Christian America*, pp. 95–101, 110–16.

8. Among historians rooted in the older mainstream point of view, Martin Marty has paid a good bit of attention to other peoples' ethnicity, but little to the ethnic quality of the mainstream. For instance, see Marty, *Ethnic and Non-Protestant Themes* and "Ethnicity: The Skeleton of Religion."

9. Leading historians of American religion tend to see religious meaning as migrating from churches to culture, but not as arising in the culture itself. Newer interpretations are typically informed by Clifford Geertz's definition of religion as a "model of and for behavior" and Victor Turner's "social process" approach. Geertz, *Interpretation of Culture*; Turner, *Dramas, Fields, and Metaphors*. Making a full anthropological turn often results in richer interpretations of churchly phenomena by pointing to their embeddedness in both culture and ethnicity, as in Orsi, *Madonna of 115th Street*.

10. For a discussion of the "genteel" literary establishment, see Tomsich, *Genteel Endeavor*.

11. Aldrich, "Unguarded Gates," 2: 72.

12. See, for instance, Bushnell, *Barbarism the First Danger*.

13. Bushnell, *Work and Play*, pp. 118–19.

14. Morrison, *Chautauqua*; Raymond, *About Chautauqua*, pp. 38–39; Hurlbutt, *Story of the Chautauqua*, pp. 170, 196–208.

15. Carter, *Spiritual Crisis of the Gilded Age*, pp. 39–65.

16. Hutchison, *American Protestant Thought*, pp. 1–14; Hutchison, *Modernist Impulse*, pp. 1–11.

17. Wiebe, *Search for Order*, pp. 45–52.

18. Insofar as the idea of the "Victorian" is applicable to the United States, the general tendency to vacillate between optimism and despair has been treated in Houghton, *The Victorian Frame of Mind*, pp. 27–89. The idea of American Victorianism has been used in an interpretation of the appropriation of Buddhist-like ideas by U.S. intellectuals in Tweed, *American Encounter with Buddhism*, pp. xxii–xxiv. I have avoided the term because I wanted to emphasize the fusion of Greco-Roman and Judeo-Christian elements in a mainstream myth, position the Exposition nearer the end of a discrete historical era, and draw attention to the sybaritic qualities, both material and rhetorical, of the Columbiad. All in all, the Exposition and Parliament seemed more characteristically Gilded than Victorian. See also Jenkyns, *The Victorians and Ancient Greece*.

19. Higham, *Strangers in the Land*, pp. 19–34.

20. In Cronon, *Nature's Metropolis*, pp. 41–43.

21. Trachtenberg, *Incorporation of America*, pp. 209, 213–18.

22. Eliade, *Sacred and Profane*, pp. 58–62.

23. Kirkland *Story of Chicago*, 2: 18; Besant, "First Impression," p. 533.

24. Johnson, *History of the World's Columbian Exposition*, 1: 171–72. For an excellent selection of photographs, see Appelbaum, *The Chicago World's Fair*.

25. For inscriptions, see Arnold, *Official Views*, Plate 13 "Peristyle and Quadriga"; Johnson, *History of the World's Columbian Exposition*, 1: 164.

26. For dedicatory rites, see *Report of the President*, pp. 155–66; Joint Committee on Ceremonies, *Dedicatory and Opening Ceremonies*, pp. 133–42; Johnson, *History of the World's Columbian Exposition*, 1: 258–306.

27. In Johnson, *History of the World's Columbian Exposition*, 1: 295–306.

28. Cronon, *Nature's Metropolis*, p. 42.

29. Van Rensselaer, "Artistic Triumph," pp. 528, 538–40.

30. Van Brunt, "Columbian Exposition," pp. 577, 581, 588.

31. *New York Times*, 28 March 1893; Gilder, "White City," pp. 201–202.

32. Swing, "Significance of the World's Fair," pp. 84, 92.

33. Morgan, "Signs of the Times," p. 69.

34. M., H. W, "Impression of the White City," pp. 1200–1201.

35. Gunsaulus, "Ideal of Culture," pp. 59–61.

36. Noble, "Meaning and Opportunities," pp. 58, 62–63.

37. Besant, "A First Impression," p. 538.

38. Rydell, *All the World's a Fair*, p. 46.

39. Bellah, "Civil Religion in America," pp. 21–41.

40. "Official Program," pp. 446–47.

41. Mowry, "Columbus Day in Salem" pp. 8–9.

42. Wells, *Wisconsin Columbian Circular*, pp. 23, 28.

43. *Celebration of Columbus Day*, pp. 4–8.

44. Ibid., pp. 34, 36.

45. Lincoln, *Discourse and the Construction of Society*, pp. 10, 21.

46. Olsen, "American Sunday," pp. 70–75; Druyvesten, "World's Parliament of Religions," pp. 98–107; Johnson, *History of the World's Columbian Exposition*, 1: 359–67; Redman, "Sabbatarian Accommodation," pp. 495–523.

47. Quoted in Druyvesten, "World's Parliament of Religions," p. 102.

48. Quoted in Barrows, Mary, *John Henry Barrows*, pp. 266–67.

49. Downey, "Tradition and Acceptance: American Catholics and the Columbian Exposition," *Mid-America* 63 (April-July 1981): 79–92.

50. Muldoon, "Sermon of Welcome," pp. 10–13.

51. Gibbons, "Address," pp. 16–17.

52. Golomb, "The 1893 Congress of Jewish Women"; *Papers of the Jewish Women's Congress*.

53. Editorial Notes, *Reform Advocate*, 22 July 1893: 421.

54. Hirsch, "Spiritual Results of the World's Fair," pp. 202–05.

55. Hirsch, "Lessons of the World's Columbian Exposition," pp. 205–206.

56. Rydell, *All the World's a Fair*, pp. 52–55; Weimann, *Fair Women*, pp. 35, 123.

57. *The White City*, Plate "The Sleeping Fisherman," n. p.

58. Rydell, *All the World's a Fair*, pp. 54–55

59. Ibid., p. 53.

60. Douglass and Wells, *The Reason Why*, pp. 3–4.

61. Quoted in Weimann, *Fair Women*, p. 123.

2. The Midway Plaisance and the Magic of the White City

1. Rydell, *All the World's a Fair*, pp. 55–60, 62–3. While Rydell casts his discussion globally, he does not discuss the religious, that is the "great tradition," aspect of the evolutionary perspective. Nor does he nuance his discussion in terms of ethnic issues in the United States, but casts his discussion in terms of a white, western utopian vision in contrast to the rest of the world.

2. Rydell, *All the World's a Fair*, p. 65.

3. There are numerous contemporary descriptions of the Midway, but the most authoritative is found in Johnson, *History of the World's Columbian Exposition*, 1: 75–80, 2: 315–57, 3: 433–50.

4. Johnson, *History of the World's Columbian Exposition*, 2: 337–38, 3: 441–43; Ives, *Dream City*, Plate "Javanese Settlement" and Plate "Javanese Orchestra."

5. Johnson, *History of the World's Columbian Exposition* 2: 338, 3: 441; Wah Mee Exposition Company, *Guide to the Joss House*, pp. 1–2; Ives, *Dream City*, Plate "Chinese Joss House" and Plate "Chinese Theater."

6. Johnson, *History of the World's Columbian Exposition*, 1: 75–76, 2: 235–37, 3: 438–41; Ives, *Dream City*, Plate "Temple of Luxor."

7. Johnson, *History of the World's Columbian Exposition*, 2: 333–37, 3: 443–44, 449–50. Cullins's observations are in 2: 337. See also Ives, *The Dream City*, Plate "Esquimoe Village" and Plate "The Aztecs."

8. Johnson, *History of the World's Columbian Exposition*, 1: 79, 2: 342, 3: 444; Ives, *Dream City*, Plate "Persian Palace"; Hawthorne, "Foreign Folk at the Fair," p. 570.

9. Lewi, "Yom Kippur on the Midway," 2: 1693–94.

10. Hawthorne, "Foreign Folk at the Fair," p. 571.

11. Ralph, *Harper's Chicago*, pp. 206–12.

12. Dockarty, *The Midway Plaisance*, pp. 176, 211.

13. Burnham, *Sweet Clover*, pp. 395–96.

14. Buel, *Magic City*, Plate "Dahomey Cannibals" and Plate "Javanese Village." In my grandfather's diary, in which he recounted his own trip to the White City as a young man, he reported that a hand-written sign at the Samoan Village announced: "Do not ask these people about cannibalism, as it annoys them."

15. Ibid., Plate "Hindostanee Delegates to the Congress of Religions."

16. Putnam, *Portrait Types of the Midway Plaisance*.

17. Higham, *Strangers in the Land*, pp. 122–23. In much the same fashion, Milton Singer wrote about civic rituals in which the status of representatives from immigrant communities was measured by their proximity or distance to Anglo-Americans in the course of ceremonials. Singer, "The Melting Pot".

18. Johnson, *History of the World's Columbian Exposition*, 1: 421–2, 433–34, 457–58.

19. Ibid., 1: 437–38; "The Convocation of Druids Ceremony," *Los Angeles Times*, 20 September 1893.

20. Johnson, *History of the World's Columbian Exposition*, 1: 411–12; *Chicago Tribune*, 15 June 1893.

21. Johnson, *History of the World's Columbian Exposition*, 1: 478–481. For notice of the balls, see *Chicago Herald*, 9 September 1893.

22. *Chicago Tribune*, 18 June 1893.

23. Johnson, *History of the World's Columbian Exposition*, 1: 478.

24. Johnson, *History of the World's Columbian Exposition*, 1: 417–19; *Chicago Tribune*, 4 July 1893.

25. *Chicago Tribune*, 4 July 1893.

26. For details of and reactions to the Midway/White City Fourths, see *Chicago Trbune*, 5 July 1893.

27. Eliade, *The Sacred and the Profane*, p. 92.

28. Davis, "Last Days of the Fair," p. 1002.

29. Gilder, "The Vanishing City," pp. 202-204.

30. Robinson, "The Fair as Spectacle," 1: 494–5, 510.

31. Buel, *Magic City*.

3. Chicago's Pentecost

1. Downey, "Tradition and Acceptance," p. 80. For an introduction to issues in American Catholicism at this time, see Dolan, *American Catholic Experience*, pp. 303–20.

2. King, "Rediscovering Women's Voices at the World's Parliament of Religions," pp. 325–43.

3. The ideological connection between the Exposition and Parliament has in-

formed a number of different discussions of the East/West encounter, most powerfully in Kitagawa, "The 1893 World's Parliament of Religions"; Druyvesten, "The World's Parliament of Religions"; Ziolkowski, "Heavenly Visions and Worldly Intentions"; Ketelaar, "Strategic Occidentalism"; and McRae, "Oriental Verities."

4. Turner, *Image and Pilgrimage*, pp. 249–50, *From Ritual to Theatre*, pp. 68–73, *Dramas, Fields, and Metaphors*, 17, 23–58.

5. Bonney, "A World's Congress at the World's Fair," p. 45.

6. *Report of the President*, "Appendix A," p. 325–27.

7. Ibid., pp. 327–35.

8. Burg, *Chicago's White City*, p. 282.

9. Bonney, "Genesis of the World's Religious Congresses," pp. 81, 90–93; Graham, "Jenkin Lloyd Jones," pp. 62–81.

10. *Programme of the World's Religious Congresses*, p, 20.

11. Bonney, "Genesis of the World's Religious Congresses," pp. 82–83.

12. Ibid., 87–89. For a general comparison with the ground rules of the 1993 centennial of the Parliament, see the address delivered by Paulos Mar Gregorios at the Inaugural Ceremonies of the Centennial in November, 1989, Beversluis, ed. *Sourcebook for the Community of Religions*, pp. 15–18.

13. Henrotin, "Great Congress," pp. 626, 632.

14. The statistical breakdown is based on an analysis of the papers and other presentations reproduced in Barrows, checked against those in other publications of the Parliament papers. These figures are close approximations.

15. In 1844, Baird assessed the religious forces that dominated American society, clustering on one side the "evangelical" churches—Episcopalians, Congregationalists, Presbyterians, Baptists, Methodists, and Lutherans. Approximately 18 million strong, these combined denominations were characterized by Baird as parts of one organic whole and "divisions of one vast army" in whose hands rested the nation's destiny. On the other side, Baird assembled the "nonevangelicals"—Catholics, Unitarians, Universalists, Jews, sectarians, atheists, and socialists. Of this smaller group, he concluded, "they present no insurmountable barrier to the advance of Truth." Baird, *Religion in America*, pp. 249–53, 257–58, 275–77.

16. *Chicago Tribune*, 13 September 1893.

17. *Chicago Tribune*, 12 September 1893.

18. In Seager, *Dawn of Religious Pluralism*, p. xiv.

19. Carus, "Charles Carroll Bonney," pp. 517–19; Bonney, "Genesis of the World's Religious Congresses," pp. 75, 93–94.

20. Graham, "Jenkin Lloyd Jones," pp. 62–81; Jenkin Lloyd Jones, "Books on the Parliament," pp. 274–75, *Chorus of Faiths*, pp. 25–26, "Triumph of the Parliament," p. 66.

21. Barrows, "Religious Possibilities of the World's Fair," p. 560.

22. Barrows, Mary, *John Henry Barrows*, pp. 262–63.

23. Barrows, *World's Parliament of Religions*, 1: 3, 2: 1578.

24. Bacon, *History of American Christianity*, pp. 416–20.

25. Philip Schaff, "The Reunion of Christendom," in Barrows, *World's Parliament of Religions* (hereafter cited as Barrows), 2: 1192, 1195–96, 1200–1201.

26. Race, *Christians and Religious Pluralism*, pp. 10–13.

27. William Wilkinson, "The Attitude of Christianity toward Other Religions," in Barrows, 2: 1249; James Dennis, "The Message of Christianity to Other Religions," in Barrows, 2: 1254–55; Joseph Cook, "Strategic Certainties of Comparative Religion," in Barrows, 1: 536, 538–40.

28. *Daily Inter-Ocean*, 9 September 1893, Second Section.

29. George Pentecost, "The Invincible Gospel," in Barrows, 2: 1166, 1172.

30. Race, *Christians and Religious Pluralism*, pp. 38–45, 56–61; Knitter, *No Other Name?*, p. 121.

31. John Keane, "The Incarnation Idea in History and in Jesus Christ," in Barrows, 2: 882, 884–5, 888.

32. John Gmeiner, "Primitive and Prospective Religious Union of the Human Family," in Barrows, 2: 1265–66.

33. Lyman Abbott, "Religion Essentially Characteristic of Humanity," in Barrows, 1: 500; Charles Briggs, "The Truthfulness of Holy Scripture," in Barrows, 1: 661, 650.

34. James W. Lee, "Christ the Reason of the Universe," in Barrows, 2: 856, 860.

35. Henry Drummond, "Evolution and Christianity," in Barrows, 2: 1317, 1322, 1325; A. B. Bruce, "Man's Place in the Universe," in Barrows, 2: 941; W. A. P. Martin, "America's Duty to China," in Barrows, 2: 1138.

36. H. Pereira Mendes, "Orthodox or Historical Judaism," in Barrows, 1: 535; Kaufmann Kohler, "Brotherhood as Taught in the Religions Based on the Bible," in Barrows, 1: 373.

37. Emil Hirsch, "Elements of Universal Religion," in Barrows, 2: 1305, 1308.

38. Thomas Wentworth Higginson, "The Sympathy of Religions," in Barrows, 1: 781–84; Paul Carus, "Science as a Religious Revelation," in Barrows, 2: 980; W. L. Tomlins, "Religion and Music," in Barrows, 2: 1303.

39. *Chicago Herald*, 27 September 1893.

40. Julia Ward Howe, "What is Religion?" in Barrows, 2: 1250–51.

41. Daniel Offord, "The Doctrine and Life of the Shakers," in Barrows, 2: 1380; Marion Murdock, "A New Testament Woman," in Barrows, 1: 799; Adolph Brodbeck, "Idealism the New Religion," in Barrows, 1: 340.

42. E. L. Rexford, "The Religious Intent," in Barrows, 1: 509–10, 19–20.

43. Ibid., pp. 518–20, 522.

44. John Keane, "The Ultimate Religion," in Barrows, 2: 1331.

45. Ibid., pp. 1331–32, 1334, 1336–38.

46. George Dana Boardman, "Christ the Unifier of Mankind," in Barrows, 2: 1338.

47. Ibid., p. 1339.

48. Ibid., pp. 1339, 1341–42, 1346.

49. Ibid., p. 1346.

4. On Mars Hill

1. The analogy between Mars Hill and the Parliament was drawn with varying theological nuances by liberals and conservatives, all of which accrued to Christian interpretations of the meaning of the Parliament. See, for example, William Wilkinson, "Attitudes of Christianity toward Other Religions," in Barrows, 2: 1247–49; George Pentecost, "The Invincible Gospel," in Barrows, 2: 1171–72; Barrows, "Welcome to the Parliament," 1: 78–79; Barrows, Mary, *John Henry Barrows*, p. 262; Bonney, "Genesis of the World's Religious Congresses," p. 77.

2. Barrows, 2: 1556.

3. William C. Wilkinson, "The Attitude of Christianity toward Other Religions," in Barrows, 2: 1247–48; T. E. Slater, "The Present Religious Outlook of India," in Barrows, 2: 1173.

4. Quoted in Swing, "Building a Great Religion," p. 975.

5. Augustine Hewitt CSP, "Rational Demonstration of the Being of God," in Barrows, 1: 256–69; William Torrey Harris, "Proofs of the Existence of God," in Barrows, 1: 306–14.

6. Carter, *Spiritual Crisis*, p. 215.

7. Ida Hultin, "The Essential Oneness of Ethical Ideas among All Men," in Barrows, 2: 1003–05; Alfred Momerie, "The Essence of Religion in Right Conduct," in Barrows, 2: 1112.

8. Crawford Toy, "The Relation between Religion and Conduct," in Barrows, 2: 1009–11.

9. Walter Eliot OSP, "The Supreme End and Office of Religion," in Barrows, 1: 462–65, Laura Ormiston Chant, "The Real Religion of Today," in Barrows, 1: 591–94.

10. Ida Hultin, "The Essential Oneness of Ethical Ideas among All Men," in Barrows, 2: 1003; Crawford Toy, "The Relation Between Religion and Conduct," in Barrows, 2: 1010.

11. Hutchison, *Modernist Impulse*, p. 131.

12. Exceptions are found in Barrows. See Annis F. F. Eastman, "The Influence of Religion on Women," in Barrows, 1: 752–58; and Marion Murdock, "A New Testament Woman," in Barrows, 1: 799.

13. Murdock, p. 1:800.

14. *Daily Inter-Ocean*, 12 September 1893.

15. Kaufmann Kohler, "Brotherhood as Taught in the Religions Based on the Bible," in Barrows, 1: 366.

16. C. D. D'Harlez, "The Comparative Study of the World's Religions," in Barrows, 1: 621.

17. David Burrell, "What Christianity Has Wrought for America," in Barrows, 2: 1159.

18. Fannie Williams, "What Can Religion Further Do to Advance the Condition of the American Negro," in Barrows, 2: 1114–15; Lady Somerset, "Letter," in Barrows, 2: 926–27; James Dennis, "The Message of Christianity to Other Religions," in Barrows, 2: 1256.

19. Walter Eliot OSP, "The Supreme End and Office of Religion," in Barrows, 1: 465; Laura Ormiston Chant, "The Real Religion of Today," in Barrows, 1: 593.

20. Barrows, 1: 138, 129, 112, 120, 67, 186, 113.

21. Jordan, *Comparative Religion*, pp. 392–93; Kitagawa, "Humanistic and Theological History of Religions," pp. 553–63; Carter, *Spiritual Crisis*, pp. 199–221; Jackson, *Oriental Religions*, pp. 243–67.

22. Sharpe, *Comparative Religion*, pp. 27–71 passim, 136–40; Hutchison, *Errand to the World*, pp. 102–108.

23. Kitagawa, "Humanistic and Theological History of Religions," pp. 553–55; Sharpe, *Comparative Religion*, pp. 138–39. Sharpe notes that the Parliament was an encouragement to the emergent science of religion because it showed the degree to which earlier intolerance was being overcome and was a danger because "it tended to associate at least some comparative religionists . . . with an idealistic programme of world peace and understanding." For a recent descussion see Ziolkowski, *A Museum of Faiths*, pp. 1–57.

24. *Daily Inter-Ocean*, 14 September 1893; Dionysius Latas, "The Greek Church," in Barrows, 1: 358–59.

25. Jean Réville, "Principles of the Scientific Classification of Religions," in Barrows, 2: 1367–69.

26. C. P. Tiele, "On the Study of Comparative Theology," in Barrows, 1: 589.

27. Albert Réville, "Conditions and Outlook for a Universal Religion," in Barrows, 2: 1363–67.

28. J. Estlin Carpenter, "The Need for a Wider Conception of Revelation, or Lessons for the Sacred Books of the World," in Barrows, 2: 842, 849.

29. F. Max Müller, "Greek Philosophy and the Christian Religion," in Barrows, 2: 935–36.

30. Eliza R. Sunderland, "Serious Study of All Religions," in Barrows, 1: 622, 638.

31. Merwin-Marie Snell, "The Relations of the Science of Religion to Philosophy," in Barrows, 2: 1375; "Service of the Science of Religion to Unity and Mission Enterprise," in Barrows, 2: 1347.

32. Hutchison, *Errand to the World*, p. 105.

33. Milton Valentine, "Harmonies and Distinctions in the Theistic Teaching of the Various Historical Faiths," in Barrows, 1: 289.

34. Conrad von Orelli, "The General Belief in the Need of Vicarious Sacrifices," in Barrows, 2: 1045.

35. T. E. Slater, "Concessions to Native Ideas, Having Special Reference to Hinduism," in Barrows, 1: 457, 459.

36. "Words of Welcome," in Barrows, 1: 74.

37. Said, *Orientalism*, p. 6.

38. As noted in an earlier footnote, all statistics are based on an analysis of the papers and other presentations reproduced in Barrows, checked against those in other publications of the Parliament papers.

39. Hutchison, *Errand to the World*, pp. 91–102.

40. Mardiros Ignados, "The Mission of Protestantism in Turkey," in Barrows, 2: 1258–61.

41. Minas Tcheraz, "The Armenian Church," in Barrows, 2: 932.

42. Horiuchi Kozaki, "Christianity in Japan, Its Present and Future Condition," in Barrows, 2: 1012–14.

43. Nobuta Kishimoto, "Future of Religion in Japan," in Barrows, 2: 1283.

44. Mr. Haworth, "Criticism and Discussion of Missionary Methods," in Barrows, 2: 1099–2000.

45. *Chicago Tribune*, 14 September 1893.

46. See Ketelaar, "Strategic Occidentalism," p. 48.

47. Kinzo Riuge M. Hirai, "The Real Position of Japan Towards Christianity," in Barrows, 1: 448–49.

48. *Chicago Herald*, 14 September 1893; Houghton, *Neely's History*, p. 157.

49. H. Dharmapāla, "Criticism and Discussion of Missionary Methods," in Barrows, 2: 1093.

50. B. B. Nagarkar, "The Work of Social Reform in India," in Barrows, 1: 777–78 and "The Spiritual Ideals of the Brahmo-Somaj," in Barrows, 2: 1229.

51. Pung Kwang Yu, "Confucianism," in Barrows, 1: 425, 438.

52. B. Fay Mills, "Christ the Savior of the World," in Barrows, 2: 999–1000.

53. George Candlin, "The Bearing of Religious Unity on the Work of Christian Missions," in Barrows, 2: 1187.

54. Francis E. Clark, "Christianity as Seen by a Voyage Around the World," in Barrows, 2: 1237–38.

55. Barrows, 1: 20–22. The complete letter is found in Pipe, "The Parliament of Religions," p. 385.

56. Henry Harris Jessup, "The Religious Mission of the English Speaking Nations," in Barrows, 2: 1122–26.

57. Vivekananda, "Hinduism," in Barrows, 1: 972, 974, 977.

58. Pung Kwang Yu, "Confucianism, Supplement Second," in Barrows, 1: 430–31.

59. B. B. Nagarkar, "Spiritual Ideas of the Brahmo-Somaj," in Barrows, 1: 1229.

60. Dharmapāla, "The World's Religious Debt to Buddha," in Barrows 1: 868.

61. Virchand A. Gandhi, "The Philosophy and Ethics of the Jains," in Barrows, 2: 1224.

62. Manilal N. D'Vivedi, "Hinduism," in Barrows, 1: 317-18.

63. Vivekananda, "Closing Remarks," in Barrows, 1: 170-71.

64. Narasima Charya, "Criticism and Discussion of Missionary Methods," in Barrows, 2: 1094.

65. *San Francisco Examiner*, 26 September 1893.

66. *Chicago Tribune*, 26 September 1893.

67. Quoted in Barrows, 1: 144-45.

68. *Chicago Tribune*, 26 September 1893.

5. "A Rapt Gaze into the Millennium"

1. Rydell, *All the World's a Fair*, pp. 2-4, 235-37.

2. The text signaling this development is Herberg, *Protestant, Catholic, Jew.*

3. McNeill, *A World History*, pp. 405-407.

4. Hay, *Asian Ideas of East and West*, pp. 4-6, 330.

5. Ketelaar, "Strategic Occidentalism," pp. 38-40.

6. Candlin, "Results and Mission of the Parliament," p. 373.

7. Ibid., pp. 371-73.

8. Carus, "World's Religious Parliament Extension," pp. 350-53.

9. Candlin, "The Parliament of Religions," pp. 35-36.

10. Ibid., p. 36.

11. Hutchison, *Modernist Impulse*, pp. 119-32.

12. Frye, *Great Code*, p. xviii.

13. J. Sanna Abou Naddara, "The Koran and Other Scripture," in Barrows, 2: 1146-48.

14. Alexander Russell Webb, "The Influence of Islam on Social Conditions, in Barrows, 2: 1046; "The Spirit of Islam," in Barrows, 2: 994.

15. George Washburn, "The Points of Contact and Contrast between Christianity and Mohammedanism," in Barrows, 1: 579-80.

16. "Taoism," in Barrows, 2: 1355-58.

17. Reuchi Shibata, "Shintoism," in Barrows, 1: 451-54.

18. P. Goro Kaburagi, "The Shinto Religion," in Barrows, 2: 1373-74.

19. Takayoshi Matsugama, "Origins of Shinto," in Barrows, 2: 1373.

20. Virchand A. Ghandi, "The Philosophy and Ethics of the Jains," in Barrows, 2: 1222-26.

21. Yoshigiro Kawai, "A Declaration of Faith and the Truth of Buddhism," in Barrows, 2: 1290-93.

22. S. Parthasarathy Aiyangar, "The Tenkalai S'ri Vaishnava, or Southern Ramanuja Religion," in Barrows, 2: 1376-78.

23. Herant Kiretchijian, "A Voice from the Young Men of the Orient," in Barrows, 2: 1276-77.

24. Little, "Parliament of Religions," p. 211.

25. Pung Kwang Yu, "Confucianism," in Barrows, 1: 375–78.

26. Ibid., 1: 428, 436–39.

27. Jinanji Jamshedi Modi, "The Religious System of the Parsees," in Barrows, 2: 906–909.

28. Ibid., 2: 909, 912, 920.

29. Manilal N. D'Vivedi, "Hinduism," in Barrows, 1: 317–18; 325.

30. Ibid., 1: 326–27.

31. Ibid., 1: 331–32.

32. Kitagawa, "The World's Parliament of Religions," pp. 5–8.

33. Hutchison, *Modernist Impulse*, pp. 2–3; Little, "Parliament of Religions," p. 212.

34. A good deal of incidental information suggestive of the complex reform networks in South Asia at about this time can be found in officer lists, letters, and announcements in the early numbers of the *Journal of the Maha Bodhi Society*. See especially 1 (March and June 1892).

35. Sangharakshita, *Flame in Darkness*, pp. 39–75.

36. Kopf, *The Brahmo-Samaj*, pp. 204–205; Schwab, *Oriental Renaissance*, pp. 244–48; *Journal of the Maha Bodhi Society* 1 (October 1892). Kopf's is the most accessible treatment of the Brāhmo-Samāj, but he overemphasizes the importance of Unitarians. Compare his treatment to Naravane, *Modern Indian Thought* and Kotnala, *Raja Ram Mohun Roy*.

37. Ketelaar, "Strategic Occidentalism," pp. 47–50.

38. *St. Louis Observer*, 21 September 1893, quoted in Barrows, 1: 95.

39. H. Dharmapāla, "The World's Religious Debt to the Buddha," in Barrows, 2: 862–64.

40. Ibid., 2: 863, 866–68, 872.

41. Nath, *New Hindu Movement*, pp. 2–9, 130–40.

42. Barrows, 1: 101–102.

43. *Daily Inter-Ocean*, 20 September 1893. *Indian Mirror*, 9 March 1894, quoted in Burke, *Swami Vivekananda in the West*, p. 85.

44. Vivekananda, "Hinduism," in Barrows, 2: 969, 972.

45. Ibid., 2: 974, 976–77.

46. Kopf, *The Brahmo-Samaj*, pp. 268–86.

47. Sen, *Lectures in India*, pp. 381, 390–98, 400–401.

48. *Daily Inter-Ocean*, 18 September 1893.

49. B. B. Nagarkar, "The Work of Social Reform in India," in Barrows, 1: 767–79.

50. B. B. Nagarkar, "Spiritual Ideals of the Brahmo-Samaj," in Barrows, 2: 1226–28.

51. Ibid., 2: 1229.

52. Mozoomdar, *The Oriental Christ*, pp. 47–56.

53. P. C. Mozoomdar, "The Brahmo-Samaj," in Barrows, 1: 345–51.

54. Little, "Parliament of Religions," p. 211.

55. P. C. Mozoomdar, "The World's Religious Debt to Asia," in Barrows, 2: 1083–86.

56. Ibid., 2: 1087–88.

57. Ibid., 2: 1089–90.

58. Ibid., 2: 1090–92.

59. H. Dharmapāla, "Closing Remarks," in Barrows, 1: 169–70.

60. Kinza Riuge M. Hirai, "The Real Position of Japan towards Christianity," in Barrows, 1: 450.

61. Reuchi Shibata, "Closing Address," in Barrows, 1: 168.

62. Vivekananda, "Hinduism," in Barrows, 2: 977–78.

63. B. B. Nagarkar, "The Work of Social Reform in India," in Barrows, 1: 779.

64. P. C. Mozoomdar, "The Brahmo-Samaj," in Barrows, 1: 351.

65. Barrows, 1: 173–74, 182, 184, 181–82.

66. Barrows, 1: 184–85.

6. Acts of Apostles

1. *Chicago Tribune*, 29 October 1893.

2. *Report of the President to the Board*, 1: 487–492.

3. *Chicago Tribune*, 30 October 1893.

4. Ginger, *Altgeld's America*, p. 92.

5. *Chicago Tribune*, 9 January 1894.

6. *Chicago Tribune*, 9 January 1894; Burnham, *Sweet Clover*, p. 410.

7. Trachtenberg, *Incorporation of America*, p. 208.

8. *San Francisco Examiner*, 28 September 1893.

9. Shaku "Universality of Truth," pp. 161–62.

10. Müller, "Real Significance of the Parliament," p. 1.

11. "First American Congress of Liberal Religious Societies," pp. 135–36; Thomas quoted in "Union of Liberal Religious Forces," p. 340.

12. Jones, "Parliament's Challenge to the Unitarians," pp. 306–307.

13. Ibid., p. 306.

14. Quoted in "Union of Liberal Religious Forces," p. 340.

15. Hirsch, "After the Parliament, What?" p. 398.

16. Ibid., pp. 399–400.

17. Ibid., p. 400.

18. Carus, "World's Religious Parliament Extension," pp. 353, 345.

19. Carus, "Dawn of a New Religious Era," pp. 18–19.

20. Snell, "Religion of Science," p. 3801

21. Quoted in Ahern, *Catholic University*, pp. 93–94.

22. Bonney, "World's Parliament of Religions," pp. 322–23.

23. Mercer, "Swedenborg and the Harmony of Religions," pp. 117–123.

24. For brief accounts of the controversy over the Parliament, see Ahern, *Life of John J. Keane*, pp. 147–49 and Ahern, *Catholic University*, pp. 142–43.

25. "Bishop Keane on the World's Parliament of Religions," p. 4.

26. Editorial Notes, *Catholic World*, pp. 141–42.

27. "World's Parliament of Religions," *American Catholic Quarterly*, pp. 670–71.

28. Ahern, *The Life of John J. Keane*, pp. 147–49; Ahern, *Catholic University*, pp. 142–42.

29. Hewitt, "Christian Unity," pp. 152, 156, 155, 161.

30. Hewitt, "Lesson of the 'White City,'" pp. 772–73, 779.

31. Ibid., pp. 77–78, 82.

32. Editorial, *Biblical World*, pp. 242–45.

33. Abbott, "Lesson from the Parliament of Religions," pp. 222–23.

34. Gladden, *Recollections*, p. 359.

35. Swing, "Building a Great Religion," pp. 976–79.

36. Little, "Chicago Parliament," pp. 208–209, 220.

37. Ibid., pp. 209, 212–13.

38. Ibid., pp. 213–16.

39. Ibid., pp. 216–20.
40. Marsden, *Fundamentalism*, pp. 55–56.
41. Pierson, "The Columbian Exposition at Chicago." pp. 3, 7–8.
42. Pierson, "Parliament of Religions," pp. 882, 890, 887, 884.
43. Ibid., pp. 890, 892.
44. Ibid., pp. 881, 883, 886–87, 891.
45. Anagarika Dharmapāla, "Opening Address," in Barrows, 1: 96.
46. Mary Barrows, *John Henry Barrows.*, pp. 313–18; Barrows, *Christianity: the World-Religion*, pp. 9–11; Barrows, *Christian Conquest of Asia* p. 223.
47. Barrows, *Christianity: The World-Religion*, pp. 26–37, 201.
48. Barrows, *World-Pilgrimage*, pp. 327, 332–34.
49. Barrows, *Christian Conquest of Asia*, pp. 62, 69.
50. Barrows, *World-Pilgrimage*, pp. 337–38.
51. Barrows, *Christian Conquest of Asia*, pp. xii-xiii, 63–64, 66, 82, 75–76.
52. Ibid., pp. 90–91.

7. Beyond the White City

1. Braybrooke, *Interfaith Oganizations*, p. 8.
2. Barrows, "Results of the Parliament," p. 1.
3. Barrows, "World's First Parliament," passim.
4. Kitagawa, "The World's Parliament of Religions," p. 1.
5. Boorstin, *The Image*, pp. 3–6, 7–9, 57–61.
6. Kallen, "Democracy Versus the Melting Pot"; Dahl, *Who Governs?*; Moynihan, *Beyond the Melting Pot*; James, *The Pluralist Universe*; Van Buren, "Dissolution of the Absolute"; Gilkey, *Naming the Whirlwind*.
7. Trumbull, "Parliament of Religions," pp. 333, 343–45, 335.
8. Ibid., pp. 334–36, 350, 353–54.
9. Allen, "Alleged Sympathy of Religions," pp. 311–12.
10. Ibid., pp. 313–18.
11. Ibid., pp. 319–20.
12. Chadwick, "Universal Religion," pp. 402–16.
13. Ibid., pp. 410–11.
14. Telang, "Christian Missionaries," pp. 481–82.
15. Quoted in "Triangular Debate," pp. 269–74.
16. Howe, "Victorian Culture in America," pp. 16–17.
17. Bose, *Life of Protap Chunder Mozoomdar*, 2: 185–88, 202–03.
18. Ibid., 2: 193–202.
19. Ibid., 2: 269–70, 274–75, 272.
20. Ibid., 2: 278.
21. Ibid., 2: 279.
22. Ibid., 2: 278.
23. Ibid., 2: 296–97.
24. Ibid., 2: 375–77.
25. Malachi Martin, in his 1987 invective against Jesuit liberalism in the wake of the Second Vatican Council, went so far as to hold Vivekananda's performance at the Parliament responsible for the success of what he called "the winsome doctrine," the compound of humanism, agnosticism, materialism, and progressivism that he saw as dominating popular religiosity in contemporary society. Martin, *The Jesuits*, pp. 259–63.

26. Burke, *Swami Vivekananda*, pp. 680–82.

27. Ibid., pp. 95–129; Eastern and Western Disciples, *Life of Swami Vivekananda*, pp. 335–70.

28. Burke, *Swami Vivekananda*, pp. 132, 138, 184.

29. Ibid., pp. 22, 316.

30. Burke, *Swami Vivekananda*, p. 68, Vivekananda, *Raja Yoga*, pp. 3–6.

31. "Proceedings of the Public Meeting of the Hindu Community"; Eastern and Western Disciples, *Life of Vivekananda*, pp. 444–451, 452–478, 745–758.

32. For details of Dharmapāla's tour, see Fields, *How the Swans Came to the Lake*, pp. 129–135. Miscellaneous information is found throughout in *Maha Bodhi* 2 (October-December), 1893.

33. For the 1896–1897 tour, see Sangharakshita, *Flame in a Darkness*, pp. 87–88 and Dharmapāla, "Diary Leaves," *Maha Bodhi* 64–66 (1956-1958).

34. For the comment on the impact of Vivekananda's teaching, see Dharmapāla, "Diary Leaves," p. 346. For the comment on Christians, see Sangharakshita, *Flame in Darkness*, p. 88.

35. Sangharakshita, *Flame in Darkness*, pp. 93, 100-111; Gunaratna, "Venerable Anagarika Dharmapāla's Work," pp. 305-306.

36. Quoted in Ketelaar, "Occidentalist Strategy," pp. 46-51.

37. Quoted in Senzuki, *Like a Dream Like a Fantasy*, p. 109.

38. Fields, *How the Swans Came to the Lake*, pp. 135, 169-174; Sōen, *Sermons of a Buddhist Abbot*, pp. 53, 79, 170.

39. John McRae suggests this may be a result of D. T. Suzuki's editing of Sōen's comments in order to tailor them for an American audience (McRae, "Oriental Verities," p. 26).

40. Shaku, *Sermons of a Buddhist Abbot*, pp. 38-48.

41. Fields, *How the Swans Came to the Lake*, pp. 136-40, 195-224.

42. *Chicago Tribune*, 17 September 1893.

43. *Chicago Tribune*, 24 September 1893.

Afterword

1. Tracy, *Plurality and Ambiguity*, pp. 1-27.

2. Weimann, *The Fair Women*, provides an useful beginning to such an analysis.

3. Tweed, *American Encounter with Buddhism*, pp. 133-56.

4. Turner, *Without God, Without Creed*, pp. 141-67. George Santayana wrote of mainstream Protestant religious sensibilities around the turn of the century that "the very heart of orthodoxy melted, has absorbed the most alien substances, and is ready to bloom into anything that anybody finds attractive." Santayana, "Moral Background," p. 85.

5. Barrows, Mary E. *John Henry Barrows*, pp. 281-83.

6. Ibid., p. 293.

7. *Daily Inter-Ocean*, 14 September 1893.

8. Rydell gives some attention to the way in which the Midway and its residents functioned as a subliminal outlet for repressed sexual desire. Rydell, *All the World's a Fair*, pp. 67-68.

9. Pierson, "The Parliament of Religions," p. 882.

10. Ibid., pp. 393-436, 437-67; Vivekananda quoted in Eastern and Western Disciples, *Life of Vivekananda*, p. 387; Student interviews are found in *Brahmavadin* 1 (June 1896): pp. 234, 243.

11. Winslow, "A Pen Picture of the Parliament," pp. 223, 228.

12. Ketelaar, "Strategic Occidentalism: Meiji Buddhists at the World's Parliament of Religions." *Buddhist-Christian Studies* 11 (1991): pp. 37–56.

13. Braybrooke, *Interfaith Organizations*, pp. 7–8.

14. Kitagawa, "World's Parliament of Religions," p. 1.

15. Augusta Chapin, "Words of Welcome," in Barrows, 1: 81–82.

16. Kitagawa, "World's Parliament of Religions." This line of interpretation is also influenced by Toulmin, *Cosmopolis: the Hidden Agenda of Modernity*.

17. Meyer, "American Intellectuals and the Victorian Crisis of Faith," pp. 59–77. Chadwick, *Secularization of the European Mind*, pp. 21–47.

18. Albanese, "Religion and the American Experience"; Bellah, *Habits of the Heart*, pp. 232–35; 245–48.

19. I borrow the phrase from Peter Berger, Berger, *Sacred Canopy*.

BIBLIOGRAPHY

Abbott, Lyman. "Lesson from the Parliament of Religions." In *Christian Thought: Papers on Philosophy, Christian Evidence, and Biblical Elucidation*, edited by Charles Weemes. New York: Wilbur Ketcham, 1893–1894.

Ahern, Patrick Henry. *The Catholic University of America, 1887–1896.* Washington, D.C.: Catholic University Press of America, 1948.

———. *The Life of John J. Keane: Educator and Archbishop, 1839–1918.* Milwaukee: Bruce Publishing Co., 1954.

Albanese, Catherine. "Religion and the American Experience: A Century After." *Church History* 57 (1988): 337–51.

———. *Sons of the Fathers: the Civil Religion of the American Revolution.* Philadelphia: Temple University Press, 1976.

Aldrich, Thomas Bailey. "Unguarded Gates." In *Poems of Thomas Bailey Aldrich.* 2 vols. New York: Houghton Mifflin, 1907.

Allen, Joseph Henry. "The Alleged Sympathy of Religions." *New World* 4 (June 1895): 310–21.

Appelbaum, Stanley. *The Chicago World's Fair of 1903: A Photographic Record.* New York: Dover, 1980.

Arnold, C. D., and H. D. Higinbotham. *Official Views of the World's Columbian Exposition.* Chicago: Press Chicago Photo-gravure Co., 1893.

Bacon, Leonard Woolsey. *A History of American Christianity.* New York: The Christian Literature Co., 1897.

Baird, Robert. *Religion in America*, edited by Henry Warner Bowden. New York: Harper and Row, 1970.

Barrows, John Henry. *The Christian Conquest of Asia.* New York: Charles Scribner's Sons, 1899.

———. *Christianity: the World-Religion.* Chicago: A. C. McClurg, 1897.

———. "The Religious Possibilities of the World's Fair." *Our Day* 10 (August 1892): 560.

———. "Results of the Parliament of Religions," Reprint. *Forum* (September 1894): 1–14.

———. *The World's First Parliament of Religions: Its Christian Spirit, Historic Greatness, and Manifold Results.* Chicago: Hill and Shuman, 1895.

———. *A World-Pilgrimage*, edited by Mary Eleanor Barrows. Chicago: A. C. McClurg, 1897.

———. ed. *The World's Parliament of Religions: An Illustrated and Popular Story of the World's Parliament of Religions, Held in Chicago in*

Connection with the World's Columbian Exposition. 2 vols. Chicago: Parliament Publishing Co., 1893.

Barrows, Mary Eleanor. *John Henry Barrows: A Memoir.* Chicago: Fleming H. Revell, 1904.

Bellah, Robert. "Civil Religion in America." In *American Civil Religion,* edited by Russell E. Richey and Donald G. Jones. New York: Harper and Row, 1974.

———. *Habits of the Heart.* New York: Harper and Row, 1985.

Berger, Peter L. *The Sacred Canopy: Elements of a Sociological Theory of Religion.* Garden City: Doubleday, 1967.

Besant, Walter. "A First Impression." *Cosmopolitan* 15 (September 1893): 528–39.

Beversluis, Joel, ed. *A Sourcebook for the Community of Religions.* Chicago: Council for a Parliament of the World's Religions, 1993.

"Bishop Keane on the World's Parliament of Religions," *Boston Pilot,* 14 October 1893, p. 4.

Bonney, Charles Carroll. "The Genesis of the World's Religious Congresses of 1893." *New-Church Review* 1 (January 1894): 73–100.

———. "A World's Congress at the World's Fair." In George F. Dole, *With Absolute Respect: The Swedenborgian Theology of Charles Carroll Bonney.* Swedenborg Studies, no. 3 (1993), 45–47. Monographs of the Swedenborgian Foundation. West Chester, PA.

———. "The World's Parliament of Religions." *Monist* 5 (April 1895): 321–343.

Boorstin, Daniel J. *The Image: A Guide to Pseudo-Events in America.* New York: Atheneum, 1987. Originally published as *The Image: Or What Happened to the American Dream.* New York: Atheneum, 1962.

Bose, Churesh Chunder. *The Life of Protap Chunder Mozoomdar.* (2 vols. in 1). Calcutta: Nababidhan Trust, 1940.

Braybrooke, Marcus, *Inter-Faith Organizations, 1893–1979: An Historical Directory.* New York: Edwin Mellen Press, 1980.

Brooklyn Museum, *The American Renaissance, 1876–1979.* New York: Brooklyn Museum, 1979.

Buel, J. W. *The Magic City: A Massive Portfolio of Original Photographic Views of the Great World's Fair.* St. Louis: Historical Publishing Co., 1894.

Burg, David. *Chicago's White City of 1893.* Lexington: University Press of Kentucky, 1976.

Burke, Marie Louise. *Swami Vivekananda in America: New Discoveries.* Calcutta: Advaita Ashrama, 1958.

Burnham, Clara Louis. *Sweet Clover: A Romance of the White City.* Boston: Houghton Mifflin, 1895.

Bushnell, Horace. *Barbarism the First Danger: A Discourse for Home Missions.* New York: Printed for the American Home Missionary Society, 1847.

———. *Work and Play.* New York: Charles Scribner's Sons, 1866.

Candlin, George. "The Parliament of Religions." *Chinese Recorder* 25 (January 1894): 35–36.

———. "Results and Mission of the Parliament of Religions." *Biblical World* n.s., 5 (1895): 371–73.

Carter, Paul. *The Spiritual Crisis of the Gilded Age.* Dekalb, Ill.: Northern Illinois University Press, 1971.

Carus, Paul. "Charles Carroll Bonney." *Open Court* 17 (September 1903): 516–19.

———. "The Dawn of a New Religious Era." Appendix, *Monist* 4 (April 1894): 1–20.

———. "The World's Religious Parliament Extension." *Monist* 5 (April 1895): 345–353.

Celebration of Columbus Day, October 21,1892, at Columbia, South Carolina, with the Address of Hon. LeRoy F. Youmans. Columbia, South Carolina: C. A. Calvo Jr., 1893.

Chadwick, John White. "Universal Religion." *New World* 3 (September 1894): 401–18.

Council for the Parliament of the World's Religions. *Parliament of the World's Religions.* n.p. 1993.

Craig, Lois, and the staff of the Federal Architecture Project. *The Federal Presence: Architecture, Politics, and Symbols in United States Government Buildings.* Cambridge and London: MIT Press, 1978.

Cronon, William. *Nature's Metropolis: Chicago and the Great West.* New York: W. W. Norton, 1991.

Dahl, Robert A. *Who Governs? Democracy and Power in an American City.* New Haven: Yale University Press, 1961.

Davis, Richard Harding. "The Last Days of the Fair." *Harper's Weekly,* 21 October 1893, p. 1002.

Dharmapāla, Anagarika. "Diary Leaves of the Late Ven. Anagarika Dharmapāla," edited by Sri D. Valisinha. *Maha Bodhi* 64–66 (1956–1958).

Dockarty, A. J. *The Midway Plaisance: The Experience of an Innocent Boy from Vermont on the Famous Midway.* Chicago: Chicago World Book, 1894.

Dolan, Jay P. *The American Catholic Experience.* Garden City: Doubleday, 1985.

———, ed. *The World's Columbian Catholic Congresses and Educational Exhibit. 1893.* Reprint. New York: Arno Press, 1978.

Douglass, Frederick, and Ida Wells. *The Reason Why the Colored American Is Not in the World's Columbia Exposition.* n.p., 1893.

Downey, Dennis. "Tradition and Acceptance: American Catholics and the Columbian Exposition." *Mid-America* 63 (April-July 1981): 79–92.

Druyvesten, Kenten. "The World's Parliament of Religions," Ph.D. diss., University of Chicago, 1976.

Dybwad, G. L., and Joy V. Bliss. *Annotated Bibliography: World's Columbian Exposition, Chicago 1893.* Albuquerque, NM: The Book Stops Here, 1992.

Eastern and Western Disciples. *The Life of Swami Vivekananda*. Calcutta: Advaita Ashrama, 1965.

Editorial, *Biblical World* n.s., 2 (October 1893): 241–46.

Editorial Notes, *Catholic World* 58 (October 1893): 141–42.

Editorial Notes. *Reform Advocate*, 22 July 1893, pp. 421–22.

Eliade, Mircea. *The Sacred and the Profane: The Nature of Religion*. Translated by Willard R. Trask. New York: Harcourt, Brace, 1959.

Fields, Rick. *How the Swans Came to the Lake: A Narrative History of Buddhism in America*. Boulder: Shambala, 1980.

"The First American Congress of Liberal Religious Societies." *Unity* 33 (May 1894): 135–36.

Frye, Northrop. *The Great Code: The Bible and Literature*. New York: Harcourt Brace, 1982.

Geertz, Clifford. *The Interpretation of Culture*. New York: Basic Books, 1973.

Gibbons, J. E. Cardinal. "Address." In *The World's Columbian Catholic Congresses and Educational Exhibit*, edited by Jay P. Dolan, 1893. Reprint, New York: Arno Press, 1978.

Gilder, Richard Watson. "The White City," and "The Vanishing City." In *The Poems of Richard Watson Gilder*. Boston: Houghton Mifflin, 1908.

Gilkey, Langdon Brown. *Naming the Whirlwind: The Renewal of God-Language*. Indianapolis: Bobbs-Merrill, 1969.

Ginger, Ray. *Altgeld's America: The Lincoln Ideal Versus Changing Realities*. New York: Funk and Wagnalls, 1958.

Gladden, Washington. *Recollections*. Boston: Houghton Mifflin, 1909.

Golomb, Deborah Grand. "The 1893 Congress of Jewish Women: Evolution or Revolution in American Jewish History?" *American Jewish History* 70 (September 1980): 52–67.

Graham, Thomas. "Jenkin Lloyd Jones and the World's Columbian Exposition of 1893," *Association for Liberal Religious Studies: Collegium Proceedings* 1 (1979): 62–81.

Gunaratna, Francis. "Venerable Anagarika Dharmapala's Work for Ceylon and India." *Maha Bodhi* 56 (September 1948): 304–306.

Gunsaulus, F. W. "The Ideal of Culture." *Chautauquan*, 16 (October 1892): 59–64.

Handy, Robert T. *A Christian American: Protestant Hopes and Historical Realities*. London: Oxford University Press, 1971.

Hanson, J. W., ed. *The World's Congress of Religions: The Addresses and Papers Delivered before the Parliament*. Chicago: W. B. Conkey, 1894.

Hawthorne, Julian. "Foreign Folk at the Fair." *Cosmopolitan* 15 (September 1893): 567–76.

Hay, Stephen N. *Asian Ideas of East and West: Tagore and His Critics in Japan, China, and India*. Cambridge: Harvard University Press, 1970.

Hecht, S. "The Lessons of the World's Columbian Exposition." *Reform Advocate*, 11 November 1893, pp. 205–206.

Henrotin, Ellen M. "The Great Congress at the World's Fair." *Cosmopolitan* 3 (March 1893): 626–32.

Herberg Will. *Protestant, Catholic, Jew: An Essay in American Religious Sociology*. Garden City: Doubleday, 1955.

Hewitt, Augustine. "Christian Unity in the Parliament of Religions," *Catholic World* 59 (May 1894): 152–63.

———. "The Lesson of the 'White City.'" *Catholic World* 59 (September 1894): 770–79; 60 (October 1895): 73–82.

Higham, John. *Strangers in the Land: Patterns of Nativism, 1860–1925*. New Brunswick, NJ: Rutgers University Press, 1955.

Hirsch, Emil. "After the Parliament, What?" *Reform Advocate*, 3 February 1894, pp. 398–400.

———. "The Spiritual Results of the World's Fair." *Reform Advocate*, 11 November 1893, pp. 202–205.

Horowitz, Helen Lefkowitz. *Culture and the City: Cultural Philanthropy in Chicago from the 1880s to 1917*. Lexington: University Press of Kentucky, 1976.

Houghton, Walter, ed. *Neely's History of the Parliament of Religions and Religious Congresses at the World's Columbia Exposition*. Chicago: Neely, 1894.

Houghton, Walter Edwards. *The Victorian Frame of Mind, 1830–1870*. New Haven: Published for Wellesley College by Yale University, 1957.

Howe, Daniel Walker. "Victorian Culture in America." In *Victorian America*, edited by Daniel Walker Howe, pp. 3–28. Philadelphia: University of Pennsylvania Press, 1976.

Hurlbutt, Jesse. *The Story of the Chautauqua*. New York: G. P. Putnam's Sons, 1921.

Hutchison, William R. *American Protestant Thought in the Liberal Era*. Lanham: University Press of America, 1968.

———. *Errand to the World: American Protestant Thought and Foreign Missions*. Chicago: University of Chicago Press, 1987.

———. *The Modernist Impulse in American Protestantism*. Cambridge: Harvard University Press, 1976.

———. "A Moral Equivalent for Imperialism: Americans and the Promotion of Christian Civilization, 1880–1910." *Indian Journal of American Studies* 1 (January 1893): 55–67.

Ives, Halsey. *The Dream City: Photographic Views of the World's Columbian Exposition*. St. Louis: N. D. Thompson, 1893.

Jackson, Carl T. *The Oriental Religions and American Thought: Nineteeth Century Explorations*. Westport: Greenwood Press, 1981.

James, William. *A Pluralistic Universe*. Cambridge: Harvard University Press, 1977.

Jenkyns, Richard. *The Victorians and Ancient Greece*. Cambridge: Harvard University Press, 1980.

Johnson, Rossiter, ed. *A History of the World's Columbian Exposition held in Chicago in 1893*. 4 vols. New York: D. Appleton, 1898.

Joint Committee on Ceremonies. *Dedicatory and Opening Ceremonies of the World's Columbian Exposition.* Chicago: Stone, Kastler, and Painter, 1893.

Jones, Howard Mumford. *Age of Energy: Varieties of American Experience, 1865-1915.* New York: Viking, 1971.

———. *O Strange New World: American Culture—The Formative Years.* New York: Viking, 1964.

Jones, Jenkin Lloyd. "Books on the Parliament." *Unity* 32 (January 1894): 274-275.

———. *A Chorus of Faiths as Heard in the Parliament of Religions.* Chicago: Unity Publishing Co., 1893.

———. "The Parliament's Challenge to the Unitarians." *Unity* 32 (January 1894): 306-307.

———. "Triumph of the Parliament." *Unity* 32 (October 1893): 66-67.

Jordan, Louis. *Comparative Religion: Its Genesis and Growth.* Edinburgh: T. & T. Clark, 1905.

Journal of the Mahabodi Society. Calcutta: Mahabodi Society, 1 (March, June, and October, 1892); 2 (October–December, 1893).

Kallen, Horace. "Democracy Versus the Melting Pot: A Study of American Nationality." *Nation* 100 (February 1915): 190-4; 217-20.

Kennedy, Roger G. *Greek Revival America.* New York: Stewart, Tabori, and Chang, 1989.

Ketelaar, James E. "Strategic Occidentalism: Meiji Buddhists at the World's Parliament of Religions." *Buddhist-Christian Studies* 11 (1991): 37-56.

King, Ursula. "Rediscovering Women's Voices at the World's Parliament of Religions." In *A Museum of Faiths: Histories and Legacies of the 1893 World's Parliament of Religions,* edited by Eric Ziolkowsky, pp. 325-43. American Academy of Religion Classics in Religious Studies, No. 9. Atlanta: Scholars Press, 1993.

Kirkland, Joseph, and Caroline Kirkland. *The Story of Chicago.* 2 vols. Chicago: Dibble Publishing Co., 1894.

Kitagawa, Joseph. "Humanistic and Theological History of Religions with Special Reference to the North American Scene." In *Traditions in Contact and Change: Selected Proceedings of the XIVth Congress of the International Association for the History of Religions,* edited by Peter Slater and Donald Wiebe. Waterloo, Ontario: Wilfred Laurier University Press, 1983.

———. "The World's Parliament of Religions and Its Legacy." Eleventh John Nuveen Lecture. Chicago: Privately printed by the University of Chicago Divinity School, 1983.

Knitter, Paul F. *No Other Name?: A Critical Survey of Christian Attitudes Toward the World Religions.* Maryknoll: Orbis Books, 1985.

Kopf, David. *The Brahmo-Samaj and the Shaping of the Modern Indian Mind.* Princeton: Princeton University Press, 1979.

Kotnala, M. C. *Raja Ram Mohun Roy and Indian Awakening.* New Delhi: Gitanjali Prakashan, 1975.

Lavan, Spencer. *Unitarians in India: A Study in Encounter and Response.* Boston: Beacon Press, 1977.

Lewi, Isidore. "Yom Kippur on the Midway." In *Report of the Commitee on Awards of the World's Columbian Exposition*. 2 vols. Chicago: Rand McNally, 1901.

Lincoln, Bruce. *Discourse and the Construction of Society: Comparative Studies of Myth, Ritual, and Classification*. New York: Oxford University Press, 1989.

Little, Charles. "The Parliament of Religions." *Methodist Review* 76 (March 1894): 208–220.

M. H. W. "Impression of the White City." *Outlook* 47 (June 1893): 1200–1201.

McClung, E. Fleming. "The American Image as Indian Princess, 1765–1783." *Winterthur Portfolio* 11 (1965): 65–81.

———. "From Indian Princess to Greek Goddess: The American Image, 1783–1815. *Winterthur Portfolio* III (1967): 37–66.

McNeill, William Hardy. *A World History*. 2nd ed. New York: Oxford University Press, 1980.

McRae, John R. "Oriental Verities on the American Frontier: The 1893 World's Parliament of Religions and the Thought of Masao Abe." *Buddhist-Christian Studies* 11 (1991): 7–36.

Manieri-Elia, Mario. "Toward an 'Imperial City': Daniel Bunham and the City Beautiful Movement." In *The American City: from the Civil War to the New Deal*, edited by Giorgio Ciucci et al. Translated from the Italian by Barbara Luigia La Penta. Cambridge: MIT Press, 1979.

Marsden, George M. *Fundamentalism and American Culture*. New York: Oxford University Press, 1980.

Martin, Malachi. *The Jesuits: the Society of Jesus and the Betrayal of the Roman Catholic Church*. New York: Linden Press, Simon & Schuster, 1987.

Marty, Martin, editor. *Ethnic and Non-Protestant Themes*. Munich and New York: K. G. Saur, 1993.

———. "Ethnicity: The Skeleton of Religion in America." *Church History* 41 (March 1972): 5–21.

———. *Modern American Religion*, vol. 1: *The Irony of It All*. Chicago: University of Chicago Press, 1986.

———. Pilgrims in Their Own Land: 500 Years of Religion in America. Boston: Little, Brown, 1984.

May, Henry F. *The End of American Innocence: A Study of the First Years of Our Own Time, 1912–1917*. New York: Knopf, 1959.

———. "Religion of the Republic." In *Ideas, Faiths, and Feelings: Essays on American Intellectual and Religious History, 1952–1982*, edited by Henry F. May, pp. 163–186. New York: Oxford University Press, 1983.

Mercer, Lewis P. "Swedenborg and the Harmony of Religions." In *The New Jerusalem in the World's Religious Congresses of 1893*. Chicago: Western New-Church Union, 1894, pp. 117–123.

Meyer, D. H. "American Intellectuals and the Victorian Crisis of Faith."

In *Victorian America*, edited by Daniel Walker Howe. Philadelphia: University of Pennsylvania Press, 1976.

Morgan, Charles. "Signs of the Times." In *World's Fair Sermons by Eminent Divines at Home and Abroad*, edited by J. B. McClure. Chicago: Rhodes and McClure, 1893.

Morrison, Theodore, *Chautauqua*. Chicago: University of Chicago Press, 1974.

Mowry, William Augustus. "Columbus Day in Salem". Reprint. Essex Institute, *Historical Collection* 30 (January-March 1893).

Moynihan, Daniel Patrick, and Nathan Glazer. *Beyond the Melting Pot: The Negroes, Puerto Ricans, Jews, Italians, and Irish of New York City*. Cambridge: MIT Press and Harvard University Press, 1963.

Mozoomdar, Protap Chunder. *The Oriental Christ*. Boston: George Ellis, 1883.

Muldoon, P. J. "Sermon of Welcome." In *The World's Columbian Catholic Congresses and Educational Exhibit*, edited by Jay P. Dolan, 1893. Reprint, New York: Arno Press, 1978.

Müller, F. Max. "The Real Significance of the Parliament of Religions." *Arena* 61 (December 1894): 1-14.

Nath, Rakhal Chandra. *The New Hindu Movement, 1886-1911*. Calcutta: Minerva, 1982.

Naravane, Vishwanath S. *Modern Indian Thought*. New Delhi: Orient Longmans, 1978.

Noble, Frederick. "Meaning and Opportunities of the World's Fair." In *World's Fair Sermons by Eminent Divines at Home and Abroad*, edited by J. B. McClure. Chicago: Rhodes and McClure, 1893.

"Official Program: The National Public School Celebration of Columbus Day, October 21, 1892." Reprint. *Youth's Companion* 65 (September 1892): 466-67.

Olsen, Frederick. "The American Sunday, 1865-1900." Honors Thesis, Harvard University, 1938.

Orsi, Robert Anthony. *The Madonna of 115th Street: Faith and Community in Italian Harlem, 1880-1950*. New Haven: Yale University Press, 1986.

Papers of the Jewish Women's Congress. Philadelphia: Jewish Publication Society of America, 1894.

Persons, Stow. *The Decline of Gentility*. New York: Columbia University Press, 1973.

——. *Free Religion: An American Faith*. New Haven: Yale University Press, 1947.

Pierson, A. T., "The Columbian Exposition at Chicago." *Missionary Review of the World* n.s., 7 (January 1894): 1-10.

——. "The Parliament of Religions: A Review." *Missionary Review of the World* n.s., 7 (December 1894): 881-91.

Pipe, William. "The Parliament of Religions." *The Outlook* 26 (August 1893), p. 385.

Programme of the World's Religious Congresses of 1893. Preliminary edition. n.p., n.d.

Putnam, Frederic W. *Oriental and Occidental, Northern and Southern Portrait Types of the Midway Plaisance.* St. Louis: N. D. Thompson, 1894.

Race, Alan. *Christians and Religious Pluralism: Patterns in the Christian Theology of Religion.* London: SCM Press, 1983.

Ralph, Julian. *Harper's Chicago and the World's Fair.* New York: Harper, 1893.

Raymond, Emily. *About Chautauqua.* Toledo: Blade Printing and Paper Co., 1886.

Redman, Barbara J. "Sabbatarian Accommodation in the Supreme Court." *Journal of Church and State* 33 (Summer 1991): 495–523.

Reinhold, Meyer. *Classica Americana: The Greek and Roman Heritage in the United States.* Detroit: Wayne State University Press, 1984.

Report of the Committee on Awards of the World's Columbian Exposition. 2 vols. Washington: Government Printing Office, 1901.

Report of the President to the Board of Directors of the World's Columbian Exposition. Chicago: Rand McNally, 1898.

Robinson, Charles Mulford. "The Fair as Spectacle." In *A History of the World's Columbian Exposition,* edited by Rossiter Johnson, pp. 493–512. New York: D. Appleton, 1898.

Rydell, Robert. *All the World's a Fair: Vision of Empire at American International Exhibitions, 1876–1916.* Chicago: University of Chicago Press, 1984.

Said, Edward W., *Orientalism.* New York: Random, Vintage Books, 1979.

Sangharakshita, Maha Sthavira. *Flame in Darkness; The Life and Sayings of Anagarika Dharmapāla.* Puna: Triratna Grantha Mala for Trailokya Bauddha Mahasangha Sahayaka Gana, 1980.

Santayana, George. "The Moral Background." In *The Genteel Tradition: Nine Essays by George Santayana,* edited by Douglas L. Wilson. Cambridge: Harvard University Press, 1967.

Schorske, Carl E. *Fin de Siècle Vienna: Politics and Culture.* New York: Knopf, 1979.

Schwab, Raymond. *The Oriental Renaissance: Europe's Discovery of India and the East, 1680–1880.* Translated by Gene Patterson-Black and Victor Reinking. New York: Columbia University Press, 1984.

Seager, Richard Hughes, ed. *The Dawn of Religious Pluralism: Voices from the World's Parliament of Religions, 1893.* LaSalle, IL: Open Court Publishing Co., 1993.

———. "Pluralism and the American Mainstream: The View from the World's Parliament of Religions." *Harvard Theological Review* 82 (1989): 301–24.

Sen, Keshub Chunder. *Lectures in India.* Calcutta: Navavidhan Publication Committee, 1954.

Senzuki, Nyogen. *Like a Dream Like a Fantasy: The Writings and Trans-*

lations of Nyogen Senzuki, edited by Eido Shimano. Tokyo: Japan Publications, 1978.

Shaku Sōen. *Sermons of a Buddhist Abbott*. Chicago: Open Court, 1906.

———. "The Universality of Truth." *Monist* 4 (January 1894): 161–62.

Sharpe, Eric. *Comparative Religion: A History*. London: Duckworth, 1975.

Singer, Milton. "The Melting Pot: Symbolic Ritual or Total Social Fact?" In *Symbolizing America*, edited by Herve Varenne, pp. 97–117. Lincoln: University of Nebraska Press, 1986.

Snell, Merwin-Marie. "The Religion of Science as a Basis for Universal Religious Union." *Open Court* 7 (September 1893): 3799–3801.

Swing, David. "Building a Great Religion." In *Neely's History of the Parliament of Religions and Religious Congresses at the World's Columbian Exposition*, edited by Walter R. Houghton, pp. 974–79. Chicago: Neely, 1894.

———. "The Significance of the World's Fair." In *World's Fair Sermons by Eminent Divines at Home and Abroad*, edited by J. B. McClure. Chicago: Rhodes and McClure, 1893.

Telang, Purushotam Rao. "Christian Missionaries As Seen by a Brahman." *Forum* 18 (Sept. 1894–Feb. 1895): 481–89.

Tomsich, John. *A Genteel Endeavor: American Culture and Politics in the Gilded Age*. Stanford: Stanford University Press, 1971.

Toulmin, Stephen Edelston, *Cosmopolis: the Hidden Agenda of Modernity*. New York: Free Press, 1990.

Trachtenberg, Alan. *The Incorporation of America: Culture and Society in the Gilded Age*. New York: Hill and Wang, 1982.

Tracy, David. *Plurality and Ambiguity: Hermenuetics, Religion, and Hope*. San Francisco: Harper and Row, 1987.

"A Triangular Debate Before the Nineteenth Century Club of New York." *Monist* 5 (January 1895): 269–74.

Trumbull, M. M. "The Parliament of Religions." *Monist* 5 (April 1894): 335–54.

Turner, James. *Without God, Without Creed: The Origins of Unbelief in America*. Baltimore: The Johns Hopkins University Press, 1985.

Turner, Victor. *Dramas, Fields, and Metaphors: Symbolic Action in Human Society*. Ithaca: Cornell University Press, 1974.

———. *From Ritual to Theatre: The Human Seriousness of Play*. New York: Performing Arts Journal Publications, 1982.

Turner, Victor, and Edith Turner. *Image and Pilgrimage in Christian Culture: Anthropological Perspectives*. New York: Columbia University Press, 1978.

Tuveson, Ernest Lee. *Redeemer Nation: The Idea of America's Millennial Role*. Chicago: University of Chicago Press, 1968.

Tweed, Thomas A. *The American Encounter with Buddhism, 1844–1912: Victorian Culture and the Limits of Dissent*. Bloomington: Indiana University Press, 1992.

"The Union of Liberal Religious Forces," *Unity* 32 (February 1984): 340–41.

Van Brunt, Henry. "The Columbian Exposition and American Civilization." *Atlantic Monthly* 71 (May 1893): 577–88.

Van Buren, Paul M. "The Dissolution of the Absolute." *Religion in Life*. 35 (Summer 1965), 335–42.

Vance, William L. *America's Rome*. 2 vols. New Haven: Yale University Press, 1989.

Van Rensselaer, Mrs. Schuyler. "The Artistic Triumph of the Fair-Builders." *Forum* 14 (December 1892): 528–40.

Vivekananda. *Raja-Yoga*. New York: Ramakrishna-Vivekananda Vedanta Center, 1982.

Wah Mee Exposition Company. "Guide to the Joss House, Temple of China." n.d., n.p.

Weber, Eugen. *France, Fin de Siècle*. Cambridge: Belknap Press of Harvard University Press, 1986.

Weimann, Jeanne Madeleine. *The Fair Women*. Chicago: Academy Chicago, 1981.

Wells, Oliver, ed. *Wisconsin Columbian Circular Containing Patriotic and Historical Sections for October 21, 1892*. Madison: Democratic Printing Co., State Printer, 1892.

White City: Chicago, 1893. n.p. 1893.

Wiebe, Robert H. *The Search for Order, 1877–1920*. New York: Hill and Wang, 1967.

Wilson, John Frederick. *Public Religion in American Culture*. Philadelphia: Temple University Press, 1979.

Winslow, Florence E. "A Pen Picture of the Parliament." In *Christian Thought: Lectures and Papers on Philosophy, Christian Evidence, and Biblical Elucidation*. New York: Wilbur Ketcham, 1893–1894.

"The World's Parliament of Religions." *American Catholic Quarterly* 19 (July 1894): 670–71.

Ziolkowski, Eric J. "Heavenly Visions and Worldly Intentions: Chicago's Columbian Exposition and World's Parliament of Religions." *Journal of American Culture* 13 (Winter 1990): 9–15.

Ziolkowsky, Eric, ed. *A Museum of Faiths: Histories and Legacies of the 1893 World's Parliament of Religions*. American Academy of Religion Classics in Religious Studies, No. 9. Atlanta: Scholars Press, 1993.

INDEX

Abbott, Lyman: 15, 148, 155; address of, 55; his reactions to Parliament, 134–35

Abdul Hamid II, Sultan, 27, 101

Abhayananda, Swami, 155

Abou Naddara, J. Sanna, 101

African-Americans: xix, 28, 66, 119, 168; and the Gilded Age crisis, 9; and the Columbian myth, 21–22, 23, 39; their general contribution to Parliament, 45

Aiyangar, S. Parthasarathy, 103

Akbar, 95

Aldrich, Thomas Bailey, 6–7, 8, 10, 161

Allen, Joseph Henry, 146–47

Arnett, Bishop Benjamin, 21, 119

Arnold, Sir Edwin, 156

Arnold, Matthew, 70

Ashmore, William, 138, 158

Asoka, 95

Bacon, Leonard, 53

Baird, Robert, 50, 182n15

Banryū, Yatsubuchi, 109

Barrows, John Henry: 34, 47, 66, 67, 99, 119, 124, 173; *World's Parliament of Religions: An Illustrated and Popular History*, xvi; his remarks on the White City, 19; his expectations for the Parliament, 48, 52–53; Asian tour of, 140–42; *Christian Conquest of Asia*, 141–42; his reactions to the Parliament, 166

Barrows, Samuel J., 151, 177n4

Barrows Lectureship in Asia, 140

Bellah, Robert N., 16

Bellamy, Francis, 16

Besant, Walter, 16

Blavatsky, Helena, 109

Board of Lady Managers, 13, 164

Boardman, George Dana: 64, 108, 119; address of, 60–62

Bonney, Charles Carroll: 98, 132, 156; his leadership of World's Congress Auxiliary, xx, 46; his expectations for Parliament, 51–52; his reactions to Parliament, 119–20, 130–31

Boorstin, Daniel J., 143

Brāhmo-Samāj: 109, 112; ideals of, 114; and F. Max Müller, 151–52

Braybrooke, Marcus, 143, 169

Briggs, Charles, 55

Brodbeck, Adolph, 58–59

Brown, Theron, 16

Brownell, William Crary, 14

Bruce, A. B., 56

Buddhism: 43, 74, 76, 96–97; western delegates' estimation of, 57, 61, 128, 129, 136, 138–39; Vivekananda on, 80; presentation of Nicheren sect, 103; delegation from, 109; major presentation of, 110–11. *See also* Dharmapāla, Anagarika; Sōen, Shaku

Buel, J. W.: 26; *The Magic City*, 38

Burnham, Clara: *Sweet Clover: A Romance of the White City*, 28, 125

Burnham, Daniel, 13, 14

Burrell, David, 66

Burton, J. R., 35, 39

Bushnell, Horace, 7–8, 161

Candlin, George: 103, 116–17; address of, 77; his reactions to the Parliament, 97–100

Carpenter, J. Estlin, 69–70, 71

Carter, Paul, 9, 65

Carus, Paul: 126, 148, 149, 156, 158; address of, 57–58; his reaction to the Parliament, 129; D. T. Suzuki and, 159

Catholics: xv, xvii, xxviii, xxx–xxxi, 39, 157; and immigration, 10; and the Columbian myth, 19; their goals at the Parliament, 44; addresses of, 54–55, 60, 70; their reactions to the

RICHARD HUGHES SEAGER is an Associate of the Committee on the Study of Religion at Harvard University and an Assistant Professor at Hamilton College. He is the editor of *The Dawn of Religious Pluralism: Voices from the World's Parliament of Religions, 1893*.